I0019827

# Leading Issues in Social Media

For researchers, teachers and students

Edited by

*asher Rospigliosi and Sue Greener*

Leading Issues in Social Media

Note to readers: Some papers have been written by authors who use the American form of spelling and some use the British. These two different approaches have been left unchanged.

ISBN: 978-1-910810-22-4 (print)
978-1-910810-23-1 (e-Pub)
978-1-910810-24-8 (Kindle)

Printed by Lightning Source POD

Published by: Academic Conferences and Publishing International Limited, Reading, RG4 9AY, United Kingdom, info@academic-publishing.org
Available from www.academic-bookshop.com.

Available from www.academic-bookshop.com.

# Contents

# About the editors

asher Rospigliosi is a principal lecturer in e-business, digital marketing and management information systems. He has researched and taught at Brighton Business School since 2001 and has developed successful modules in e-commerce, mobile innovations, big data and digital marketing. asher has research interests in the history, impact and nature of higher education, graduate employability and how graduates might best be served by university. He is associate editor of the research journal Interactive Learning Environments. He also writes and talks on e-commerce, digital marketing, big data and digital entrepreneurship.

Prince Pericles 'asher' Rospigliosi
*Brighton Business School, University of Brighton*

Before joining the University of Brighton asher was a project manager at CNet / ZDNet developing commercial e-commerce publishing systems, working with developers across Europe, the USA and Singapore. He had six years at ZDNet and was web master to the a number of successful properties including PC Magazine, The Computer Channel, IT Week and founded Gamespot UK, which won the PPAi consumer web site award in 1999.

Away from the Business School asher is excited by sustainable and low impact living, tipis and fire. He has been helping keep the fire in the tipi field at Glastonbury Festival since the early nineties.

Dr Sue Greener BA, MBA, EdD, FHEA,
Chartered Fellow CIPD
*Brighton Business School, University of Brighton*

Sue Greener is a Principal Lecturer at Brighton Business School, University of Brighton, UK. She conducts research in the fields of technology enhanced learning, blended learning and reflective learning and is particularly interested in developing teachers' and trainers' interest and competencies in these areas. She is editor of the research journal Interactive Learning Environments.

Sue leads university Business and Management programmes, teaches blended and fully online courses in Research Methods and is Subject Examiner for a Business distance learning programme.

Her publications can be found at:
https://sueg1.wordpress.com/sueg-publications-and-presentations/

# List of Contributing Authors

**Mehbub Anwar**, SMART Infrastructure Facility, University of Wollongong, Australia

**Patricia Alejandra Behar**, Graduate Program in Computer Education (PPGIE) at Federal University of Rio Grande do Sul (UFRGS), Av. Paulo Gama, Porto Alegre, Brazil

**Johan Breytenbach**, Department of Information Systems, University of the Western Cape, Bellville, South Africa

**Leona Craffert**, Western Cape CoLab for eInclusion and Social Innovation, University of the Western Cape, Bellville, South Africa

**Nurdilek Dalziel**, Henry Grunfeld Foundation, ifs University College, London, United Kingdom

**Suzanne Elayan**, Centre for Information Management, Loughborough University, UK

**Nick Ellison**, Department of Social Policy and Social Work, University of York, York, UK

**Evridiki Fioratou**, University of Dundee School of Medicine, Dundee, UK

**Eleanor Hothersall**, University of Dundee School of Medicine, Dundee, UK

**Nazerin Ibrahim**, Multimedia University, Malaysia

**Ismawati Noor Jaafar**, Department of Operations and Management Information Systems, Faculty of Business and Accountancy, University of Malaya, Kuala Lumpur, Malaysia

**Thomas Jackson**, Centre for Information Management, Loughborough University, UK

**Anelise Jantsch**, Graduate Program in Computer Education (PPGIE) at Federal University of Rio Grande do Sul (UFRGS), Av. Paulo Gama, Porto Alegre, Brazil

**Jaroslava Kubátová**, Palacký University, Olomouc, Czech Republic

**Natalie Lafferty**, University of Dundee School of Medicine, Dundee, UK

**A. von Lunen**, Centre for Information Management, Loughborough University, UK

**Leticia Rocha Machado**, Graduate Program in Computer Education (PPGIE) at Federal University of Rio Grande do Sul (UFRGS), Av. Paulo Gama, Porto Alegre, Brazil

**Annalisa Manca**, University of Dundee School of Medicine, Dundee, UK

**Andrew McCusker**, SMART Infrastructure Facility, University of Wollongong, Australia

**Ann O'Brien**, Centre for Information Management, Loughborough University, UK

**Johanne Orchard-Webb**, School of Environment and Technology, University of Brighton, UK

**Pascal Perez**, SMART Infrastructure Facility, University of Wollongong, Australia

**Tenku Putri** Norishah Tenku Shariman, Multimedia University, Malaysia

**Alisdair Smithies**, University of Dundee School of Medicine, Dundee, UK

**Kardi Somerfield**, University of Northampton, United Kingdom

**Ainin Sulaiman**, Department of Operations and Management Information Systems, Faculty of Business and Accountancy, University of Malaya, Kuala Lumpur, Malaysia

**Martin Sykora**, Centre for Information Management, Loughborough University, UK

**Othman Talib**, University Putra Malaysia, Malaysia

**José Valdeni de Lima**, Graduate Program in Computer Education (PPGIE) at Federal University of Rio Grande do Sul (UFRGS), Av. Paulo Gama, Porto Alegre, Brazil

**Kobus Visser**, Faculty of Economic and Management Sciences, University of the Western Cape, Bellville, South Africa

**Anne Marie Warren**, Department of Operations and Management Information Systems, Faculty of Business and Accountancy, University of Malaya, Kuala Lumpur, Malaysia

**Piotr Wiśniewski,** Department of Corporate Finance, Warsaw School of Economics, Poland

# Introduction to Leading Issues Social Media

## Preface

Social media is a field of growing importance in our understanding of society, business and education. Emerging from the rapid adoption of internet technologies, social media is liable to grow even more ubiquitous, as the smart phone, tablet and other mobile platforms proliferate. Social media is of intense interest to business, the public sector, educators and analysts both as an exciting way of harnessing technology and widening participation, but also as the generator of big data – which offers a wealth of content for analysis.

Leading Issues in Social Media seeks to further our appreciation of the impact of social media by gathering papers presented by a range of academic voices. The volume came about as a result of the editors, Sue Greener and asher Rospigliosi, hosting the first European Conference on Social Media at the University of Brighton in 2014.

From those three days in which academics and practitioners gathered, debated, discussed and learned and the ensuing conversations there emerged these exciting papers that further our thinking about the leading issues in social media.

# Introduction to Leading Issues in Social Media for Business

**by Asher Rospigliosi**

Social media is accelerating the pace of change. The long term impacts of technological change, ICT change and internet change are all made most immediate in social media. It is the touch point between technologies, and the way we live.

For business, accelerating change brings opportunities and threats, and we can see the business impact of social media writ large in the dramatic valuations of Facebook, Instagram and Twitter. But these changes go deep into the nature of how firms understand and respond to their environment, how they communicate with customers and staff and the ideas they have access to.

The first wave of information systems transformation of business was business process re-engineering. This allowed the automation of many repetitive record keeping systems and the access to data across business processes, typified by the installation of enterprise resource planning systems.

The second wave, was the dot.com boom and the dramatic growth of e-business, which brought the opportunities of the internet to the attention of business. With e-business came a new role for customer input, increased choice and reduced transaction costs. Eventually there was much disintermediation (particularly of parts of the retail economy), and the emergence of the new super intermediaries of Amazon and Google.

Now we are well into the third wave, the social wave. Firms that recognise the central role that customers play in creating, curating and sharing content are finding great benefits from user generated value. Taking Instagram as an example, the users of Instagram are authors and consumers of digital content created and shared for free.

Away from the purely digital beneficiaries of the social media revolution, firms like Airbnb and Uber are harnessing the demand for personalised services and increased choice and using the power of social networks to recommend and share. Airbnb and Uber manage assets as physical as cars and houses using social media and social networks.

In the papers in this volume, we have sought to offer insight into areas of business transformation that will let the reader investigate where the increasing impact of social media may take business. Beyond the most dramatic emergence of high value companies driven by social media there are many quieter changes taking place. We have identified four changes to investigate.

The first change to consider is how firms share knowledge and learn. Social media allows easy access to questions, answers and comments from inside and from outside firms. This digitisation of "the conversation" allows a goal of knowledge management theorists to be realised: the externalisation of tacit knowledge.

The second change is to look at the impact of social media on how to sell and publicise. While digital marketing is well on the way to being the definitive means of marketing (in much the same way as e-business is becoming synonymous with business), the ways that social media allow individuals to market their assets are less well explored, and the case study of artists sharing pictures presents a dramatic example.

The third area explored in this business section is responding to customer complaints. The banking sector has faced a lot of bad publicity since the global financial crisis arose, and the study contained here, of how Barclays use social media to respond to customers raises a range of concerns and implications for firms who are facing complaint in a visible and networked social environment.

The fourth investigation is an analysis of the value that can be found in mining social media for intellectual capital. By reframing the perspective, the conversations between customers, employees and competitors can be seen as a rich seam of ideas.

We hope that it is this capacity to reframe the debate that will give the reader of this volume a dynamic sense of the leading business issues in social media.

# Better Understanding the Effect of Social Networking on Organisational Success

## Mehbub Anwar, Andrew Mccusker and Pascal Perez

SMART Infrastructure Facility, University of Wollongong, Australia

Originally published in the proceedings of ICICKM 2014

## Editorial Commentary

For business organisations, the goal of improved communications, internal and external has a great attraction. The need for flexibility in an organisation's response to the fast changing environment, is directly related to how employees share knowledge and learn. In this paper, Anwar et al reframe important knowledge management concerns, in the light of the affordances of social networks. Drawing on recent studies they propose two rich models, integrating 14 key variables. These models allow us to explore the influence of social networks on organisational performance. Key outcomes of individual competence and the resultant organisational learning are evaluated for how they support growth in knowledge sharing and an increase in organisational flexibility.

If organisations are to respond to the increased speed of change in the market and the impact of customer networks and the impact of word of mouth, they will need to find ways to bring understanding from outside the organisation into the learning within the organisation. Anwar's models offers a plausible way to consider the key criteria.

**Abstract:** Social networking (SN) is widely believed to offer business and organisations a powerful means to improve communication with customers, internal processes and overall performance. Unfortunately, there is only limited and anecdotal evidence about the way SN can durably influence various components and functions within an organisation. Thus, this paper aims to develop a conceptual model of influence based on a comprehensive literature review. Our model states that organisational success strongly depends upon socialisation and collaboration amongst individuals within an organisation while individual successes combine to form a permanent adaptation capability within the organisation. The adaptation capability itself proceeds to organisational success through knowledge transfer and sharing of a wide range of competencies that can respond to the changing environment. Based on these premises, a recursive impact model (without feedback effect) is proposed. Then, this model is extended to a non-recursive impact model to understand feedback effects of key variables on SN and organisational performance. The recursive and non-recursive models contribute to a better understanding of the effect of SN on organisational success. This understanding may give decision-makers new insights into an effective use of SN as part of a customer-centric service strategy. Therefore, the contribution of this paper is two-fold: (i) it demonstrates a better understanding of SN from the perspective of organisational performance; and (ii) it models an impact relationship between SN and organisational performance through knowledge management and organisational learning considered with and without feedback effect.

**Keywords:** social network, knowledge management, adaptation capability, flexible strategy, organisational performance, competency building

# 1. Introduction

Today most organisations use internal social networks (SN) to share knowledge, experience and expectations amongst employees. These platforms also have the ability to link internal and external social networks. The speed at which the shared information travels is beyond the control of the organisation. Every employee, customer and supplier has become a reflection on how the organisation functions and operates. For better or for worse, power has shifted from what an organisation wants to relay to the public (social communication), to what employees, customers and suppliers say about the company (social engagement). This transfer of power has impacted organisations on all levels. Early adapters of SN have accepted the power shift and harnessed the influence of social networks to their advantage.

In practice, SN expands the number of business or social contacts by making connections through individuals and groups across the organisation and beyond. Today, the ubiquitous spread of the internet has helped SN to become the most powerful means to improve communication of information, knowledge sharing and, ultimately, overall performance (Martin and Bavel 2013; Andriole 2010).

Albeit a growing corpus of anecdotal evidence about the benefits of SN, many organisations still fail to take advantage of it due to their limited understanding of the relationships between SN's characteristics and organisational performance. Therefore, this paper aims to (i) demonstrate a better understanding of SN from the perspective of organisational performance; and (ii) develop a conceptual model of influence (with and without feedback) between SN and organisational performance, through knowledge management and organisational learning.

# 2. Past studies

SN equips employees with knowledge and skills and thus play very important role in improving the performance of 21st century organisations. Essence of these variables is becoming very popular for managerial performance study in recent years described in Table 1.

Table 1    Summary of studies related to SN, knowledge management and organisational performance

| Issues/dimensions | Findings | Sources |
|---|---|---|
| SN and organisation | Individual's competence varies on the shape and size of his/her SN and it (competence) plays role to manage organisation efficiently and become more profitable. | Zyl (2008) |
| SN and knowledge management in supply chains | The SN model that establishes a relationship among the companies along with supply chain, exchanges the knowledge to create specific capabilities in organisational management. | Capo-Vicedo et al. (2011) |
| CEO's SN and organisational performance | CEOs' SN capability influences the organisational positive performance through knowledge and strategic flexibility. | Fernandez-Perez et al. (2012a) |
| Knowledge conversion and SN in team performance | Interaction through SN between team members and intra-organisational networks contribute to team performance and ultimately organisational performance. | Janhonen and Johanson (2011) |

*(Continued)*

Table 1    (*Continued*)

| Issues/dimensions | Findings | Sources |
|---|---|---|
| Social capital, knowledge transfer and performance | Knowledge transfer acts as an instrument for developing social capital and organisational positive performance. | Maurer et al. (2011) |
| Knowledge management in small and medium enterprises | Social capital and motivation-opportunity-ability models are useful to investigate the human factors to characterise knowledge sharing from both social and technological dimensions perspective. | Chen et al. (2012) |
| Networks in firm performance | Strong and heterogeneous network improve innovation towards performance. | Gronum et al. (2012) |
| Knowledge management and firm performance | An intensive application of knowledge available in firms and obtained from external sources impacts positively on performance. | Vaccaro et al. (2010) |
| SN and organisational knowledge sharing | SN motivates a person to wish to exchange the knowledge that contributes to the organisational performance. | Chow and Chan (2008) |
| Knowledge sharing and firm innovation capability | Individual factors such as enjoyment in helping others and knowledge self-efficacy and the organisational factor such as top management support influence knowledge-sharing processes significantly and thus improve innovation capability of the firms. | Lin (2007) |
| Strategic flexibility and SN | The size of SN can affect strategic flexibility positively and the effects vary if previously the organisation is involved in a process of strategic change. | Fernandez-Perez et al. (2012b) |

# 3. Motivating of understanding

According to most studies above, SN connections enable collaborative work and allow sharing of ideas, knowledge and information among the members of these social groups. In turn this kind of sharing behaviour plays an important role in generating solutions and identifying problems or opportunities. Hence, SN can be regarded as a potential key contributor to organisational performance.

Jonhonen and Johanson (2011) argue that SN plays an increasing role in knowledge creation and individual competency, leading to improved performance for the organisation. Knowledge creation provides an intangible resource that enhances organisational capability to adapt to the changing environment (Nonaka et al. 2006). Knowledge creation and management is becoming a very important and popular tool in the measuring of organisational success (Kilduff and Brass 2010) Sharing and transferring knowledge are key aspects of effective organisational management in mission achievement. Organizations should create the situation where SN can act as a tool to enhance individual competence to the positive benefit of organisational performance (Salas et al. 2008).

SN provides robust links for information and complex knowledge which is difficult to transfer (Hansen 1999). The ability of process to transfer and share knowledge gained from SN becomes critical. Therefore, there are some researchers who have emphasised the importance of organisational integration mechanisms to enable knowledge dissemination from outside and inside the organisation (Fernandez-Perez et al. 2012a; Van den Bosch et al. 1999). As a result, individual capability can be enriched through knowledge acquisition and creation that can be transferred, shared and exploited to achieve adaptation within the organisation. Therefore employees' participation in learning networks structured along SN lines should be encouraged as the developing capability and adaptive capacities accrued by the individual can be valuable to organisational performance.

Basically, adaptation capability synthesises current and acquired knowledge to enhance individual development beyond present requirements. The knowledge gained by individuals acts to boost business agility. The flexible strategy option is an organisational ability to respond to the changing environment and thus organisational performance can be enhanced (Hitt et al. 1998). New information and knowledge are critical to be adopted in appropriate ways. Therefore, knowledge should be structured and disseminated with a view to build individual's capability in a manner that supports rapid application by the organisation. These capabilities can provide the organisation with multiple assessments of the value of its own information and knowledge, explaining why some organisations move more quickly into new strategic actions (Eisenhardt and

Martin 2000). Shimizu and Hitt (2004) claimed that flexible strategy can be a key response to changing environment and an important contributor to the existence of firms or organisations within the competitive market. It is a strong indicator that a wide range of flexible strategies can support organisations and individuals to perform effectively and ultimately, success.

# 4. A conceptual model of influence

In this section, we present a recursive model (without feedback effect) of influence of SN on organisational performance mediated through individual competency and organisational learning. Figure 1 shows the connections between 14 key variables and their relationships, stated as 17 hypothetical propositions.

## 4.1. SN and knowledge creation

Firms or organisations should be active actors in the process of knowledge creation by promoting the interaction between and among individuals and groups for developing new capabilities (Farshchi and Brown 2011). Despite the relative ease of knowledge creation at an individual level, the greater challenge is in the ways that the organisation can promote SN/interactions among individual as well as groups, not only to facilitate the transfer of explicit knowledge but also to create tacit knowledge.

The development of SN within and outside organisations is necessary for the creation of individual competence and hence innovation. Many researchers refer to SN as an important source of knowledge creation and acquisition (Nonaka 2007). In addition, several authors have established a relationship between knowledge creation and network connections (Kleijnen et al. 2009). Thus, the flow of information from the SN may determine the knowledge creation capability. In the line of this discussion, the following proposition can be proposed:

*P1 – P2: SN is positively related to knowledge acquisition and creation.*

## 4.2. Knowledge creation and adaptation capability

Once knowledge is acquainted and created by employees, organisational capability is improved, defined as *adaptation capability* in this paper. This capability

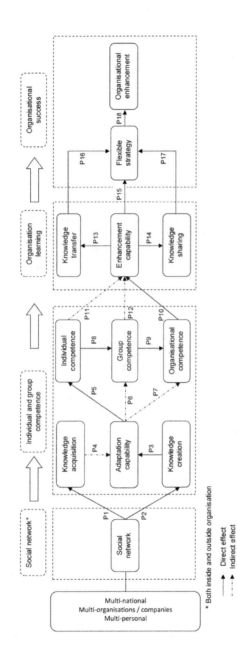

Figure 1 Recursive model showing the impact of social network on organizational performance

enables dissemination and transfer of the current and obtained knowledge (Eisenhardt and Martin 2000). To facilitate this kind of knowledge building process, organisations should establish intra and inter organisational mechanisms or systems that support the employees to acquire the knowledge to be disseminated throughout the organisation. Employees must disseminate their personal knowledge (Kogut and Zander 1992) including related to job nature and other than job into the organisational management process to increase the adaptation capability. Todorova and Durisin (2007) argued that the employees of organisation are powerful actors who influence knowledge building and sharing process to achieve organisational mission. Thus, employees are the main players in knowledge acquisition within the organisation (Jansen et al. 2005) and by the mean of this environment, the acquired knowledge can be disseminated throughout the organisations and adapted with the existing information and knowledge (Zahra and George 2002; Gupta and Govindarajan 2000). In this way, knowledge obtained from SN and other means can contribute to enrich the capability of employees to achieve the organisational goals as a whole. Thus, we propose that:

*P3-P4: Knowledge acquisition and creation has a positive effect on organisational adaptation capability.*

## 4.3. Adaptation and enhancement capability

When an organisation displays the Capability to readily adapt to it's environment it is an indication of organisational enhancement. That means, organisational adaptation capability promotes organisational enhancement capability. Sirmon et al. (2007) explains that a firm's adaptation capacity to environmental dynamism is very important to enhance organisational capability and it increases new knowledge which when applied leads to organisational success. The use of social integration process marks a line between adaptation and transformation and thus increased enhancement capability (Zahra and George 2002). This process may impact on strategic formulation consensus and indicate strategic priorities. Employees are encouraged to discuss and exchange conflicting views and demands associated with organisational performance. Such conflicting argument helps to resolve conflicting situations related to organisational strategies (Jansen et al. 2009). Thus, adaptation capability is being treated as an organisational determinant of the level of enhancement capability. Jansen et al. (2005) observes that organisational adaptation ability can contribute to enhance organisational ability. However, we propose that adaptation capability contributes to improve the individual competence which again promotes group competence and finally organisational competence is increased as a whole. So the following proposition is derived:

> P5-P12: *Adaptation capabilities are positively related to enhancement capability via the development of individual, group and organisational competence.*

## 4.4. Enhancement capability and knowledge transfer and sharing

Currently, knowledge sharing across the organization is rising in importance. There are some researches that focus how the technological development can play role in knowledge management (Alavi and Tiwana 2003) and also some describe how managers and supervisors can play a critical role in knowledge management and knowledge sharing (Carmeli et al. 2011; Carmeli and Waldman 2010; Bryant 2003). Researches related to the role of employees in knowledge management suggest that the effectiveness of knowledge sharing depend on the capability of the employee themselves. (Carmeli et al. 2011; Srivastava et al. 2006). Troy et al. (2001) understood that an open and flexible communication system could lead to greater knowledge sharing. Similarly, groups that had cooperative norms were more likely to share knowledge and develop better and more innovative solutions (Tjosvold et al. 2009). An enhanced capable employee (i.e. organisational leader) is more instrumental in developing an environment that help to cultivate the knowledge transfer and sharing practice in appropriate way for organisational betterment.

Organisational leaders carefully attend to the need for facilitating knowledge creation and sharing process to enhance organisational creativity and innovation (Collins and Smith 2006). Specifically, organisations constantly seek ways to facilitate and enhance creative and innovative behaviours among their employees (Carmeli et al. 2013) and Chowdhury (2005) has pointed to the importance of knowledge sharing between employees within, across and outside organisation to enhance the capability of an organisation. Thus, for transferring or sharing the knowledge, employees should be developed so that they can be capable to do that in effective way. Therefore, employees, who are capable in modelling knowledge sharing, need to be motivated to exchange information, views and ideas with others within and outside the organisation. On the line of this discussion, the following proposition can be assumed:

*P13-P14: The enhancement capability influences the knowledge transfer and sharing motivation in positive way.*

## 4.5. Enhancement capability and flexible strategy

Flexible strategy formulation may be defined as the capacity of an organisational capability to identify the changes environment and to respond them appropriately from a wide range of strategy options (Shimizu and Hitt 2004). Sanchez (1995) has interpreted that organisations in flexible nature demonstrate both diversity in strategic response and quick shift from one to another strategy. Thus, strategic flexibility refers to an organisational ability to respond to uncertainties by adjusting its objectives and strategies with the support of information, knowledge and capabilities. The organisation must transfer knowledge acquired from the source and edit to make it understandable, appropriate and useful to the organisation (Fernandez-Perez et al. 2012b). In this sense, organisational capability can be enhanced by the adaptation capacity of organisations through knowledge creation, sharing and transfer. So, the enhancemed capacity then contributes to the flexible strategy where applicable and thus, we propose that:

*P15: Enhancement capabilities positively contribute to flexible strategy.*

## 4.6. Knowledge transfer and sharing and flexible strategy

Knowledge is a critical organisational resource that provides a sustainable competitive advantage in a dynamic economy (Wang and Noe 2010). To achieve the competitive advantage, employees are required to be trained to enrich their capabilities. Organisations should also emphasise on an effective way to exploit the acquired knowledge that already exist within the organisation (Damodaran and Olphert 2000). Knowledge transfer and sharing between employees and within and across divisions/teams is exploited and capitalised as resource-based resource (Cabrera and Cabrera 2005). There is evidence in extant researches that knowledge transfer and sharing has positive impact on team performance, firm innovation capabilities, and firm performance (Mesmer-Magnus and DeChurch 2009; Lin 2007; Collins and Smith 2006; Arthur and Huntley 2005). Flexible strategy is one of the effective mechanisms to improve the organisational performance due to ability to cope with changing environment and the knowledge sharing and transfer are relevant to organisational performance and therefore, we assume that:

P16-P17: *The impact of knowledge transfer and sharing is positively related to flexible strategy*

### 4.7. Flexible strategy and organisational enhancement

Volberda (1996) indicated flexible strategy formulation as a strong variable that indicates the capability of an organisation to perform efficiently. Nadkarni and Narayaanan (2007) pointed out that strategic flexibility can contribute to a firm's performance significantly. Firms are strategically flexible in using their resources (Raff 2000) produce flexible strategic opportunities which push the organisation up the success ladder. These opportunities can help the organisations to formulate sustainable strategy for superior performance. Studies show that the lining up between strategy and changing environment can create a competitive environment and this competitive situation provides advantages for the organisational performance (Zajac et al. 2000). Thus, we propose that:

P18: *Flexible strategy has positive impact on organisational enhancement*

The model illustrated in Figure 1 does not maintain the feedback effect but undoubtedly there are some relevant feedback relationships that can enrich the understanding about the impact of SN on organisational performance. Accordingly, the recursive model is extended to a non-recursive impact model showing feedback effect in the following section.

# 5. Non-recursive impact model

For a better understanding of the impact of SN on organisational performance, a graphical notation (Figure 2) called non-recursive model showing the feedback impact is introduced in this section. This model follows the conceptual model described in Figure 1.

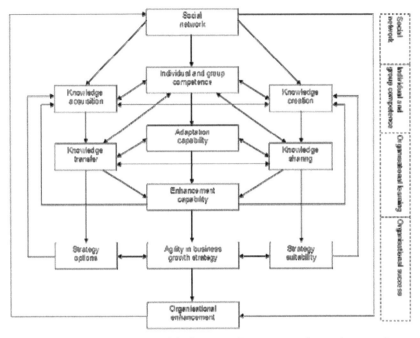

Figure 2   Non recursive model showing the impact of social network on organizational performance

SN acts as an input of knowledge creation as well as improvement of individual competence that is also impacted by the quality of knowledge acquisition and creation. On the other hand, individual competence may direct appropriate knowledge hunting. That means, knowledge acquisition and creation and development of individual competence as well as group competence are reciprocal to each other. Knowledge acquisition and creation may have a direct effect to knowledge sharing and transfer at organisational level. At the same time, the ability of individual and group competence influences how to share and create the knowledge and vice-versa. Thus, adaptation capability is influenced by individual and group competence too.

Once adaptation capability is improved, the consequence of it is to make enhancement capability better. Simultaneously, knowledge transfer and sharing contribute to the capability enhancement. Enhancement capability may offer feedback to knowledge acquisition and creation if enhancement capability is moderate or poor in terms of effectiveness for the performance. Thus, enhancement capability can also be revised or improved again through knowledge management and adaptation capability.

Knowledge transfer, knowledge sharing and enhancement capability have direct impact on strategy options, strategy values and flexible strategy respectively. Quality of knowledge acquisition and creation booster the strategy options with suitability that influence flexible strategy at the end. Flexible strategy may be enriched by a wide range of strategy options and suitability and vice-versa. Knowledge acquisition can also be influenced by strategy option directly to redesign it as per requirement. Similarly, knowledge creation is affected by the direct influence of strategy suitability.

Finally, a wide range of strategy options can play crucial role for the organisational success because of its ability to respond to the changing environment. Thus, flexible strategy contributes significantly to the improvement of organisational performance. If desirable performance is not achieved, it should be connected with SN networks at the top as a feedback and then mediated throughout all variables described above.

# 6. Implications of models for business practitioners

Our proposed conceptual model of influence can give the organisational decision makers (i.e. managers) new insight into the SN structures within the organisation, leading to more effective information management and organisational learning. Today's era of digital society requires managers who can confront customer-focused services based on perceived knowledge and foster strategic flexibility to achieve improvements in organisational performance. The knowledge can be nourished and updated by social media such as Facebook, Twitter etc. However, managers sometimes may fail to achieve sustainable competitive advantage due to their limited understanding related to the influence of knowledge (perceived via social media) and strategic flexibility (wide range of options) in the relation between SN and organisational performance. Thus, the models have several implications for business practitioners. *First,* organisations must foster SN that is appropriate to their competitive interests or needs. The 'right' manager with 'right' SN could access relevant and new information and knowledge, ultimately contributing to improvement of organisational performance. *Second,* the manager should encourage knowledge acquisition, implementation and transformation and use of new relevant knowledge through adaptation and enhancement capabilities. It encourages modern organisational structures and stimulates organisational flexibility to inspire better knowledge transfer. *Third,* managers can make adaptation to the changing environment and establish positive dynamics to encourage collaborative actions through flexible strategy. *Finally,* due to the increased speed of change in market environments, higher competition, and narrower profit margins, the concept of flexibility of strategy option has emerged. Both efficient performance and flexibility become an important source of competitive advantage to organisations. Therefore, organisational managers can be realised by our proposed models that how high-performing organisations can be built by adopting a mixed strategy of flexibility by examining SN knowledge management. In turn, this kind of co-creation behaviour plays an important role in generating solutions and identifying problems or opportunities in organisational domain. Hence, our model of influence can be regarded as a potential key pathway to organisational performance which is the expectation of managers indeed.

Concisely, in providing valued products and customer service, managers, with the aid of interfacing social network tools, can engender greater relevance in deliberation on customer needs within their organisations. Our model will assist managers to track that the customer view penetrates deep within their organisations, that lessons and learned and that knowledge on the customer views permeates the whole organisation and leads to rapid up take within their culture. Agility in responding to customer needs is a key success factor today and our model allows an understanding to be gained on the depth and breadth of activity in relation to knowledge and learning of customer opinion.

# 7. Conclusions

The two models presented above rely upon four inter-related components: (i) SN; (ii) individual and group competency; (iii) learning organisation; and (iv) organisational success. The models indicate SN as a foundation to achieve organisational objective via knowledge management and organisational learning. It is also noted that SN cannot contribute directly to the organisational success unless adaptation and enhancement capability are established through other strategic variables described in the models. Thus, this study investigated a better understanding of SN that influences the process of organisational success. Eighteen propositions have been indicated in the models. It is believed that the propositions would help business managers to identify the motivational elements that could encourage organisation to work on it. These propositions introduce organisational learning initiatives in order to strengthen the SN as an input of organisational self-learning competence towards organisational success.

# References

Alavi, M. and Tiwana, A. (2003) "Knowledge Management: The Information Technology Dimension". In M. Easterby-Smith and M. Lyles (Eds.), *Organizational Learning*, Blackwell Press, London, pp 103–120.

Andriole, S.J. (2010) "Business Impact of Web 2.0 Technologies", *Communications of the ACM*, Vol. 53, No. 12, pp 67–79.

Arthur, J.B. and Huntley, C.L. (2005) "Ramping Up the Organizational Learning Curve: Assessing the Impact of Deliberate Learning on Organizational Performance under Gainsharing", *The Academy of Management Journal*, Vol. 48, No. 6, pp 1159–1170.

Bryant, S.E. (2003) "The Role of Transformational and Transactional Leadership in Creating, Sharing and Exploiting Organizational Knowledge", *Journal of Leadership & Organizational Studies*, Vol. 9, No. 4, pp 32–44.

Cabrera, E.F. and Cabrera, A. (2005) "Fostering Knowledge Sharing Through People Management Practices", *The International Journal of Human Resource Management*, Vol. 16, No. 5, pp 720–735.

Capo-Vicedo, J., Mula, J. and Capo, J. (2011) "A Social Network-Based Organizational Model for Improving Knowledge Management in Supply Chains", *Supply Chain management: An International Journal*, Vol. 16, No. 5, pp 379–388.

Carmeli, A., and Waldman, D. A. (2010) "Leadership, Behavioral Context and the Performance of Work Groups in a Knowledge-Intensive Setting", *Journal of Technology Transfer*, Vo. 35, No. 4, pp 384–400.

Carmeli, A., Atwater, L. and Levi, A. (2011) "How Leadership Enhances Employees' Knowledge Sharing: The Intervening Roles of Relational and Organizational Identification", *Journal of Technology Transfer*, Vol. 36, No. 3, pp 257–274.

Carmeli, A., Gelbard, R. and Reiter-Palmon, R. (2013) "Leadership, Creative Problem-Solving Capacity, and Creative Performance: The Importance of Knowledge Sharing", *Human Resource Management*, Vol. 52, No. 1, pp 95–122.

Chen, C.W. Chang, M.L. and Tseng, C.P. (2012). "Human factors of knowledge-sharing intention among taiwanese enterprises: A model of hypotheses", *Human Factors and Ergonomics in Manufacturing & Service Industries*, 22 (4), pp. 362–371.

Chow, W.S. and Chan, L.S. (2008) "Social Network, Social Trust and Shared Goals in Organizational Knowledge Sharing", *Information & Management*, Vol. 45, No. 7, pp 458–465.

Chowdhury, S. (2005) "The Role of Affect-And Cognition-Based Trust in Complex Knowledge Sharing", *Journal of Managerial Issues*, Vol. 17, No. 3, pp 310–326.

Collins, C.J. and Smith, K.G. (2006) "Knowledge Exchange and Combination: The Role of Human Resource Practices in the Performance of High-Technology Firms", *The Academy of Management Journal*, Vol. 49, No. 3, pp 544–560.

Damodaran, L. and Olphert, W. (2000) "Barriers and Facilitators to the Use of Knowledge Management Systems", *Behaviour & Information Technology*, Vol. 19, No. 6, pp 405–413.

Eisenhardt, K.M. and Martin, J.A. (2000) "Dynamic Capabilities: What are They?", *Strategic Management Journal*, Vol. 21, No. 10–11, pp 1105–1121.

Farshchi, M.A. and Brown, M. (2011) "Social Networks and Knowledge Creation in the Built Environment: A Case Study", *Structural Survey*, Vol. 29, No. 3, pp 221–243.

Fernandez-Perez, V., Garcia-Morales, V.J. and Bustinza-Sanchez, O.F. (2012a) "The Effects of CEOs' Social Networks on Organizational Performance through Knowledge and Strategic Flexibility", *Personnel Review*, Vol. 41, No. 6, pp 777–812.

Fernandez-Perez, V., Fuentes-Fuentes, M.D.M. and Bojica, A. (2012b) "Strategic Flexibility and Change: The Impact of Social Networks", *Journal of Management and Organization*, Vol. 18, No. 1, pp. 2–15.

Gronum, S., Verreynne, M.L. and Kastelle, T. (2012) "The Role of Networks in Small and Medium-Sized Enterprise Innovation and Firm Performance", *Journal of Small Business Management*, Vol. 50, No. 2, pp 257–282.

Gupta, A.K. and Govindarajan, V. (2000) "Knowledge Flows Within Multinational Corporations", *Strategic Management Journal*, Vol. 21, No. 4, pp 473–496.

Hansen, M.T. (1999) "The Search-Transfer Problem: The Role of Weak Ties in Sharing Knowledge Across Organization Subunits", *Administrative Science Quarterly*, Vol. 44, No. 1, pp 82–111.

Hitt, M.A., Keats, B.W. and DeMarie, S.M. (1998) "Navigating in the New Competitive Landscape: Building Strategic Flexibility and Competitive Advantage in the 21st Century", *The Academy of Management Executive*, Vol. 12, No. 4, pp 22–42.

Janhonen, M. and Johanson, J.E. (2011) "Role of Knowledge Conversion and Social Networks in Team Performance", *International Journal of Information Management*, Vol. 31, No. 3, pp 217–225.

Jansen, J.J.P., Tempelaar, M.P., Van den Bosch, F.A.J, and Volberda, H.W. (2009) "Structural Differentiation and Ambidexterity: The Mediating Role of Integration Mechanisms", *Organization Science*, Vol. 20, No. 4, pp 797–811.

Jansen, J.J.P., Van Den Bosch, F.A. and Volberda, H.W. (2005) "Managing Potential and Realized Absorptive Capacity: How Do Organizational Antecedents Matter?",

*Academy Management Journal*, Vol. 48, No. 6, pp 999–1015.

Kilduff, M. and Brass, D.J. (2010) "Job Design: A Social Network Perspective", *Journal of Organizational Behaviour*, Vol. 31, No. 2–3, pp 309–318.

Kogut, B. and Zander, U. (1992) "Knowledge of the Firm, Combinative Capabilities, and the Replication of Technology", *Organization Science*, Vol. 3, No. 3, pp 383–97.

Lin, H.F. (2007) "Knowledge Sharing and Firm Innovation Capability: An Empirical Study", *International Journal of Manpower*, Vol. 28, No. 3/4, pp 315–332.

Martin, A. and Bavel, R.V. (2013) *Assessing the Benefits of Social Networks for Organizations*, Publications Office of the European Union, Spain.

Maurer, I., Bartsch, V. and Ebers, M. (2011) "The Value of Intra-Organizational Social Capital: How It Fosters Knowledge Transfer, Innovation Performance, and Growth", *Organization Studies*, Vol. 32, No. 2, pp 157–185.

Mesmer-Magnus, J.R. and DeChurch, L.A. (2009) "Information Sharing and Team Performance: A Meta-Analysis", *Journal of Applied Psychology*, Vol. 94, No. 2, pp 535–546.

Kleijnen, M. Lievens, A. Ruyter, K. de and Wetzels, M. (2009) "Knowledge Creation through Mobile Social Networks and its Impact on Intentions to Use Innovative Mobile Services", *Journal of Service Research*, Vol. 12, No. 1, pp 15–35.

Nadkarni, S. and Narayanan, V.K. (2007) "Strategic Schemas, Strategic Flexibility, and Firm Performance: The Moderating Role of Industry Clockspeed", *Strategic Management Journal*, Vol. 28, No. 3, pp 243–270.

Nonaka, I. (2007) "The Knowledge-Creating Company", *Harvard Business Review*, July-August.

Nonaka, I., Krogh, G.V. and Voelpel, S. (2006) "Organizational Knowledge Creation Theory: Evolutionary Paths and Future Advances", *Organization Studies*, Vol. 27, No. 8, pp 1179–1208.

Raff, D.M.G. (2000) "Superstores and the Evolution of Firm Capabilities in American Bookselling", *Strategic Management Journal*, Vol. 21, No. 10–11, pp 1043–1059.

Salas, E. Cooke, N.J. and Rosen, M.A. (2008) "On Teams, Teamwork, and Team Performance: Discoveries and Developments", *Human Factors: The Journal of the Human Factors and Ergonomics Society*, Vol. 50, No. 3, pp 540–547.

Sanchez, R. (1995) "Strategic Flexibility in Product Competition", *Strategic Management Journal*, Vol. 16, No. S1, pp 135–159.

Shimizu, K. and Hitt, M.A. (2004) "Strategic Flexibility: Organizational Preparedness to Reverse Ineffective Strategic Decisions", *The Academy of Management Executive*, Vol. 18, No. 4, pp 44–59.

Sirmon, D.G., Hitt, M.A. and Ireland, R.D. (2007) "Managing Firm Resources in Dynamic Environments to Create Value: Looking Inside the Black Box", *Academy of Management Review*, Vol. 32, No. 1, pp 273–292.

Srivastava, A., Bartol, K.M. and Locke, E.A. (2006) "Empowering Leadership in Management Teams: Effects on Knowledge Sharing, Efficacy, and Performance", *The Academy of Management Journal*, Vol. 49, No. 6, pp 1239–1251.

Tjosvold, D., Yu, Z. and Wu, P. (2009) "Empowering Individuals for Team Innovation in China: Conflict Management and Problem Solving", *Negotiation and Conflict Management Research*, Vol. 2, No. 2, pp 185–205.

Todorova, G. and Durisin, B. (2007) "Absorptive Capacity: Valuing A Reconceptualization", *The Academy of Management Review*, Vol. 32, No. 3, pp 774–786.

Troy, L.C., Szymanski, D.M. and Varadarajan, P.R. (2001) "Generating New Product Ideas: An Initial Investigation of the Role of Market Information and Organizational Characteristics", *Journal of the Academy of Marketing Science*, Vol. 29, No. 1, pp 89–101.

Vaccaro, A., Parente, R. and Veloso, F.M. (2010) "Knowledge Management Tools, Inter-Organizational Relationships, Innovation and Firm Performance", *Technological Forecasting & Social Change*, Vol. 77, No. 7, pp 1076–1089.

Van den Bosch, F.A.J., Volberda, H.W. and de Boer M. (1999) "Coevolution of Firm Absorptive Capacity and Knowledge Environment: Organizational Forms and Combinative Capabilities", *Organization Science*, Vol. 10, No. 5, pp 551–568.

Volberda, H.W. (1996) "Toward the Flexible Form: How to Remain Vital in Hypercompetitive Environments", *Organizational Science*, Vol. 7, No. 4, pp 359–374.

Wang, S. and Noe, R.A. (2010) "Knowledge sharing: A Review and Directions for Future Research", *Human Resource Management Review*, Vol. 20, No. 2, pp 115–131.

Zahra, S.A. and George, G. (2002) "Absorptive Capacity: A Review, Reconceptualization, and Extension", *The Academy of Management Review*, Vol. 27, No. 2, pp 185–203.

Zajac, E.J., Kraatz, M.S. and Shortell, S.M. (2000) "Modelling the Dynamics of Strategic Fit: A Normative Approach to Strategic Change", *Strategic Management Journal*, Vol. 21, No. 4, pp 429–55.

Zyl, A.S.V. (2008) "The Impact of Social Networking 2.0 on Organisations", *The Electronic Library*, Vol. 27, No. 6, pp 906–918.

# Social Media and Open Innovation – a Systemic Approach to Commercialisation of Socio-economic Solutions

**Leona Craffert[1], Kobus Visser[2] and Johan Breytenbach[3]**
[1]Western Cape Colab for eInclusion and Social Innovation, University of the Western Cape, Bellville, South Africa [2]Faculty of Economic and Management Sciences, University of the Western Cape, Bellville, South Africa [3]Department of Information Systems, University of the Western Cape, Bellville, South Africa

lcraffert@uwc.ac.za; kvisser@uwc.ac.za; jbreytenbach@uwc.ac.za

Originally published in the Proceedings of ECSM 2014

## Editorial commentary

How can companies share the cost of innovation without risking loss of intellectual property? This dynamic case study from South Africa charts a bold attempt to foster a system in which co-creation occurs in facilitated public private partnership.

Craffert et al chart the development of a CodeJam in South Africa in which companies set aside competitive concerns to address specific socio – economic challenges. Working with academics they draw in the resulting ideas to develop products in a moderated, safe incubation period. Social media was the both the means of negotiation and the instrument of moderation, giving all participants in this exercise in trust, access to a shared synergy, all too difficult to achieve in an un-mediated competitive environment.

The case offers a workable and visible model for using social media to support successful open innovation with exciting implications for cross-boundary and trans-disciplinary software development.

**Abstract:** This experimental case describes an example of a public-private partnership (PPP) to develop a collaborative model for open innovation using social media, with the purpose of addressing socio-economic challenges in the context of a developing country. Open innovation postulates the notion that ownership of processes should be acquired from other enterprises that can afford such levels of research investment, as well as utilising licensing and joint ventures to commercialise internally-generated innovations. However, this multiple channel process is often fraught with mistrust and lack of commitment amongst the participants.

This project proposes a systemic model that optimises innovation through social media and minimizes conflict in the commercialisation of open innovation. Although PPP is a fairly common and advocated approach to challenge complex socio-economic challenges, using social media adds to the complexity of dealing with intellectual property (IP) and/or commercial rights.

In an experimental process entitled "CodeJam 2013", PPP stakeholders (representing business, government, communities and academia) co-designed a collaborative process to develop and commercialise solutions for specific socio-economic challenges. Ascribing to the notion of open innovation, social media was used as the primary source of ideation. The premise for this experiment was that CodeJam 2013 could provide a safe, commercially non-threatening environment in which competitive and concurrent stakeholders could co-design optimum innovative solutions in collaboration with external (social media) and internal ideators, with the ultimate objective of establishing new paths to the market, i.e. commercialisation.

This process consisted of two distinct phases, namely a defined, neutral and shared intellectual property realm referred to as the co-creation phase, followed by a demarcated incubation phase during which partners negotiated for product development (and thus commercial/IP rights).

From the perspective of business (as a PPP partner/stakeholder) a number of outcomes related to the use of social media for open innovation have been identified, inter alia: limiting business risks typically associated with open innovation; the agreed "safe space" promoted optimal innovation as a result of reduced focus on IP rights; radical transgression of internal business boundaries as a benefit from "out"ternships; benefits for external ideators through learning that occurs as a result of intimate business engagement; realisation that problem complexity can be minimised through team participation; the diffusion of the innovation process across PPP boundaries; introducing the essence of "warm bodies" in the clinical processes of open innovation with social media; successful open innovation based on social media is reliant upon extensive co-creative collaboration, networking and shared responsibility from all stakeholders. In essence, this systemic approach to open innovation based on social media proved to be a viable model and alternative for the development and commercialisation of socio-economic solutions.

**Keywords:** Open innovation, social media, public-private partnerships, intellectual property, socio-economic challenges, commercialisation.

# 1. Background

## 1.1. Historical development

South Africa is lagging behind with respect to the level of digital competence of e-Readiness. According to the 2012 WEF Networked Readiness report of 142 countries, South Africa is at the 72nd place and not yet leveraging the potential benefits offered by ICT. This has serious implications for the country's ability to remain competitive within the global knowledge economy and to capitalise on the advantages posed by the digital economy.

Given the fact that South Africa follows the same "mobile and social media first" ICT development trajectory as other developing countries (Dutta & Bilbao-Osorio, 2012), various stakeholders representing government, business, academia and the community agreed to form a collaborative PPP to develop skills and capacity in the area of social innovation leveraging off social media and mobile technologies. As change-makers (Phills, Deiglmeier & Miller, 2008) the PPP agreed to co-design a new model, in an experimental manner, to address socio-economic challenges. The main principles that guided the process were shared ownership and shared responsibility based on relationships of trust.

# 2. Purpose of this paper

The purpose of this paper is to present a systemic model of work-in-progress that optimises innovation through social media and to report on the outcomes that minimizes conflict in the commercialisation of open innovation. Based on the work of Altman, Nagle and Tushman (2013) the innovation process observed and described here impacts on organisational openness, user innovation, community engagement, social media, all which have implications for organisations.

We propose a novel and systemic approach, as postulated by Sautet (2013) for open innovation in business (based on social media) to address socio-economic challenges. Our approach seeks to incorporate the structure of systemic processes (Visser & Craffert, 2013) in the context of a developing country, not only to generate interest in and support for the acquisition of digital knowledge, skills and competencies, but also that it may present opportunities for, *inter alia*, learning, experimentation, wealth creation, employment in a developer ecosystem.

The envisaged approach to a systemic model aims to follow a process almost diagonally opposed to the traditional methodology of developing solutions to challenges. A key initiative of the mentioned PPP is to leverage social innovation and human skills development off mobile technology and social media. Mitra and Abubakar (2011) refer to such initiatives as processes of "capacity creation", not only in the context of development and growth, but also in moving from levels of low to high productivity, the creation and adoption of new goods and services, developing new skills and creating new knowledge. In a South African context, the approach envisaged in this experiment is (in all probability) the first manifestation of a redirection of resources into human development.

The democratic nature of social media allows for the maximisation of idea generation and solution development as it accommodates cross-boundary interaction and collaboration of (internal and external) ideators in a non-threatening and commercially-safe environment. In this model, innovation precedes the negotiation of commercial rights. In other words, a developer ecosystem (Altman, Nagle & Tushman, 2012) acts as a framework in which an impartial environment is created wherein PPP stakeholders, including competing business organisations, create products/solutions that clients (and communities) may acquire through the marketplace (to address socio-economic challenges).

# 3. Literature review

Our proposed model (see Figure 1, section 4.2) builds on a diverse selection of topics from literature, including open innovation theory, public private partnerships (PPP), ownership and IP rights within innovation processes, and the use of social media and crowdsourcing as vehicles for co-operative innovation.

Open Innovation and PPP (Steps A-E of our model): Innovation processes are enhanced by the co-operation of competing stakeholders; co-opetition (Mention, 2011). Such co-operation, for the purpose of mutual commercial benefit, requires both public and private stakeholders to step outside traditional ownership boundaries (Altman, Nagle & Tushman, 2013). Open innovation theory, as postulated by Chesbrough, Vanhaverbeke and West (2008), allows for such public-private co-operation – including various levels of community engagement, but limits the usefulness of such arrangements to instances that draws innovation into the research and develop-

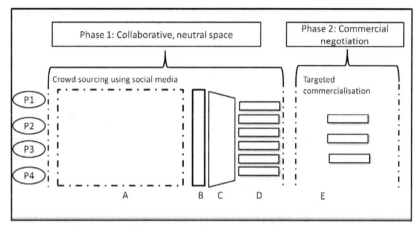

Figure 1    The phases of the outbound open innovation process

**Legend:**

P1-P4: Identified socio-economic problems to be addressed through social innovation; facilitating B2C interaction

Step A: Ideas composition "window" period of two weeks using crowd sourcing through social media

Step B: Period of evaluating and assessing opportunities using social media with full participation of PPP

Step C: Face-to-face ideation workshop with full participation of PPP

Step D: Teamwork based on solution-refinement, case development, apps development and prototyping

Step E: Commercial negotiation – still to be refined

ment processes of a large firm(s) – referred to as inbound open innovation (Dahlander & Gann, 2010). Examples of such inbound open innovation processes include the crowdsourcing of innovative solutions through ideas competitions, which results in a novelty driven competitive advantage for the co-operating stakeholders (Leimeister et al, 2009).

The problematic assumption underpinning co-operative inbound open innovation is that participating stakeholders will share (be able to contract on) the ownership of any resulting intellectual property (IP) product, or process (see Altman, Nagle & Tushman, 2013). As new fields of study, the relationships between: (i) ownership-related friction, (ii) the level of community engagement within innovation processes, and (iii) innovation processes targeted towards solving socio-economic problems have not been adequately addressed in literature.

Altman, Nagle and Tushman (2013) contend that a lack of clarity regarding IP laws and the effect of IP laws on ownership boundaries may have a negative impact on co-operative open innovation. Several IP researchers share concerns regarding the complexity of IP laws within multi-stakeholder processes that extend beyond the boundaries of the firm, as opposed to traditional shareholder ownership, as argued by Klein et al (2012).

The traditional view of open innovation, as being inbound and governed by ownership agreements, is reviewed in this article (see the descriptions of Steps A-D of our model in section 4.2).

Ownership conflict within open innovation processes: Moving closer to our model for minimizing conflict during open innovation and the commercialisation of socio-economic solutions, we note that a further cause of conflict within such PPP relationships is the tension between the various agendas (i.e. the internal strategies) of stakeholders. Drnevich and Croson (2013) observe that as stakeholders struggle internally to embed technology driven innovation as a strategy within their business models, whereas Wang, Yeung, and Zhang (2011) state that innovation processes within organizational boundaries are often deflated by issues of trust and ownership. Moreover, when stepping outside organizational boundaries into an open innovation space (see Steps A-D of our model), the multi-stakeholder and multi-disciplinary character of open innovation processes heighten this conflict.

Optimizing innovation using crowdsourcing via social media (Steps B and C of our model): Crowdsourcing via social media is a recognized form of inbound open innovation (Leimeister et al, 2009; Majchrzak & Malhotra, 2013). Libert and Spector (2010) describe open innovation as a proven method for optimizing innovation within firms. However, Spithoven, Clarysse and Knockaert (2011) warn that the innovation potential of social media can only be harnessed if the firm's innovation processes can absorb the large amount of input generated by this approach (refer to step B of our model).

Measuring the materialised results (impact) of crowdsourcing on innovation remains a complex challenge (Orlikowski & Scott, 2014).

Our model accommodates and contributes to the elements as discussed in the literature above, i.e. innovation through public private partnerships (PPP), ownership conflict and IP rights within innovation processes, and the use of social media and crowdsourcing as vehicles for co-operative innovation.

# 4. Method, structure and approach

## 4.1. Towards CodeJam 2013

CodeJam 2013 is a substantially revised version of CodeJam 2012, which was the first iteration of an experimental approach amongst a limited number of PPPs to develop (mobile) solutions for socio-economic and business (enterprise) challenges, by means of open innovation based on social media. It was conceptualised as an inbound social innovation process in which ideas/solutions developed by the community were to become part of the internal product development process of the business partner. The 2012 process required the upfront negotiation (contracting) of commercial rights with strict terms and conditions guiding the process. The limited success of the 2012 model as an inbound innovation process was the result of: the application of "strict business rules" (i.e. commercial process and rights) to an explorative 'sandbox environment"; solutions too narrowly defined for commercialisation; and, a lack of follow-through for good ideas. Apart from the development of skills in ideation, use of social media and mobile apps development, the 2012 process did not result in any solution that could be commercialised, or applied to address socio-economic challenges. However, the positive potential of the 2012 process motivated the PPPs to invest energy and resources to further develop and explore the model into a next round, referred to as CodeJam 2013.

As extracted from the literature, the CodeJam 2012 pre-agreement on ownership proved to be problematical, as too much focus was put on commercialisation at the expense of idea generation and idea development. The first lesson learned from our initial 2012 process, was that more investment was required to grow, develop and mature ideas, instead of stifling the process with ownership discussions and agreements; for example, the legal documentation of the first round is still under consideration by the various stakeholders.

Whereas the first round of CodeJam focused on idea generation for generic enterprise and community solutions, a clear lesson learned was that the open innovation process had to be embedded in the reality of the socio-economic context. Given the scarcity of resources in a developing country context, the

PPP realised that the challenges to be solved had to be present in, and had to be real for communities or community representatives.

This article focuses on the description of the CodeJam 2013 model.

The CodeJam PPP responsible for the 2013 model consisted of representatives of provincial and local government, an NGO (representing a large community), three universities, students and community members, 2 ICT vendors and 4 companies (of which 2 are listed on the local stock exchange). To become part of the PPP, stakeholders had to commit to participate in and contribute towards Phases 1 and 2 of the process. Phase 1 of the CodeJam process consisted of the neutral, collaborative (almost "educational") phase in which all stakeholders participated in the outbound social innovation process. Phase 2 (i.e. the competitive, business aspect of the process) focused on the selection of and investment in ideas/solutions for commercial purposes.

The precondition for CodeJam 2013 participation was based on the premise that participants would waive their conditions for IP and commercial rights during the first phase of the process, i.e. no contracting would take place before or during the innovation phase of the 2013 process. It was generally agreed that the terms for the eventual commercialisation of resultant solutions were to be postponed to Phase 2 of the process.

## 4.2. Description of the CodeJam 2013 approach/model

The two-phased CodeJam 2013 process is presented in Figure 1.

For the experiment, as briefly delineated above, our emphasis during Phase 1 was on creating an environment free from the conflicts typically associated with similar multi-stakeholder innovation processes, whereas Phase 2 was concerned with the processes of targeted commercialisation of the successful outcomes of Phase 1.

The "internal dynamics" of Phase 1 are briefly described below:

- Representatives of the government and the NGO sectors identified four real-life socio-economic challenges (P1-P4 in Figure 1) in the surrounding community which required innovative solutions. The challenges ranged from addressing transport difficulties to support for young job seekers. The representatives of the government departments (local and provincial) and the NGO committed themselves to take the refined ideas (mobile solution) forward. In principle this could require the provision of sponsorship for the incubation of ideas, acquiring venture capital, or to deploy the solution in their particular portfolio. This elicited the appetite from business as it provided them with an ideal opportunity to obtain insight into community (consumer) problems and community-developed solutions (social or open innovation). It has huge potential for business as this can facilitate and inform the B2C business strategy and provide fresh input/ sources into the innovation process.

- Based on the principles of crowd sourcing, community members between the ages of 18 - 25 were invited to propose solutions for these problems using the custom-build social media platform (see step A in Figure 1). In the guise of an 'ideas competition' the social media idea portal was open for 2 weeks for postings.

- Using the same idea portal, ideators were then afforded the opportunity to vote for and give a weighting to "popular" or feasible ideas. The stakeholders (PPP) participated in this process by adding to ideas, sharing research information to support or redirect ideas, or simply by indicating support for a particular line of thinking in this neutral, open innovation space (step B in Figure 1). The democratic nature of social media as platform made it possible for stakeholders to contribute across sector boundaries (business, community academia and government), as postulated by Phills, Deiglmeier and Miller (2008). Typically, this selection and refinement of ideas would happen within the internal R&D processes of a company.

- Given the magnitude of the ideas sourced via the social media platform, a face-to-face ideation workshop was introduced with the main objective being the optimal development and refinement of the ideas. Ideators had the choice to work in self-selected teams or as individuals. This step addressed the absorption capacity challenge posed by crowd sourcing (Spithoven, Clarysse and Knockaert, 2011). Atypical to crowd sourced inbound innovation (Leimeister et al, 2009), this step of the innovation process, happened "outside" the internal boundaries of the PPP further enhancing cross-boundary participation. As the result of the dilation of organisational boundaries during step B of the process - given the democratic nature of social media - cross-boundary participation followed naturally during this face-to-face workshop (step C).

- Step D required ideators/participants to work in teams to refine their solutions, build a business case for the solution, and translate the case into a mobile app, or a prototype for a mobile app. Participants were motivated to work in teams as CodeJam 2012 clearly demonstrated that innovation (and related learning, knowledge creation) is enhanced by multi-disciplinary collaboration (see Hearn & Bridgstock, 2009). As in steps B and C, ideators had open access to stakeholders for guidance and support.

- During steps A - D of the model, the stakeholders provided training to participants on mobile apps development (iOS, Android, prototyping), design thinking and business case development - a concept we referred to as *outernships*.
- Phase 1 of the CodeJam 2013 process was concluded with the presentation of the ideas to an evaluation panel comprising of the CodeJam 2013 PPP (stakeholders), to identify those solutions that best addressed the challenges. The entire first phase happened in a neutral, collaborative space (virtual and physical) outside the boundaries of any of the stakeholders' ownership; hence the reference to this model as an outbound open innovation process.

Although outside of the framework of this paper, the internal dynamics of Phase 2 are briefly described below:

- This phase of the CodeJam 2013 process is still unfolding - it is an area that requires detailed attention in the months to come. As agreed at the onset of the process, stakeholders could exercise the right to choose a particular solution with the view of commercialisation. The latter choice implies that commercial and IP right negotiations have occurred in a limited fashion, only with those individuals who formed part of the particular solution.
- In reality, the flow from Phase 1 to Phase 2 is not as linear as anticipated. The generated solutions varied in magnitude which calls for different methods of intervention towards commercialisation. For example, some solutions need to go into a pre-incubation phase to further develop the proposal or business case, whereas others require significant financial investment, which is the domain of venture capitalists.
- The PPP is currently in the process of developing and expanding Phase 2.

# 5. Outcomes

The addition of social media in a neutral innovation space contributed new insights and possibilities for PPPs to address socio-economic challenges in a systemic manner. These novel insights enabled the researchers to extract a number of outcomes which may impact positively on how PPPs can be structured to facilitate open innovation for socio-economic development. This also has implications for how business conducts open innovation to develop solutions. Although these outcomes have been observed and manifested in a developing country context, their impact is not restricted or limited to environments fitting that status only; rather, evidence suggests that the outcomes may be equally applicable in an industrial economy context.

The major outcomes of the study are described below:

- Applying social media in the innovation process facilitates the fusion and collaboration of PPPs (stakeholders) across boundaries, a process described by Phills, Deiglmeier and Miller (2008) as "dissolving sector (silo) boundaries." *Although parties agreed to collaborate, they still 'toil' within the boundaries of their respective silos.* The CodeJam 2013 model supports the notion that the democratic and open nature of social media as innovation platform enables parties/stakeholders to collaborate equally in an open, boundaryless space. Social media, therefore, contributes to dissolving sector boundaries amongst multiple parties in their effort to address socio-economic challenges.
- The neutral collaborative space outside the traditional stakeholder boundaries facilitated the unrestricted participation in the co-creation phase in view of creating the best solution for the problem. The CodeJam 2013 model, therefore, proposes the concept of *outbound innovation* as a potential viable model for structuring innovation initiatives. Outbound innovation as argued by Altman, Nagle and Tushman (2013), leaves the innovation outside the internal R&D sphere of individual stakeholders, which is in contrast to the typically observed classic open innovation (i.e. inbound innovation) that draws innovation into the firm.
- Outbound innovation, as proposed in this model, is a viable option under the condition that the collaborative space (steps A, B and C in Figure 1) is not restricted by IP and commercial requirements. As experienced during CodeJam 2013 the reduced focus on IP rights created a safe space free from the pressures of the profit motive which contributed to the pursuit of the primary objective, i.e. innovation (Altman, Nagle & Tushman, 2013). We argue that the cohesion of stakeholders during this process can be attributed to trust relationships and the commitment to be change makers (see: Wang, Yeung & Zhang, 2011; Phills, Deiglmeier & Miller, 2008).

- Open innovation based on social media can be significantly enhanced by allowing ideators to engage in face-to-face situations for idea development and refinement (step D - warm bodies in addition to cyber bodies/ideas). This argument counters the capacity absorption dilemma of companies to deal with the scope/magnitude of ideas generated by means of social media (Spithoven, Clarysse & Knockaert, 2011). This face-to-face interaction, open for participants and representatives of the PPP, provided the additional opportunity for stakeholders to add depth and wisdom to the idea refinement process. This agrees with the observation by Phills, Deiglmeier and Miller (2008) who state that *"thought leaders generate the kind of knowledge that can truly support the development of social innovation."*
- The safe, neutral space (provided in steps A-D) not only contributed towards the innovation process, but facilitated the stepping out of the typical silo mentality into an education-focused arena of transdisciplinarity (Hearn & Bridgstock, 2009) which is required for the development of solutions to complex problems.
- The radical transgression of silo (business and disciplinary) boundaries also enabled stakeholders to develop confidence in cross-boundary and transdisciplinary collaboration (e.g. co-operation, networking, and partnership formation, impact of synergistic allegiances and alliances) - a core skill that stands them in good stead in the growth and survival of their own businesses/endeavours.

# 6. Conclusions

This systemic approach to open innovation based on social media proved to be a viable model and alternative for the development and commercialisation of socio-economic solutions. The approach followed by the researchers was an attempt to present an alternative method of "doing things", i.e. novel combinations of skills, competencies and resources to achieve the desired/anticipated outcome: an optimised social innovation process, enriched by mobile and social media technologies, without the restrictions of ownership contracts.

Successes attributed to this approach are: (i) the ability of our model to promote the quality and social impact of innovation as the highest priority in a developing country context, with ownership, IP rights, and the internal strategies of stakeholders being managed as secondary concerns in a separate post-innovation contracting phase; and, (ii) the model's support for the notion that social media can be used to build multi-stakeholder partnerships, break down traditional silos of ownership, optimise innovation, and increase the absorption capacity of the innovation process.

This research project showed that a multi-stakeholder partnership (PPP) consisting of business, academia, government and the community not only creates a full array of positive outcomes manifested in new opportunities, business growth, individual advancement, but more so the commercialisation of hitherto profitable solutions for socio-economic challenges. Future avenues of research include the development of detailed guidelines for the second (contracting and commercialisation) phase of our model.

With its objective of proposing an implementable, systemic model that optimises innovation through social media and which minimizes conflict in the commercialisation of open innovation, this South African PPP moves us with clarity into a new direction that correlates with the literature, namely that innovation (social and otherwise) is optimised outside the boundaries of the firm, enriched by multi-stakeholder participation, and enhanced through social media.

# Acknowledgements

We wish to express our sincere gratitude to the CodeJam PPP for the opportunity to co-create, co-design and learn from this journey; in particular, our sincere appreciation goes to the following students who managed the CodeJam process on behalf of the PPP: Jignesh Patil, Chiunde Mwanza, Conal da Costa, Ziyaad Parker and Chad Williams.

# References

Altman, E.J. Nagle, F. and Tushman, M.L. (2013) Innovating without Information Constraints: Organizations, Communities, and Innovation When Information Costs Approach Zero, Working Paper 14-043, Harvard Business School, Boston.

Chesbrough, H., Vanhaverbeke, W. and West, J. (Eds.). (2008) *Open Innovation: Researching a New Paradigm,* Oxford University Press, Oxford .

Dahlander, L. and Gann, D. M. (2010) How open is innovation? *Research Policy,* Vol 39, No. 6, pp 699–709.

Drnevich, P. L. and Croson, D. C. (2013) Information Technology and Business-Level Strategy: Toward an Integrated Theoretical Perspective, *Management Information Systems Quarterly,* Vol 37, No. 2, pp 483–509.

Dutta, S. and Bilbao-Osorio, B. (2012) *The Global Information Technology Report 2012, Living in a Hyperconnected World*, World Economic Forum and INSEAD, Geneva.

Hearn, G. and Bridgstock, R. (2009). Educating for innovation, networks and transdisciplinarity in the knowledge economy, *ICERI2009 Proceedings*, p 463.

Klein, P.G., Mahoney, J.T., McGahan, A.M. and Pitelis, C.N. (2012) Who is in charge? A property rights perspective on stakeholder governance, *Strategic Organization*, Vol 10, No. 3, p 304.

Leimeister, J.M., Huber, M., Bretschneider, U. and Krcmar, H. (2009) Leveraging crowdsourcing: activation-supporting components for IT-based ideas competition, *Journal of Management Information Systems*, Vol 26, No. 1, pp 197–224.

Libert, B. and Spector, J. (2010) *We are smarter than me: how to unleash the power of crowds in your business*, Pearson Education, Upper Saddle River, New Jersey.

Majchrzak, A. and Malhotra, A. (2013) Towards an information systems perspective and research agenda on crowdsourcing for innovation, *The Journal of Strategic Information Systems*, Vol 22, No. 4, pp 257–268.

Mention, A.L. (2011) Co-operation and co-opetition as open innovation practices in the service sector: Which influence on innovation novelty? *Technovation*, Vol 31, No. 1, pp 44–53.

Mitra, J. and Abubakar, Y.A. (2011) Knowledge creation and human capital for development: the role of graduate entrepreneurship, *Education + Training*, Vol 53, No. 5, pp 462–479.

Orlikowski, W.J. and Scott, S.V. (2014) The Algorithm and the Crowd: Considering the Materiality of Service Innovation, *Management Information Systems Quarterly*, forthcoming 2014.

Phills, J.A., Deiglmeier, K. and Miller, D.T. (2008) Rediscovering social innovation, *Stanford Social Innovation Review*, Vol 6, No. 4, pp 34–43.

Sautet, F. (2013) Local and Systemic Entrepreneurship: Solving the Puzzle of Entrepreneurship and Economic Development, *Entrepreneurship Theory and Practice*, Vol 37, No. 2, pp 387–402.

Spithoven, A., Clarysse, B. and Knockaert, M. (2011) Building absorptive capacity to organise inbound open innovation in traditional industries, *Technovation*, Vol 31, No. 1, pp 10–21.

Visser, K. and Craffert, L. (2013) Social innovation and entrepreneurialism as co-producers of systemic entrepreneurship in a university-based intervention, 3rd Colloquium on Systemic Entrepreneurship, Institute of Applied Entrepreneurship, Coventry University, Coventry UK, March 5–6.

Wang, L., Yeung, J.H.Y. and Zhang, M. (2011) The impact of trust and contract on innovation performance: The moderating role of environmental uncertainty. *International Journal of Production Economics*, Vol 134, No. 1, pp 114–122.

# Enabling the Casual Entrepreneur: Artists and Artisans on Social Media

## Kardi Somerfield

University of Northampton, United Kingdom

Kardi.somerfield@northampton.ac.uk

Originally published in the Proceedings of ECSM 2014

## Editorial commentary

Social media as a contributor to the marketing mix is a topic attracting much attention in the business community, the increased emphasis on earned media and 'the conversation' highlighting the more participatory nature of much commercial content shared this way. But what impact is that having on the casual entrepreneur such as artists seeking a market for their work? In this closely focused paper Somerfield charts the participation of around 200 UK artists in a collaborative sharing and promotion of their art via twitter. From a simple premise, of posting and hashtagging a picture a day for a month emerged a complex and dynamic set of online and offline responses, including the planning of a physical exhibition.

Somerfield's case study focuses on the motivation and reward of participation and offers insight into the relationship between creativity, social media participation and emerging entrepreneurship. For the creative individual, this juxtaposition may herald new routes to market.

**Abstract:** Much has been made of the digital marketing mix and the way in which brands are moving from 'Paid' and 'Owned' digital media into 'Earned' (for example social media and online PR). We will consider the way in which individuals have used social media as their entry point to commercial activity. Furthermore the desire to share and possibly sell artworks and other made objects can be a catalyst for individuals to engage with social media for the first time. Using a case study approach, the research examines the fascinating case of #DrawingAugust on Twitter; over 200 artists, amateur and professional tweeting one drawing per day throughout August

2013. Some artists were seasoned Twitter users, while for others #DrawingAugust represented their first experience of this social media platform. The research examines the social, economic and unexpected consequences of the artists' participation in the event. The reach and influence of those taking part is considered using metrics such as retweets, favourites, mentions and follows. We go on to consider the traits of the entrepreneur and the role of social media in facilitating entrepreneurial behaviour among the respondents in this virtual community. An interesting aspect of the research is the extent to which the event facilitated both global and local relationships. At a local level we studied a group of artists from meeting through Twitter, then meeting in reality on the last day of August, through to planning a joint exhibition. An example of the internet 'acting as a kind of glue bringing communities together in all sorts of wonderful new ways' as Carswell discussed in his article (2013).

**Keywords:** social media, art social media, Twitter, virtual community

# 1. Introduction

Author and politician Douglas Carswell recently argued that 'The web is bringing society together, not tearing it apart' (2013). In the face of widespread cultural pessimism – 'We are constantly invited to believe that the country is going to the dogs' - he holds the belief that the internet is making the world a better place.

If we believe that our creative capital has value in our society, the visual arts and crafts make for an interesting lens through which to examine the impact of social media. Pictures have the particular quality of overcoming language boundaries, thereby making a global point of view possible. For many, their creative endeavour represents a passion or even a compulsion.

Much has been made of the digital marketing mix and the way in which brands are moving from 'Paid' and 'Owned' digital media towards 'Earned' - for example social media and online PR (Chaffey & Ellis-Chadwick, 2012). We will consider the way in which individuals have used social media as their entry point and are moving in the opposite direction – towards commercial activity. Furthermore the desire to share and possibly sell artworks and other made objects can be a catalyst for individuals to engage with social media for the first time – for some it answers the question 'What is Twitter for?'

Using a case study approach, the research examines the fascinating case of #DrawingAugust on Twitter; over 200 artists, amateur and professional tweeting one drawing per day throughout August. Some artists were seasoned Twitter users, while for others #DrawingAugust represented their first experience of this social media platform.

The research considers the role of social media in facilitating entrepreneurial behaviour among the respondents in this virtual community by mapping against entrepreneurial traits identified in the academic literature in this field. The study examines the social, economic and unexpected consequences of the artists' participation in the event. The depth of engagement with the online forum #DrawingAugust is measured using metrics such as retweets, favourites, mentions and follows. Further, the artists were surveyed on economic factors such as commissions and sales.

Soft measures were also considered including collaborations, friendships, feedback and confidence both in the use of Twitter and as an artist. Respondents were also surveyed about negative factors such as trolling and other unwelcome dialogue.

An interesting aspect of the research is the extent to which the event facilitated both global and local relationships. The global reach of artists through #DrawingAugust is discussed. At a local level we studied a group of artists from meeting through Twitter, then meeting in reality on the last day of August, through to planning a joint exhibition. An example of the internet 'acting as a kind of glue bringing communities together in all sorts of wonderful new ways' as Carswell discussed in his article (2013).

# 2. Background to #Drawing August

Early in 2013 two artists resolved to set themselves an artistic challenge. Deciding to commit to doing a drawing every day for a month, they considered when they would be able to devote this much time to such an enterprise. They agreed that August seemed the ideal month to do so.

"There are times in your life when you wish you had the chance to give some focus to a skill that you're trying to develop or refine. And a chance conversation with Wales Arts Review's Design Editor Dean Lewis (@OlderthanEvil) on Twitter was all it took to provide the idea for Drawing August." says DrawingAugust co-founder Jean Stevens (Wales Arts Review, 2013).

As early as May 2013 Dean Lewis started using the hashtag #DrawingAugust on Twitter as he and Jean Stevens (@JeanStevens4) started to promote the idea of a Twitter-based event whereby artists would post a photograph of their drawing every day throughout August. The Tweets would contain the searchable hashtag #DrawingAugust thereby creating a forum.

"It's great to see social media used for a positive purpose where people can provide a supportive environment to build networks, encourage others and help others gain confidence." Says Jean, "It's a big thing showing your drawings to the world for everyone to see, judge and potentially feedback. So, with more volunteers signing up every day, we sent out Tweets asking if anyone else wanted to join in."

As artists began to sign up by requesting that they be added to a list, they also began to promote the idea to other artists they knew, thereby creating a viral effect. By the start of August, over 200 artists had joined the initiative. During August 2013 as more and more content was posted and shared, the hashtag began to trend, and yet more artists joined in.

"We thought it would be great to get to 50 participants, then it went to 100, and so on, until we ended with 213 official participants and many more using the hashtag to comment on the work and the project as a whole" said Jean.

As can be seen in *Figure 1*, at its peak there were 1,216 instances of use of the hashtag in one day. Between 1.05.13 and 31.01.14 #DrawingAugust has been used on 33,260 occasions.

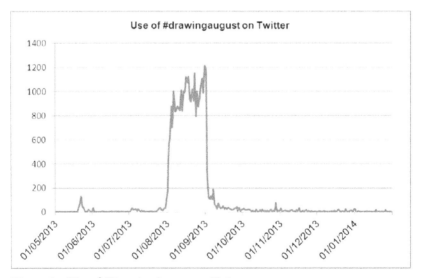

Figure 1    Use of #DrawingAugust on Twitter

#DrawingAugust was identified as a subject for a case for study as a result of direct involvement as an artist in the forum. The consequences of participation were profound, initially seeming like a trivial diversion but quickly attracting very high levels of engagement and activity on Twitter.

On the last day of August, six #DrawingAugust regulars who had not met before except online, met and drew together. The phenomenon of taking part in this online forum was discussed, and the artists resolved to put on a joint (real) exhibition in 2014. So the virtual became actual.

The experience of artwork being retweeted and favourited, as well as eliciting numerous favourable comments on a daily basis was very motivating. Furthermore, by diligently following everyone who interacted, it was possible to grow the following by over 600 in one month. As an external measure, the Kred score (a Social Media Influence metric) was monitored and was found to climb from 40 to 62. Sales to complete strangers also resulted, including some overseas.

It was this move into commercial activity that prompted the examination of the way in which engagement with this forum might have facilitated entrepreneurial behaviour in the participants.

# 3. Entrepreneurship

For the purposes of the study the emphasis has been placed on the traits of the entrepreneur. Early in attempts to define entrepreneurship, the importance of creativity and imagination were identified by writers as being key in the entrepreneurial process (Shackle 1970). Koh (1996) identified the four key traits as need for achievement, locus of control, propensity to take risks, and innovativeness. Ten years later Gurol and Atsan (2006) examined Koh's four characteristics and added another two: tolerance for ambiguity and self-confidence. In the research instances of these 8 entrepreneurial traits will be measured, although a limitation of the study is that causality is not easily captured.

The inclusion of the term 'Casual' Entrepreneur attempts to capture the concept that from the outset, it was clear from the nature of the dialogue that participants were not in the first instance using this forum on Twitter to sell their work, indeed to do so would be contrary to the etiquette of the community and would probably have been frowned upon by members had it occurred in an overt fashion.

# 4. Objectives

There were two main aims of this exploratory study;
  To better understand the way artists engaged with the #DrawingAugust forum

- Extent and depth of engagement
- Sentiment positivity / negativity

This research also attempted to establish whether or not artists participating in #DrawingAugust on Twitter were displaying entrepreneurial characteristics, and the extent to which participating in the online forum was facilitating that entrepreneurship. More specifically:

- Whether the artists are displaying entrepreneurial behaviour
- Is entrepreneurship developed through engagement in an online community?

# 5. Methodology

The research was conducted via a 40-item online questionnaire. The questionnaire was designed in GoogleForms, and the link to the online survey was distributed via Twitter.

## 5.1. Sampling

The population of interest for this research was the group of artists who had taken part in #DrawingAugust on Twitter – approximately two hundred identified themselves at the start.

The sampling strategy was part 'convenience' and part 'judgement' in that an open call to #DrawingAugust participants was published on Twitter as well as messages to named individuals known to have taken part. This effort was assisted by the support and active involvement of Dean Lewis @OlderThanEvil who was the organiser of #DrawingAugust and had the highest profile among the participants.

## 5.2. Questionnaire Design

The survey started with a screener question asking the participants whether they took part in #DrawingAugust. The next question qualified the extent of participation in terms of artwork posted to the forum – as it could be possible to consider oneself to have 'participated' by simply commenting or sharing on a post.

The next two questions related to the expectation and reality of participating in #DrawingAugust – these were designed as free text boxes to allow some data of a qualitative nature to be collected. They were also presented before any topics were discussed in order that they would constitute unprompted recall.

The third part of the survey consisted of a grid of 8 questions presented as a 5-point Likert Scale to ascertain the extent of agreement with a number of statements. These were mostly positive in nature but did include the question 'I have received negative or unpleasant dialogue about my work' in order that this possibility was taken into account.

The next section consisted of 6 questions which examine the subject's relationship with Twitter and other social media, and the extent to which that relationship changed of the course of #DrawingAugust, as well as an attempt to quantify followers and shares gained as a result of participation.

The fifth section of the survey contained classification questions such as demographic data likecourteage and gender. It also asked how they would classify themselves as an artist. Questions relating to the selling of work were in this section, and due to the sensitivity of this data options of 'prefer not to say' were introduced here and these questions were positioned near the end as recommended by Bradley (2013).

The last question allowed freetext general comments about #DrawingAugust which was to allow any factors not anticipated to come out and also as a courtesy to the organisers of drawing August.

The questionnaire piloted on a small test sample prior to launch in order to check that the questions were understood and logical, and that the answers were recorded correctly.

## 5.3. Execution

The questionnaire was disseminated to Twitter users via a link embedded in Tweets sent out by @KardiSom and the organiser @OlderThanEvil from 22nd – 31st December 2013. Responses were received up to 23rd January 2014.

The response rate was relatively pleasing. A limitation of this study is that the sample is too small to be statistically robust; however as a proportion of the population of interest, it is significant (28.5%). Conducting this survey during the Christmas Holidays may have had a negative impact on response rate.

A more likely factor is that potential subjects may simply not have seen the call for participation in their Twitter timelines.

As the Phenomenon of Interest was 'Participation in #DrawingAugust' it was not clear who was going to respond. In the event there was a spread of responses across genders. The age groups tended towards the 35-64 bands. In terms of both Twitter experience and Artistic experience, the sample spanned both ends of the spectrum – it was pleasing to get this cross section as it would facilitate cross-tabulations that are more meaningful.

## 5.4 Analysis

The data from the online forms were exported into SPSS and the findings are presented in both percentage format and through SPSS data analysis to gain insight and search for any potential correlations in the data collected. The verbatim comments were coded and analysed for themes and sentiment.

# 6. Findings

The sample consisted of 57 Twitter users, one of whom was removed from the sample as they failed the screening question.

## 6.1 Demographics

As can be seen in Figure 2, 72% of the respondents were in the age bracket 35-54 and another 18% were in the 55-64 category. No respondents were in the 18-25 group. This makes for an interesting cohort as Twitter in general has a different age demographic; 47% of 18-24 year olds use Twitter compared with 16% of 55-64 year olds (Kinetic, 2013).

When asked how they would describe themselves as artists, 5% said they were Absolute Beginners, 32% described themselves as Recreational artists, and the same number chose the description 'Semi-professional'. 23% were Professional artists and another 7% preferred a different description ranging from 'Struggling Art Student trying to make a living at it' to 'Professional but retired'.

In a bid to establish how business-oriented the participants were at the start of #DrawingAugust, they were asked what their normal sales output was.

23% of people preferred not to say. This could have been for a number of reasons; possibly they could not quantify their sales. It is common for people to call themselves professional artists while not actually being economically

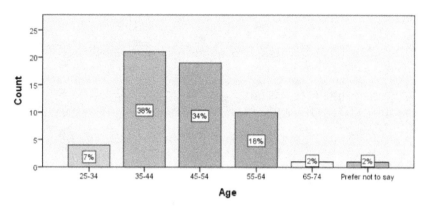

**Figure 2**    Age profile of Respondents

The gender split was biased towards female (67%) compared with male (33%)

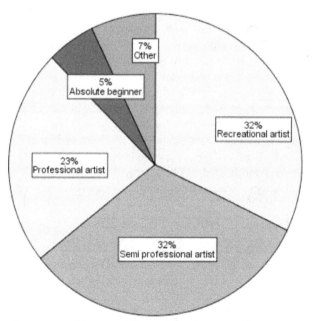

**Figure 3**    Answers to "How would you describe yourself as an Artist?"

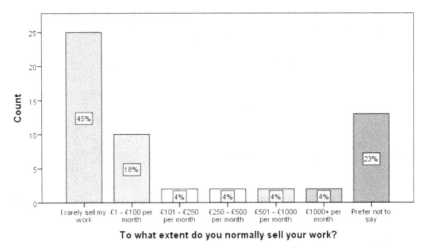

**Figure 4**   Answers to "To what extent do you normally sell your work?"

active or making a living at it. Furthermore it is the sort of activity that some-times operates in a grey market – i.e. a cash enterprise without income tax or reporting. For this reason people can be reticent to talk about it. Others may simply consider it a private matter and not wish to share it.

Of those who did select a category to describe their sales, 45% said they rarely sell their work. 18% said their sales represent £1-£100 per month. Of the other 4 categories £101-£250, £251-£500, £501-£1000 and £1000+ each had 4% which represents 2 respondents for each of those bands.

When the description is cross tabulated with the normal monthly sales value, it can be seen that the two largely corroborate one another, with the 'Profes-sional Artists' accounting for all of the larger value sales categories, while the 'Recreational Artists' account for most of the 'I rarely sell my work' category.

## 6.2. Relationship with Social Media

The subjects were asked to describe the extent of their experience with Twitter at the start of #DrawingAugust. This was to enable research into the question of whether Art could be a means to engage with Twitter as well as vice versa.

Over a third of the respondents were either Absolute Beginners or Fairly New/Inexperienced with Twitter (5% and 25% respectively). 23% described themselves as Moderate in their Tweeting habits, while 32% said they were

| | NormallySell | | | | | | |
|---|---|---|---|---|---|---|---|
| | £1 - £100 per month | £1000+ per month | £101 - £250 per month | £250 - £500 per month | £501 - £1000 per month | I rarely sell my work | Prefer not to say |
| Absolute beginner | 0 | 0 | 0 | 0 | 0 | 3 | 0 |
| Former art student struggling to be professional | 0 | 0 | 0 | 0 | 0 | 1 | 0 |
| I do not label myself | 0 | 0 | 0 | 0 | 0 | 1 | 0 |
| It is not my "day job", because I'm retired. I do, however work on a professional level, and sell. | 0 | 0 | 0 | 0 | 0 | 0 | 1 |
| Professional artist | 1 | 2 | 0 | 0 | 2 | 2 | 6 |
| Recreational artist | 2 | 0 | 0 | 0 | 0 | 15 | 1 |
| Recreational but with professional experience as a graphic designer | 0 | 0 | 0 | 0 | 0 | 1 | 0 |
| Semi professional artist | 7 | 0 | 2 | 2 | 0 | 2 | 5 |
| | 10 | 2 | 2 | 2 | 2 | 25 | 13 |

Table 5    Crosstabulation – Artist description / Estimated Monthly Sales

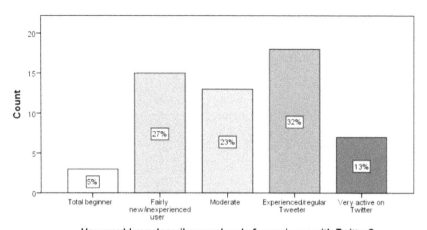

**How would you describe your level of experience with Twitter?**

**Figure 6**    Answers to "How would you describe your level of experience with Twitter?"

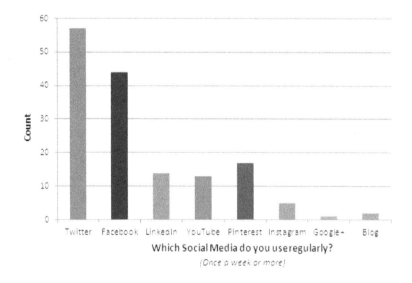

**Which Social Media do you use regularly?**

*(Once a week or more)*

**Figure 7**    Answers to "Which Social Media do you use regularly?"

Experienced/Regular Tweeters. 13% considered themselves Very Active on Twitter. This represents a good spectrum for analyses.

As well as Twitter habits, the other Social Media habits of the respondents were taken into consideration. The question asked which other Social Media they used regularly (which was defined as once a week or more).

As expected, all of the respondents said Twitter, most said Facebook. Unsurprisingly among a creative community, the more visual Social Media such as Pinterest and Instagram also featured.

## 6.3. #DrawingAugust Specific Questions

Moving towards the questions that relate specifically to participation in #DrawingAugust we first sought to quantify the level of activity / engagement of the respondents. The question asked 'How many times did you post a drawing to #DrawingAugust'. The nature of the project meant that really the maximum possible number of posts during August would be 31 (there being 31 days in the month). As 43% of the respondents answered 30+ this would indicate a very high level of engagement. As the next highest scoring category was the 20-29 posts group at 25% this means that over two thirds of our sample posted

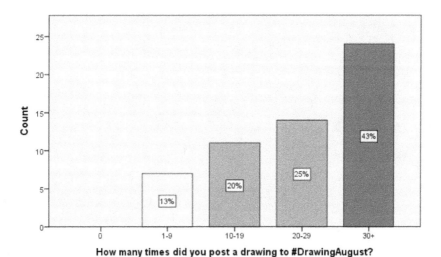

**How many times did you post a drawing to #DrawingAugust?**

Figure 8    Answers to "How many times did you post a drawing to #Drawing August?"

20 times or more to #DrawingAugust. A limitation of this statistic is that we do not know the causal relationship. It may be that those most highly engaged individuals would anyway have the highest propensity to self-select to participate in the research. As expected there are no respondents who answered '0' to this question – the earlier non-participant having been removed from the sample at the screening stage, however this option was left in as a second screening question.

Participants were then asked 'What did you expect to get out of participating in #DrawingAugust' – an unprompted free-text question. The responses were coded and the sentiments visualised in the graphic below (Figure 9). By far the biggest unprompted response was 'Make me draw every day' – 23% of all the mentions related to this. 'Challenge / Discipline' was next highest with 14% of the mentions.

Participants were then asked 'What did you actually get out of participating in #DrawingAugust?'

Overall there were twice as many responses for the 'actual' than 'expected' question, with most responses containing more than one category of response.

**Figure 9**     Answers to "What did you expect to get out of #DrawingAugust?"

The responses were coded using the same coding frame and the responses visualised in Figure 10 below. Response categories which increased in volume are indicated by ↑, a decrease is denoted by ↓ and the same number is indicated with =.

The categories most notably increasing in number of mentions from 'expectations' to 'experienced' are:

'Community, Connections, Artistic Allies' with 24 mentions compared with 8; 'Fun, Enjoyment, Excitement' with 16 compared with 6, and 'See other Artists' work' 15 compared with 5.

The biggest rise in percentage terms is 'Twitter Skills' capturing an increase in confidence with Twitter and follows/retweets. This rose from 1% to 8% of the mention.

The biggest decrease in number of mentions was observed in 'Make me draw regularly', and 'Start Drawing again' and 'Challenge/Discipline' also fell.

There were 3 new categories of response recorded – the largest of these was 'Friendship' which was observed 10 times, along with 'Support' and

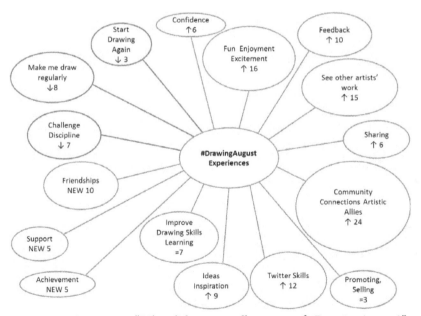

Figure 10    Answers to "What did you actually get out of #DrawingAugust?"

'Achievement' with 5 mentions each respectively. Most interesting of these is use of the word 'Friendship' which is quite an emphatic word to use in connection with only connected in the virtual space. On a few occasions this was qualified to 'Twitter Friendships', nevertheless the respondent clearly intended to indicate that a relationship of some value had been established.

There was one case in the study of a negative response which the responses to both this question and the following question recounted in some detail an ill-tempered exchange between two members of the forum. This survey respondent referred to 'bullying behaviour' and 'celebrating mediocrity'. This response was very much at odds with the rest of the data, but reflects one person's experience of participation nonetheless.

These are collated in the table below (Table 11) for ease of comparison.

Participants were asked 'Has participating in #DrawingAugust changed your perception of Twitter' – to which 46% answered No. Those that said Yes

Table 11   Answers to "What did you expect to get / actually get out of #DrawingAugust?"

| Mentions | Expected | Experienced |
|---|---|---|
| Make me draw regularly | 18 | 8 |
| Improve my drawing skills / learning | 7 | 7 |
| Promote/Sell my work | 3 | 3 |
| Start drawing again | 6 | 3 |
| Fun / enjoyment / excitement | 6 | 16 |
| Community / connections / artistic allies / belonging | 8 | 24 |
| Unsure | 4 | |
| Challenge / Discipline | 11 | 7 |
| Encouragement / motivation | | 11 |
| Feedback | 2 | 10 |
| Ideas / inspiration | 3 | 9 |
| See other artists' work | 5 | 15 |
| Sharing | 4 | 6 |
| Develop Twitter skills / followers | 1 | 12 |

| Mentions | Expected | Experienced |
|---|---|---|
| Develop confidence | 1 | 6 |
| Support | | 5 |
| Friendships | | 10 |
| Achievement | | 5 |

had the opportunity to explain why and the main sentiments expressed (in descending frequency) were:

"I view Twitter in a more positive light / Had heard so many negative comments / Much nicer and more friendly than I expected"

"Made me realise the global reach of Twitter / Appreciate the international dimension"

"A more useful medium than I realised / I discovered the power of the hashtag

"Felt a sense of community for the first time / My followers and I really communicate now"

"I thought my account would be all about my professional side – but it's all about art"

Two of the comments were more negative in tone:

"It is still a very shallow pond / Yes slightly in a negative way"

Moving to a more directly commercial question; Of the 41 respondents who answered 'To what extent did #DrawingAugust enable you to sell more of your work?" only 5 had received commissions or sales as a result, while another 10 believed that it had enabled them in an indirect way, such as creating an opportunity to put on an exhibition, or putting them in touch with a prospective customer. 7 did not believe it had any effect and 3 didn't know whether it had or not.

9 of the people who answered the question felt it was not applicable to them while 7 more pointed out that selling was not the point of #DrawingAugust.

# 7. Discussion

The purpose of this study was twofold; to better understand the way artists engaged with #DrawingAugust forum, and to examine the extent to which artists who engaged in this online community exhibited entrepreneurial behaviour.

The results indicated firstly that the extent and depth of engagement with #DrawingAugust was significant among those who answered the survey. In the volumetric measures around participation such as Posts, Followers and Shares, the group scored highly, indicating a correspondingly high level of engagement. There was an interesting contrast between what participants expected to get from taking part, and actually got. The main findings here reflect a shift in emphasis from motivation and discipline as expectations, to collaboration, friendship and fun actually experienced.

The demographic profile of the respondents indicated that, if representative of the population of #DrawingAugust participants, they were somewhat older than typical Twitter users, but covered a wide spectrum of both familiarity with Twitter and experience as artists.

When considering sentiment, the analysis from the verbatim comments best captures the mood, which is almost universally posititive. Furthermore the experience seems to have been transformative for participants in three main ways; artistic practice, sense of community and Twitter experience.

When considering whether the participants were displaying entrepreneurial behaviour, the demographic classification questions were revealing; A large proportion of the people in the sample were perhaps not predisposed to be entrepreneurial in the commercial sense with their art, either due to life stage (some were retired or otherwise out of the labour market) or due to their development as an artist. Over half of those surveyed, however, did classify themselves as being professional or semi-professional artist, and might reasonably be expected to want to sell their work.

There was limited evidence that #DrawingAugust had a direct impact on sales (this was reported in 5 instances) however a larger number of people identified indirect ways in which participation would lead to sales.

In addition to looking at direct commercial activity, the study considers whether there is any correlation between the seven character traits of the entrepreneur identified in the literature, and the experiences identified in Figure 10.

It might be assumed that community of artists would have a propensity to score highly on the attribute of 'Creativity & Imagination'. In terms of #DrawingAugust enabling this trait 'Ideas and Inspiration' were captured. Several of the participants identified a sense of 'Achievement' from participation. There is also the very tangible outcome of Retweets and Favourites – public displays of advocacy which several mentioned brought them pleasure. These factors could be mapped against 'Need for Achievement'- another of the traits of the entrepreneur identified in the literature. Part of the categorisation of innovative behaviour under the Classical School of Entrepreneurship relates to combining but also creating opportunities. (Barton & Cunningham 1991). #DrawingAugust enabled this in several ways; 'See other Artists' work', 'Ideas & Inspiration', 'Community, Connections, Artistic Allies' all enable this entrepreneurial trait. It could also be argued that those artists who have adopted Twitter and participated in an art-based forum have already demonstrated a level of opportunity identification. Several participants identified an increase in confidence as an outcome from participating in the forum. It could be argued that people with high levels of self confidence would not need an external enabler.

In summary, there is evidence that four of the seven characteristics associated with entrepreneurship have been enabled by participation in #DrawingAugust for some of the participants.

# 8. Conclusion

This paper explored the extent to which artists were enabled to behave in an entrepreneurial way by participating in a forum on Twitter. Findings from this study suggest that some of the characteristics of entrepreneurial behaviour were enabled by participation in #DrawingAugust, however there is limited evidence to suggest that this goes as far as sales for most artists surveyed.

Art as a vehicle to engage with Twitter was also researched, and for both the organisers and those surveyed, the event was deemed an important and successful use of this social medium. Some participants found that participation changed their perception of Twitter in a positive way, with a sense of community and friendship which in some cases extended beyond national boundaries being the largest unintended consequence of taking part.

#DrawingAugust was the forum examined in this paper. There have been successors #PaintSeptember #PrintOctober #PortraitNovember #StillLifeDecember #SketchJanuary #LineFebruary – many of the participants moving from one forum to the next. Arguably #DrawingAugust was the most successful – possibly because it was the first, and also the timing facilitated a high level of engagement due to being in the school holidays (it was observed during conversations that many of the participants work in education).

It would be interesting to do a longitudinal study following the development of this online community through the forums. Alternatively it would be possible to extend the research by identifying a forum in a different field and comparing the relative entrepreneurial traits with this set of data.

There are plans for #DrawingAugust to reconvene in 2014.

# References

Bradley, N. 2013. *Marketing research.* Oxford [u.a.]: Oxford Univ. Press.

Carswell, D. 2013. *The web is bringing society together, not tearing it apart –Telegraph Blogs.* [online] Available at: http://blogs.telegraph.co.uk/news/douglascarswellmp/100249159/the-web-is-bringing-society-together-not-tearing-it-apart/ [Accessed: 29 Jan 2014].

Chaffey, D. and Ellis-Chadwick, F. 2012. *Digital marketing.* Harlow: Pearson.

Cunningham, J. B. and Lischeron, J. 1991. *Defining entrepreneurship.* Journal of small business management, 29 (1), pp. 45--61.

Gurol, Y. & Atsan, N. (2006). *"Entrepreneurial characteristics amongst university students: some insights for entrepreneurship education and training in Turkey",* Education + Training, Vol. 48, No. 1, pp 25-38.

Koh, H.C. (1996). *"Testing hypotheses of entrepreneurial characteristics: a study of Hong Kong MBA students",* Journal of Managerial Psychology, Vol. 11, No. 3, pp 12-25.

Shackle, G. (1970). *Expectation, Enterprise and Profit,* George Allen and Unwin, London, cited in Lourenco, F. & Jayawarna, D. (2011). *Enterprise education: the effect of creativity on training outcomes.* International Journal of Entrepreneurial Behaviour & Research, Vol. 17, No. 3, pp. 224-244.

Kineticww.com. 2013. *Kinetic Panel UK February 2013.* [online] Available at: http://www.kineticww.com/en-gb/home/our-current-thinking/moving-minds/2013/03/06/kinetic-panel-uk-february-2013 [Accessed: 26 Jan 2014].

Wales Arts Review 2013. *Drawing August | Wales Arts Review.* [online] Available at: http://www.walesartsreview.org/drawing-august/ [Accessed: 29 Jan 2014].

# Customer Complaints and Service Recovery on Social Media: An Investigation into Barclays Bank Facebook Page

**Nurdilek Dalziel**

Henry Grunfeld Foundation, ifs University College, London, United Kingdom

ndalziel@edu.ifslearning.ac.uk

Originally published in the Proceedings of ECSM 2014

## Editorial commentary

As an increasing range of business activities move online, the role of customer care, and the handling of customer complaints becomes more visible. Social media presents platforms where complaints can be aired, responded to and left visible. Dalziel has benefited from this visible evidence trail by charting and analysing six weeks of customer complaints to Barclays bank. The evidence indicates differences between complaints about process and complaints about outcomes, with process failures giving customer complaint teams more traction to respond to than failed outcomes.

The type of complaint was not the only factor to vary the nature of the care team response. There seemed to be significant variation in the way that different members of the team answered, indicating a 'social media lottery' of care. The paper offers stimulating suggestions for the implications these variations have such as the need for greater training and clearer guidelines.

**Abstract:** Purpose: The services marketing literature recognises the importance of technology in improving service quality, customer satisfaction and providing efficient service recovery tactics. There is evidence on how technology affects consumer complaints and recovery strategies. However, academic research on social media, as an emerging technology platform, is rather scant. This is surprising since many business-es have extended their service provision to include social media platforms. The pur-pose of this paper is to extend the research on social media and provide insights into customer complaint behaviour and service recovery strategies using social media. In turn, research on outcome and process related service failures and resource-exchange theory are used to form the theoretical framework of this paper. **Methodology:** The context of this study is the banking industry. It serves as a valuable means by which to understand social media customer services because banks are using social media plat-forms as part of in their multi-delivery channels. The focus is Barclays Bank Facebook page which provides rich data for observing customer firm interactions. There were 255 customer complaints (and subsequent comments) posted in June-July 2013 that were analysed using qualitative data analysis methods. **Findings:** Evidence is present-ed on the overwhelming number of outcome-related service failures. This suggests that customers are more likely to place a complaint on firms' Facebook pages when there is a problem with the delivery of a core service. Moreover, the data extend the ap-plicability of resource-exchange theory to social media customer services. There was a fit between the type of service failure and recovery efforts. More customers with pro-cess-related service failure received an apology and empathetic response than custom-ers with outcome-related service failures. Finally, there were inconsistencies among Facebook teams in terms of the way they responded to customer complaints, which we call the *"social media lottery"*. Depending on the people who were working, some customers received a faster and more empathetic response, and some received privi-leged treatment such as the Bank's Facebook team calling the customer's branch to book an appointment on behalf of the customer. **Practical Implications:** The findings demonstrate the need for frontline social media staff to receive appropriate training and empowerment that enables them to work effectively to address service failures in a consistent way. **Originality / Value:** This research improves understanding of social media customer services by presenting empirical data on how customer complaints are managed on Facebook. More specifically, Facebook offers a good opportunity to observe the different parties interacting. In comparison with traditional service en-counters, social media encounters are more transparent involving multiple actors. In this study, there is a critical examination of how customer complaints and recovery strategies are affected in the new social media context.

**Keywords:** social media, service failure, service recovery, customer services, finan-cial services, resource-exchange theory

# 1. Introduction

Service failures are common in the services industry (Chuang *et al.* 2012) which has a direct impact on customer dissatisfaction by threatening their loyalty (Dalziel *et al.* 2011). Consequently, it is important that firms retain dissatisfied customers through appropriate service recovery strategies. There is a debate in the services marketing literature concerning what is *appropriate service recovery* for customers. Researchers approach this situation from a range of theoretical standpoints. Resource-exchange theory (RET) has recently attracted the attention of service failure researchers (such as, Mattila *et al.* 2011; Chuang *et al.* 2012; Roschk and Kaiser 2013), and is used to construct the conceptual framework of this research (Figure 1).

Developed by Foa (1971), RET suggests resources perceived as similar are more likely to be exchanged than dissimilar resources. The purpose of this research was to expand the applicability of RET to social media customer services. First, there was an investigation of whether firms' social channels were popular for certain types of service failures. Then, by using RET there was an examination of whether there was a match between the type of service failure and service recovery strategies. Drawing on prior empirical research, Figure 1 illustrates the impact of service failure and recovery strategies on relationship quality. This paper examines the interaction at the top half of the model which is shown in grey.

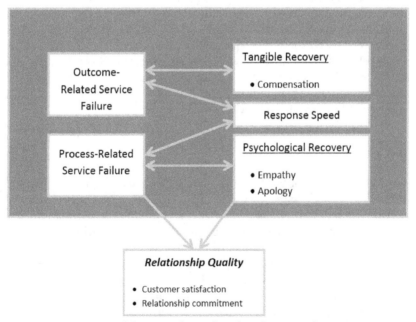

Figure 1:   Conceptual framework employed in the research process

# 2. Service failure

Service failure is defined as situations in which customers' perceptions of the service they receive fail to meet their expectations (Chuang *et al.* 2012). When customers experience problems with service delivery, this can have a significant impact on their levels of satisfaction (Dalziel *et al.* 2011), relationship commitment and word-of-mouth behaviour (Hart *et al.* 1990; Jones and Farquhar 2003; Boshoff 2007).

The services marketing literature recognises various types of service failures. Using a typology developed by Bitner (1990), Keller *et al.* (2001) and Hoffman *et al.* (1995) it is possible to categorise service failures into three types which are employee responses to service delivery system failures, implicit / explicit customer requests, and unprompted and unsolicited employee actions. Keaveney (1995) divided service failures as core service and service encounter failures. Similarly, Smith *et al.* (1999) distinguished between outcome- and process-related service failure (ORSF and PRSF). In the case of ORSF it is related to what customers actually receive from their service provider while in the case of PRSF it refers to how the service is delivered. In an ORSF, the provider fails to fulfil the basic service need or perform a core service. In PRSF, the delivery of a core service is flawed or deficient which is directly attributable to the behaviour of service employees. It is argued that ORSF is associated with an economic loss and PRSF causes social / psychological loss for the customer (Smith *et al.* 1999). Thus, ORSF typically involves a utilitarian exchange while PRSF involves symbolic exchanges.

# 3. Service recovery

Service recovery is defined as "the actions that a service provider takes to respond to service failures" (Lewis and Spyrakopoulos 2001:37). Well executed service recoveries are important for promoting customer relationships due to their impact on customer loyalty (Smith *et al.* 1999; Dalziel *et al.* 2011). In most situations it is not the initial failure to deliver the core service, but staff responses to the failure that causes dissatisfactory service encounters (Bitner *et al.* 1990). Along with solving the problem, customers want to feel that organisations care about their problems and keep their interests at heart (Lewis and Spyrakopoulos 2001; Dalziel *et al.* 2011). This caring approach needs to include acknowledging the problem, explaining why the service is faulty or unavailable, apologising, and assisting the customer in solving the problem by suggesting different options, which can all make a positive impact on the customer experience despite a service failure having occurred (Bitner et al. 1990). In turn, the tone of the response (Hart et al. 1990) and the sincerity of the apology (Mattila et al. 2011) are likely to improve the chances of success of service recovery efforts. On the other hand, a negatively perceived character or attitude of company staff (both verbal and nonverbal) has been found to cause more dissatisfaction than the deficient quality of the core service alone (Bitner et al. 1990).

In demonstrating the critical role of service interactions between the customer and their bank, it has been shown that effective communication characteristics of service delivery are different from effective service recovery attributes (Dalziel 2007). The following service recovery attributes are identified as having the potential to influence customer relationships: empathetic behaviour (1) and trust in the customer (2), apologising for mistakes (3), being proactive in dealing with mistakes (4), continuously communicating (5), adequate recovery speed (6) and whether the customer was refunded at the end of the recovery process (if relevant) (7). According to research by Miller et al. (2000), these attributes can further be categorised as tangible and psychological. Characteristics such as empathetic behaviour and apologising are viewed as psychological service recovery efforts while in tangible recovery the service is re-performed, the product is exchanged, and a monetary compensation is offered. A considerable amount of research supports the idea that customers who receive an apology following a service failure are more satisfied than customers who receive no apology (Roschk and Kaiser 2013). At the same time, Roschk and Kaiser (2013) provided empirical evidence that not only the presence or absence of an apology, but how an apology is given, is crucial in enhancing customer satisfaction. They state that the more empathetic and intense an apology in its delivery, the more satisfied customers are.

# 4. Service failures types, recovery efforts and resource exchange theory

Customers' evaluations of service failure and recovery strategies depend on the failure type (ORSF versus PRSF), failure magnitude and service recovery attributes (tangible versus psychological) (Smith et al. 1999). There is evidence that customers do not only expect a failure to be resolved to their satisfaction, but they also expect a fit between the type of service failure and the recovery efforts. Chuang *et al.(2012)* demonstrated that customers who experience ORSF are more satisfied with tangible service recovery efforts and those who experience PRSF are more satisfied with psychological recovery efforts. This is explained with reference to RET.

RET was originally developed by Foa (1971) as a psychological exchange theory. According to Foa, people prefer to exchange similar resources rather than dissimilar ones. Although RET was reported to have "fallen out of favor" at one time (Arnould 2008:22), it is still the dominant framework in the marketing literature (Mattila *et al.* 2011). Smith *et al.* (1999) demonstrated that customers preferred service recovery efforts that match the loss (e.g., monetary compensation for overbooking or empathy for a social loss). Similarly, classifying apology as a social or psychological resource, Roschk and Kaiser (2013) argue that it is more effective when a customer faced a PRSF than an ORSF situation. In another study by Mattila *et al.* (2011), it is suggested that human involvement (such as interacting with frontline staff) was more effective when the failure was caused by a human being rather than by a machine. In comparison, human involvement was less effective when a failure was caused by self-service technology. This is because consumers who choose to use self-service technologies to interact with their service providers wish to avoid customer–employee interactions.

Consequently, from this review we can infer that a match between the type of service failure and recovery efforts is likely to promote customer satisfaction. Moreover, customers who interact with their service providers primarily through self-service technologies prefer minimal human interference when a service failure occurs. Yet, there are uncertainties about how useful RET is in explaining social customer behaviour when service providers and their customers interact through social media. In a continuum from human interactions (such as talking to a member of staff in a bank branch) to technology-mediated interactions (such as online banking), it is not defined yet where social media interactions can be placed in this continuum. Drawing on RET, the aim of this paper is to provide insight into social media interactions between firms and their customers.

# 5. Research methodology

There are different social media channels, and this paper focuses on Facebook as a commonly used social media channel for customer services (Littleton 2013). The context of the study was the banking industry. It served as a valuable means to understand social media customer services since banks have started to include social media platforms in their multi-channel communication strategies. When deciding which bank to include in the research, a search was undertaken of the UK banks with an active Facebook page that allowed people to post comments and queries on its page. It was also important that the bank did not frequently delete or block customer posts. Consequently, it was decided to select Barclays Bank UK Facebook page which provided rich data enabling the observation of customer-firm interactions.

The research data consisted of customers' service failure related posts and responses by Barclays Facebook team. Due to the large number of consumer posts, it was decided to set a limit on the number of posts analysed. The data collection took place between 1st June and 15th July 2013, which resulted in the collection of 255 customer posts. The next stage comprised an emphasis on the responses by Barclays Facebook team to these posts. Comments were tracked until there were no further posts. Since the focus of the study was on customer-firm interactions, posts which were not responded to by Barclays and posts from other non-bank people commenting on a customer's query or the bank's response were excluded from the analysis of data. This data collection strategy resulted in the examination of over 800 posts which formed the base of the subsequent data analysis.

The analysis of this textual data comprised the use of qualitative data analysis methods guided by the principles underpinning content analysis. Content analysis is a technique used to obtain a systematic and objective description and explanation of textual data (Berelson 1952; Kassarjian 1977; Miles and Huberman 1994). In this case, the analysis started with an a priori set of codes that emerged from the literature review and conceptual framework. Starting with a set of codes prior to fieldwork is recommended for studies where research questions are well defined and a theoretical framework is developed. In this case, pre-structured coding is reported to facilitate the analysis by forcing the researcher to tie research questions or conceptual interests directly to the data (Miles and Huberman 1994; de Wet and Erasmus 2005). For example, there were higher-level codes such as ORSF and PRSF, and a number of first-level codes as sub-categories of these higher-level codes. Each customer post was first coded as ORSF, PFSF or both (such as a post referring to a problem with money transfer and at the same time a complaint about the waiting time on a telephone Help Line to talk to a member of staff). Then the sub-category for each code was identified (such as money transfer, problems with online / mobile banking and unavailable system for ORSF code). Similarly, responses by Barclays Facebook team were treated as recovery strategies. They were first coded as tangible or psychological recovery strategies which constituted higher-level codes. Then, they were coded into sub-categories such as response time, level of empathy and whether an apology was offered. It is important to note that the initial code list evolved along with the analysis. New codes and sub-categories emerged while some codes were redefined, removed or merged with others as more data was analysed.

Computer software programs can be used to facilitate data analysis and interpretation by providing support in storing, coding and retrieving data. In addition, computer software programs can help researchers become familiar with a large amount of data within a relatively short time frame. In this case, NVivo 10 was used to facilitate data analysis. As the dataset source, **Facebook wall posts and comments** were imported into NVivo 10 using NCapture for coding and further analysis.

# 6. Research findings

## 6.1. Service Failure Types on Barclays Facebook Page

Of the 255 customer complaints that were analysed, 163 posts (64 percent) were identified as ORSF whereas PRSF totalled at 29 posts (11 percent). Sixty three complaints (25 percent) were related to both outcome- and process-related failures. Table 1 lists the top five ORSF complaints.

The majority of ORSF complaints were related to online and mobile banking being down and hence the customer not being able to access their

Table 1    Top five outcome-related service failure complaints on Barclays Facebook page

|  | Number of complaints | Percentage |
|---|---|---|
| Unavailable service / system being down | 41 | 18% |
| Issues with transferring money / making a payment | 39 | 17% |
| Blocked / deactivated bank account | 26 | 11% |
| Account being used fraudulently | 17 | 7% |
| Service charges / fees | 16 | 7% |

account (41 complaints). This has followed by problems with transferring money and making a payment (39 complaints), blocked account or bank card (26 complaints), fraudulent use of an account (17 complaints) and service charges (16 complaints). Customers with a blocked card or account and those who felt they were charged unfairly expressed their intention to terminate their relationship with Barclays if their complaint was not resolved. This could also be related to the fact that customers had already informed Barclays through other traditional communication channels such as their branch, help line and online banking team about their problem, yet receiving no resolution to them. When customers voiced their complaint on social media, they were already stressed, feeling frustrated and had lost their trust in Barclays:

*"...I am left with 1 Option "Take it Public via the Media" as Barclays don't give a toss about me as a customer!"*

In comparison, PRSF complaints were largely related to communication quality (38 complaints) and waiting time (34 complaints). Table 2 lists the top five PRSF complaints. Scored as "1 out of 100", customers' comments on the quality of interaction with their bank staff were "dreadful", "less than helpful", "rude", "one ear doesn't know what the other ear is doing" and "as helpful as a chocolate fire guard". Call centre representatives were claimed to be "not professional", "not competent", "not caring for small customers!", "hanging up and talking down to customers" and "promising but not doing anything". It is interesting that some customers thought bank staff needed "diversity training" while a few customers kept referring to the perceived ethnicity of the help line

Table 2    Top five process-related service failure complaints on Barclays Facebook page

| | Number of complaints | Percentage |
|---|---|---|
| Issues with communication quality | 38 | 36% |
| Waiting time on Help Line | 34 | 32% |
| Staff behaviour to customers | 8 | 7% |
| Inconsistencies of information given by different Help Line representatives | 7 | 7% |
| Line being disconnected / not answered | 7 | 7% |

representatives. In their post, some customers referred to talking to an "Asian" with "an Indian accent" who "didn't even know where Exeter or Devon was in the UK", which felt like this contributed to customers' perceived poor quality of the service.

After communication quality attribute, the next common complaints were about waiting time on the help line (which changed from 15 minutes to two hours) and the customer being disconnected or transferred to another representative constantly: "Only 10% of this time was spent talking to staff, the rest was just waiting. About 2 hours." Customers also complained about the cost of the phone calls which was over £30 in some situations. In particular customers calling from abroad (9 in total) had concerns about the high cost of phone calls. Consequently, those customers requested compensation for their calls, asked for a landline number and a call-back. Of 92 PRSF complaints, the perceived communication quality was identified as the most crucial aspect of the process. Fifty-four percent of customers who threatened to switch their bank account had complaints about the poor interaction quality with Barclays.

# 7. Service Recovery Strategies by Barclays

The data analysis included the 255 customers' service failure related posts which received a reply from Barclays Facebook team. This resulted in over 800 responses and comments, which formed the base for the analysis in this section.

### 7.1.1. Tangible Recovery Strategies

Only three complaints were identified that resulted in the offered monetary compensation. In the first situation, the customer faced both outcome- and process-related service failure and was living overseas. The customer had already voiced her complaint using traditional banking communication channels with no resolution to their problem, and then used Facebook "to highlight the hassle [she] had to go through every time there was a problem with [her] account." The customer's account was credited for the phone calls incurred as a goodwill gesture by the bank. In the second case, the customer appeared to be a victim of fraud. Similarly, this complaint had already been filed by the bank. In both cases, the customers were refunded for costs incurred after they posted their complaint on Facebook. Although customers were appreciative when their problems were resolved, they were not pleased their problems were addressed because of the role of social media (and not because of having the customer's interests at heart): "I tried the usual route of phoning the fraud line, going in to my bank branch. I finally got it [the problem] sorted once I posted it on a social network site, not ideal." In the third case the customer had both outcome- and process-related service failures, and complained through phone calls to Barclays costing over £30. The bank offered a landline number stating "calls to this number are charged at a local rate and should be included in any inclusive mobile minutes."

It was disappointing that it was possible to identify only very limited number of tangible service recovery efforts. This could be due to Barclays not being willing to announce their monetary compensation strategies on a social media platform.

### 7.1.2. Psychological Recovery Strategies
In line with the literature, it was decided to examine the number of apologies, how an apology has been made and whether the bank's response was empathetic. Barclays Facebook team appeared to be paying good attention to apologising for the service failures their customers were facing. Sixty six percent of ORSF complaints (149 posts) received an apology in the first response from

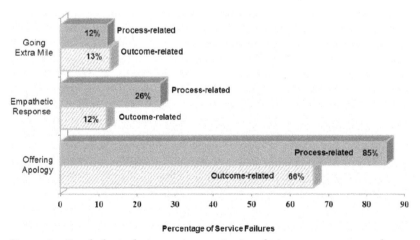

Percentage of Service Failures

Figure 2   Psychological recovery strategies in relation to outcome- and process-related service failures

the bank, and this ratio went up to 85 percent for PRSF complaints (78 posts) (Chart 1). On the other hand, it was possible to identify that not in all cases did the bank apologise for the right reason. For example, there were situations when the Bank's Facebook team apologised not for the service failure but for the delay in responding to the customer's post or customer's response to service failure: "We're sorry to hear you're thinking about leaving us." There were also instances when the bank offered a rather unemotional scripted apology: "Apologies for any inconvenience caused." When an apology had no emotional element, customers did not seem to consider the response to be sincere: "You are sorry?" These are examples of types of communication that do not depict empathy or aim to facilitate a close relationship between bank and customer.

A particular psychological service recovery attribute is empathy. Twelve percent of ORSF complaints (28 posts) received an empathetic response from Barclays Facebook team in comparison with 26 percent for PRSF complaints (24 posts). When responding to customer complaints, the bank expressed the view that they were "very sorry to hear how a customer feels about their bank" and they "certainly didn't want [their customer] to feel this way". The team offered "a sincere apology" and "appreciated the [customer's] frustration or position" in respect of a service failure and the length of time it took to resolve the problem. The bank also wanted the customer's "the next call [to Barclays] to be a better experience". There were cases when Barclays posted an empathetic response to a problem even after a customer had informed the bank they had opened an account with a competitor:

> "We're sorry to hear that you've opened your account elsewhere. It is regrettable that an appointment wasn't available sooner. We'll share your feedback with our team in [branch name]."

It was possible to identify 30 service recovery posts where Barclays made a clear attempt to introduce a personal touch that went the extra mile. For example, instead of directing the customer to another department, Facebook staff offered to pass the customer's complaint to the relevant bank team, contacted the customer's branch or business manager on behalf of the customer to book an appointment, checked the image that the customer wanted to upload for their personalised card to see whether it fits the image requirements, offered a local telephone number instead of a usual 084 number, posted a new PINsentry to customer, and offered a call back.

# 8. Individual responses by facebook team to customer complaints

This section examines whether Barclays Bank customers received a consistent service from the whole Bank Facebook team. On the whole, there was a satisfactory balance of customer posts between the members of the team. Each advisor answered around 36 posts on average. With respect to the number of apologies offered, there was a good consistency. The majority of staff offered an apology when responding to service failures.

On the other hand, there were important variations on whether the bank's response was empathetic versus unemotional, ranging from 0 to 19 percent across the team. Similarly, there was a considerable difference in whether the bank advisor went the extra mile and introduced a personal element into the service recovery effort, ranging from 0 percent to 11 percent. For example, a number of customers wanted to apply for a Barclays Bank personalised card. However, the system did not accept their photo image. When customers complained, some team members were happy to check the image whereas other team members simply directed the customer to the Barclays Bank website to check the guidelines for image uploading. Likewise, customers appeared to receive a faster response to queries depending on who answered their query, which ranged from 35 to 99 minutes on average. Other areas of important differences between the team members were whether the complaint was resolved by the Bank Facebook staff (ranging from 5 to 14 percent) or the customer was simply directed to another department (ranging from 17 to 80 percent).

Consequently, it seems that depending on who was working on a particular shift, some customers received a faster and more empathetic response than others, and some even received privileged treatment, which was seen as part of "*social media lottery*".

# 9. Conclusion and managerial implications

The service recovery strategies used by Barclays Bank Facebook team appeared to operate mostly in parallel with RET theory. Bank customers with PRSF problems seem to be more likely to receive an apology and empathetic response than customers with an ORSF complaint. However, in terms of going the extra mile, the difference between PRSF and ORSF was minor. Likewise, response speed by the bank for PRSF and ORSF posts was similar. There were limited observations of tangible recovery efforts. Yet, in all cases customers were refunded for monetary loss (phone charges and losing money fraudulently) suggesting tangible recovery strategies were used in response to ORSF queries. Thus, our data has confirmed the applicability of the RET in a social media context.

Moreover, it was possible to identify a good allocation of outcome- and process-related service failures, dominated by ORSF complaints. It emerged that social media is commonly used as a follow-up for ongoing complaints that had already been voiced using traditional banking communication channels. Customers wanted to take advantage of social media being an open communication channel with the expectation that this could speed up the service recovery process. The majority of service failure complaints were related to technology failures such as unavailable service. This is in conformity with a study by Mattila *et al.* (2011) who report that customers prefer to use technology-driven communication channels when they need to deal with a technology-related service failures.

Meanwhile, confirming the study by Roschk and Kaiser (2013) it is shown that the way an apology is offered is equally important in customers' evaluations of service recovery efforts. However, a simple apology is unlikely to be sufficient by itself. As stated by Smith and Bolton (2002):

*"Redressing service failures means more than smiles - it means delivery of core services. Thus, service employees must have a real ability to improve customers' situations." (p.20)*

Finally, considerable variations were identified in the bank's responses to customer complaints (Table 3). There were instances where the Bank's Facebook team responded satisfactorily but other times the response to a similar type of query from another customer was less helpful. There were instances when the Bank's Facebook team openly addressed a query whereas another similar type of query was directed to another banking communication channel and so on. These examples highlight issues with the training and empowerment of Barclays Bank social media staff. The bank's social media policies could be better communicated throughout the frontline team and highlights training needs for the bank's social media personnel.

Table 3    Service recovery efforts by Barclays Bank Facebook team members

| | Number of ORSF posts replied | Number of PRSF posts replied | Average response speed (in minutes) | Offering an empathetic answer (%) | Apologis- ing for failure (%) | Going the extra mile (%) |
|---|---|---|---|---|---|---|
| Facebook Team Member 1 | 34 | 20 | 86 | 7 | 9 | 4 |
| Facebook Team Member 2 | 38 | 15 | 99 | 19 | 11 | 7 |
| Facebook Team Member 3 | 21 | 5 | 66 | 0 | 42 | 0 |
| Facebook Team Member 4 | 41 | 14 | 35 | 18 | 18 | 11 |
| Facebook Team Member 5 | 37 | 11 | 52 | 8 | 19 | 4 |
| Facebook Team Member 6 | 35 | 16 | 73 | 18 | 24 | 5 |
| Facebook Team Member 7 | 29 | 14 | 64 | 2 | 23 | 1 |

# Acknowledgement

The author wishes to thank Henry Grunfeld Foundation for providing finan-cial support for this research.

# References

Arnould, E. J. (2008). "Service-dominant logic and resource theory." *Journal of the Academy of Marketing Science* 36: 21–24.

Berelson, B. (1952). *Content analysis in communication research.* Glencoe, Illinois, The Free Press Publishers.

Bitner, M. J. (1990). "Evaluating service encounters: The effects of physical surroundings and employee responses." *Journal of Marketing* 54: 69-82.

Bitner, M. J., Booms, B. H. and Tetreault, M. S. (1990). "The service encounter: Diagnosing favourable and unfavourable incidents." *Journal of Marketing* 54: 71-84.

Boshoff, C. (2007). "Understanding service recovery satisfaction from a service encounter perspective: A pilot study." *South African Journal of Business Management* 38(2): 41-51.

Chuang, S. C., Cheng , Y. H., Chang, C. J. and Yang, S. W. (2012). "The effect of service failure types and service recovery on customer satisfaction: a mental accounting perspective." *The Service Industries Journal* 32(2): 257–271.

Dalziel, N. (2007). The impact of marketing communications on customer relationships: an investigation into the UK banking sector. *The Open University Business School.* Milton Keynes, The Open University. PhD Thesis.

Dalziel, N., Harris, F. and Laing, A. (2011). "A multidimensional typology of customer relationships: from faltering to affective " *International Journal of Bank Marketing* 29(4-5): 398-432.

de Wet, J. and Erasmus, Z. (2005). "Towards rigour in qualitative analysis." *Qualitative Research Journal* 5(1): 27-40.

Foa, U. G. (1971). "Interpersonal and economic resources." *Science* 171: 345–351.

Hart, C. W. L., Heskett, J. L. and Sasser, W. E., Jr (1990). "The profitable art of service recovery." *Harward Business Review* July-August: 148-156.

Hoffman, K. D., Kelley , S. W. and Rotalsky, H. M. (1995). "Tracking service failures and employee recovery efforts." *Journal of Services Marketing* 9(2): 49-61.

Jones, H. and Farquhar, J. D. (2003). "Contact management and customer loyalty." *Journal of Financial Services Marketing* 8(1): 71-78.

Kassarjian, H. H. (1977). "Content analysis in consumer research." *Journal of Consumer Research* 4(June): 8-18.

Keaveney, S. M. (1995). "Customer switching behavior in service industries: An exploratory study." *Journal of Marketing* 59(2): 71-82.

Keller, K. L. (2001). "Mastering the Marketing Communications Mix: Micro and Macro Perspectives on Integrated Marketing Communication Programs." *Journal of Marketing Management* 17(7/8): 819-847.

Lewis, B. R. and Spyrakopoulos, S. (2001). "Service failures and recovery in retail banking: the customers' perspective." International Journal of Bank Marketing 19(1): 37-47.

Littleton, T. (2013). "Social media and customer service." eModeration Report May 2013 (http://www.emoderation.com/social-media-publications/download-a-guide-to-social-media-and-customer-service).

Mattila, A. S., Cho, W. and Ro, H. C. (2011). "The role of self-service technologies in restoring justice." *Journal of Business Research* 64: 348–355.

Miles, M. B. and Huberman, A. M. (1994). Qualitative data analysis: An expanded sourcebook. London, Sage.

Miller, J. L., Craighead, C. W. and Karwan, K. R. (2000). "Service recovery: A framework and empirical investigation "*Journal of Operations Management* 18(4): 287-400.

Roschk, H. and Kaiser, S. (2013). "The nature of an apology: An experimental study on how to apologize after a service failure." *Mark Lett* 24: 293–309.

Smith, A. K. and Bolton, R. N. (2002). "The Effect of Customers' Emotional Responses to Service Failures on Their Recovery Effort Evaluations and Satisfaction Judgments." *Journal of the Academy of Marketing Science* 30(1): 5-23.

Smith, A. K., Bolton, R. N. and Wagner, J. (1999). "A Model of Customer Satisfaction with Service Encounters Involving Failure and Recovery." *Journal of Marketing Research* XXXVI(August): 356-372.

# Intellectual Capital (IC) in Social Media Companies: Its Positive and Negative Outcomes

## Piotr Wiśniewski

Department of Corporate Finance, Warsaw School of Economics, Poland

Originally published in the proceedings of ECIC 2013

## Editorial commentary

What is the business value of the interactions that take place via social media around a firm? Among the many areas to consider, the intellectual capital of the many conversations is substantial. As Web 2.0 emerged in the last decade, many commentators recognised this, and in this paper Wisniewski attempts to classify the ways that intellectual capital might be characterised.

By recognising the differences between the interactions between firm and customers (as 'customer capital') , the employees of the firm (as human capital) and the ways this might be leveraged (as 'structural capital'), Wisniewski offers a framework to evaluate these elements. Their negative as well as positive implications are considered in an attempt to determine long term implications for how firms stimulate, respond to and draw on these rich pools of intellectual capital.

**Abstract:** Social media are becoming a vital element of intense Intellectual Capital (IC) growth. Their ultimate shape is being determined by dynamic technical innovation (involving hybrid products and services), merger and acquisition (M&A) activity among product and service innovators, as well as user behaviorisms (embodying the very social dimension of these media). Despite obvious constraints (novelty, limited research coverage), it is evident that two IC segments have come to the fore of social media expansion: Customer Capital (CC) and Structural Capital (SC). It is premature to produce a comprehensive assessment of social media sustainability and utilitarianism; however, key positives and negatives of online interconnectedness can now be outlined. Their impact analysis and interdependence should be explored in further empirically based research for which this paper might serve as a useful starting point.

**Keywords:** intellectual capital, social media, social outcomes, social responsibility

# 1. The origins, definition and significance of social media

Social media are a fairly recent phenomenon; although initial signs of their activity can be traced to the late 1960s (see Appendix 1). In earnest, their rapid ascent occurred in the late 2000s when the social media paradigm began to eclipse what had thereto been referred to as "mass media" (Appendices 1 and 2).

*"Social media are media for social interaction, using highly accessible and scalable publishing techniques" (Social Media Guys, 2010). This definition resonates with a notion formalized by Kaplan & Haenlein (2010) whereby social media are "a group of Internet-based applications that build on the ideological and technological foundations of Web 2.0 [i.e. online interactivity], and [in fact it should be "i.e."] that allow the creation and exchange of user generated content".*

The classification of social media is in a constant state of flux, yet the following key categories of Web based interconnectedness are thus far distinguishable and reasonably established (cf. taxonomy proposed by Kaplan & Haenlein, 2012).

Social media share a number of characteristics will mass (traditional) media. Certain features of social media are nevertheless unique and reflect the unprecedented character of this media resource. Among them are (cf. Social Media Guys, 2010):

- *popularity*: social media are increasingly emulating the outreach of their (by far more established) predecessors – this trend is best illustrated by the dwindling circulation of newspapers vs. booming number of social media's daily active users
- *democracy*: social media are – in essence – a grassroots movement (natural, spontaneous and driven by human individualism – opposed to the ineludible corporationism of traditional media sources)
- *credibility*: on the one hand social media are relatively uncensored, outspoken and non-partisan, on the other hand the lack of scrutiny prior to publication might result in errors, omissions, misinformation (largely unintended) or disinformation (downright deliberate)

**Table 1** Social media classification, characteristics, examples and commercial aspects

| # | Name | Subsets, characteristics | Examples | Commercial relevance |
|---|------|--------------------------|----------|----------------------|
| 1. | *Collabora-tive projects* | wikis (websites allowing users to add, remove or alter web-based content), 2) social bookmarking (group-based collection and rating of Internet resources) | 1) Wikipedia 2) Reddit | Providing free access to information, enhancing socioeconomic efficiencies, improving resource transparency, challenging copyrighted content |
| 2. | *Blogs* | Websites portraying the life experiences of individuals or groups and presented in textual, pictorial or audiovisual forms | Huffington, TMZ | Keeping in touch with consumers, keeping employees informed, enhancing website visibility (traffic) |
| 3. | *Content communities* | Platforms for sharing media content (audiovisual, photographs or other formats) among users | Youtube, Flickr | Cross-selling potential (relating to pay versions) from distributing free content, marketing |
| 4. | *Social networking* | Applications enabling users to connect via personal profiles comprising diverse personal information (photographs, audiovisual files and blogs) and featuring instant messaging and email | Facebook, Twitter | Networking with consumers and employees, enhancing brand development, |
| 5. | *Virtual worlds* | Computer-based environments allowing users to create their virtual identities (avatars) and interact online: 1) virtual game worlds: Massively Multi-player Online Role Playing Games (MMORPGs), 2) three-dimensional platforms allowing users to interact in a way similar to real (offline) life | World of Warcraft, Second Life | Promoting brands, goods and services in contexts unavailable to mainstream media |

Source: based on Miller (2011)

- *accessibility*: traditional media employ professionally trained staff and sophisticated equipment (whose costs ultimately have to be borne by end users), whereas the lion's share of social media initiatives are usually amateur and free of charge (the chief limitation of their creators and users is Internet connectivity and hosting capacity)
- *timeliness*: the very process of news gathering, verification, processing and dissemination by conventional media is time consuming, while social media are able to react instantaneously and without significant formalism
- *permanence*: in general industrial media cannot be altered following their dissemination, whereas social media are continuously and promptly editable (by their author or other online contributors), while their Internet traces are usually indelible (they can be retrieved by a skilled user)

# 2. Social media relevance to intellectual capital

Intellectual capital (IC) has to date been defined in multiple ways. The following examples illustrate IC's nomenclature in international literature at the turn of the millennium:

- "non-monetary and non-physical resources that are fully or partly controlled by the organization and that contribute to the value creation of the organization" (Roos et al., 2005)
- "knowledge that transforms raw materials and makes them more valuable" (Stewart, 2001)
- "the brainpower assets of the organization, recognizing them as having a degree of importance comparable to the traditional land, labor, and tangible assets" (Sullivan, 2000)
- "the hidden roots of value" (Edvinson & Malone, 1997)
- "the sum of everything everybody in a company knows that gives it a competitive edge" (Stewart, 1997)
- "intellect in action" (Hudson, 1993)

Despite these conceptual variations, the aforementioned definitions tend to be uniform in highlighting IC's:
- intangible form (IC ): in most in-depth references to IC, it is portrayed as a fairly abstract notion and its character is usually nonmaterial/nonphysical

- socioeconomic impact: even avowed critics of IC oriented research begrudgingly admit that IC's consequence for socioeconomic growth – although problematic in clear-cut appellation, taxonomy and measurement – is undeniable and substantial
- cross-asset synergies: the most challenging aspect of IC (besides its inherent intangibility and measurement complexity) is functional overlap in IC's segmentation and multidimensional interaction among individual IC components

Table 2 demonstrates a frequently applied and reasonably coherent segmentation model for IC, with its key drivers of socioeconomic utility and value as well as examples existing in practical circumstances:

The established record of traditional media has resulted in numerous scientific publications focused on how IC is created, enabled or facilitated by them. This contrasts with a rather scarce body of knowledge developed thus far with specific regard to social media. In consequence, it is problematic reapplying the IC segmentation philosophy to social online connectivity, yet an attempt to this effect is indispensable for any further analysis.

Figure 1 demonstrates social media concepts associated with individual IC segments as well as the reasoning behind such linkage:

Evidently, HC is a prerequisite for the existence and spread of the two other subsets of IC (CC and SC), as social media cannot operate without human creativity and its transmission. However, it is CC and SC that underlie the

Table 2    IC subsets: definitions, key drivers and examples

| IC Subset | Key drivers of utility and value | Examples |
| --- | --- | --- |
| *Customer Capital*: relationships with customers and suppliers | Interacting among users | Relationships with customers and suppliers |
| *Human Capital*: the skills and knowledge of the company's people | Disseminating creations of the human mind | Employees' knowledge, practical skills and competences |
| *Structural Capital*: Intellectual Property | Extracting value from IC | Patents, Processes, Databases, Networks etc. |

Source: based on Stewart (2001). IC subsets listed in alphabetical order

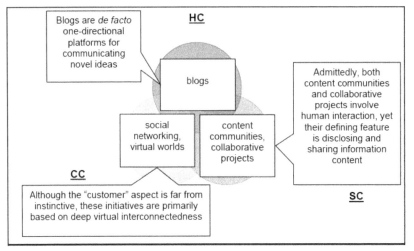

Figure 1    IC subsets (Customer Capital: CC, Human Capital: HC, Structural
            Capital: SC and) in the social media context

Source: own elaboration

commercial viability of IC embedded in social media. This happens for the
following two reasons:

- social leverage: the aggregate value represented by social media outnum-
  bers the simple sum of their components (in other words – it is social media
  interconnectedness that defines the bulk of their commercial value)
- value extraction: whereas innovation is a starting point of the social media
  value chain, its ultimate success is driven by effective commercialization

# 3. Are social media an IC asset or a liability?

To begin with, IC interpretation is gradually evolving from a notion whose
associations used to be universally positive to that whose social outcomes are
by far more nuanced (Cf. Dumay, 2012).

The socioeconomic perception of social media tends to be even more vola-
tile and controversial. Despite the intense use of social media globally, relatively few of their social impacts have been proved empirically on the basis

of statistically representative data. Table 3 encapsulates the most significant public outcomes relating to social media use along with their description and accompanying effects:

Table 3    The positives and negatives of social media activity: the practices, their character and social impacts

|  | Practice | Description | Social impacts |
|---|---|---|---|
| **Positives** | Globalization | "Globalization is a process that encompasses the causes, course, and consequences of transnational and transcultural integration of human and non-human activities" (Al-Rodhan *et al.*, 2006) | "World shrinkage": reducing distances among individuals and groups, leveraging information and promoting interpersonal activity |
| | Democratization | "The transition to a more democratic political regime. It could refer to the transition from an authoritarian regime to a full democracy, a transition from an authoritarian political system to a semi-democracy or transition from a semi-authoritarian political system to a democratic political system" (Przeworski *et al.*, 2000, Wikipedia, 2012) | Overcoming information asymmetries, widening access to information, reducing the cost of information gathering and processing |
| | Networking | Socioeconomic activity by which groups of like-minded people recognize, create, or act upon opportunities (cf. Wikipedia, 2012) | Synergies from online interaction among individuals and groups, developing and maintaining interpersonal ties |
| | Scale benefits | Adding impetus to (online or offline) scale-related business models facilitating the use of worldwide economic resources and enabling penetration of new markets and client segments | Innovation in products and services, providing access to affordable good and services |

*(Continued)*

Table 3   Continued

| Practice | Description | Social impacts |
|---|---|---|
| Functional/secondary illiteracy | "Inability to manage daily living and employment tasks that require reading skills beyond a basic level" (Schlechty, 2004) | Socioeconomic exclusion, lower micro/macroeconomic, competitiveness, inefficient socioeconomic choices |
| Intellectual Property (IP) infringement | "An intellectual property infringement is the infringement or violation of an intellectual property right. There are several types of intellectual property rights, such as copyrights, patents, and trademarks. Therefore, an intellectual property infringement may for instance be a copyright infringement, patent infringement or trademark infringement" (Wikipedia, 2012) | Theft, lower propensity to innovate by legitimate IP developers, inefficient allocation of IC |
| Behavioral addiction | "Syndromes analogous to substance addiction, but with a behavioral focus other than ingestion of a psychoactive substance" (Grant et al., 2010) | Socioeconomic exclusion, lower micro/macroeconomic, competitiveness, |
| Misinformation/ Disinformation | ""While 'misinformation' can be simply defined as false, mistaken, or misleading information, 'disinformation' entails the distribution, assertion, or dissemination of false, mistaken, or misleading information in an intentional, deliberate, or purposeful effort to mislead, deceive, or confuse" (Fetzer, 2003) | Cybercrime, distrust in online activity, reputational damage |
| Cybercrime | "Crimes committed on the Internet using the computer as either a tool or a targeted victim" (Computer Crime Research Center, 2012) | Malware, viruses, hacking, scams, fraud and theft, distrust in online activity, reputational damage, stress |

The leftmost column is labeled **Negatives** (rotated vertically).

Table 3 Continued

| Practice | Description | Social impacts |
|----------|-------------|----------------|
| Privacy breaches | "A privacy breach is the result of an unauthorized access to, or collection, use or disclosure of personal information. Such activity is 'unauthorized' if it occurs in contravention of applicable privacy legislation. Some of the most common privacy breaches happen when personal information is stolen, lost or mistakenly disclosed. A privacy breach may also be a consequence of faulty business procedure or operational breakdown" (OPC, 2012) | Reputational damage, stress, cybercrime, distrust in online activity |

Source: own elaboration based on the sources referenced

Although the positives appear to outweigh the negatives in social impact, both categories are interdependent (a great deal of positive outcomes can turn negative if abused). Such an observation might suggest the need for more scrupulous (albeit highly selective and sophisticated) regulation, and measures (e.g. in education) that would promote online accountability.

Another way of examining the public impact of social media is reviewing its performance from the global investment perspective. Given the rising trend toward passive investment and fund indexation (Cf. EFAMA, 2012), it would be ideal to use a global proxy for the entire industry. Fortunately, such a proxy has existed since late 2011 as the "Solactive Social Media Index (SOCL)" and has been tracked by the Global X Social Media Index ETF (its composition is summarized in Appendix 3).

In spite of limited history, tentative observations can be made as to the SOCL's performance vs. the widely used benchmark for the U.S. equity universe (the Standard and Poor's 500 Index, the SPX). They are indicative of social media's two major investment features (Appendix 4):

- relatively high correlation with the broad U.S. equity market returns, limited speculative characteristics: despite exposure to advanced technologies the SOCL's beta ($\beta$) of 1.15 appears exceptionally close to the SPX (the scope for autocorrelation is limited by virtue of solely one stock, Google, being shared by both benchmarks) – this underscores ongoing convergence

between social media and the general economy (interestingly, this convergence defies international borders: while the SPX is primarily focused on
the U.S., the SOCL's makeup is truly global);
- inferior performance (in absolute and relative terms): the SOCL in the
surveyed period posted a negative rate of return, whereas the SPX gained
substantially – the SOCL's risk-adjusted efficiency has been further down-
graded by other (than the $\beta$) measures of volatility (high standard deviation, semi-variance) – this is only partially explainable by the inopportune
course of Facebook's Initial Public Offering (IPO) and a wave of mistrust in
Web based business models.

Evidently, the popularity of social media has yet to be matched by solid business models that would captivate the interest of worldwide asset managers.
Addressing negative social outcomes would help lure those institutions that
are particularly sensitive to socially responsible and impact investment strategies (Cf. Falkowski & Wiśniewski).

# 4. Conclusion

Social media have grown to be a powerful public media genre (whose global
reach has begun to eclipse traditional mass media) thanks to unparalleled
mobility, accessibility, interactivity, flexibility and scalability.

Taking into account the character of currently dominant social media
concepts, whereas the precondition of their growth is attributable to Human
Capital resources, their commercial viability is primarily being driven by virtual interconnectedness (Customer Capital) and information disclosure and
sharing (Structural Capital). Social media commercial relevance will therefore
profit mostly from a greater degree of transparency with regard to their business models as well as more emphasis on efficient and legally compliant networking and content dissemination.

As with any globally potent force, social media can be both socially productive and disruptive. The future challenges to a more responsible use of
social medial lie in raising public awareness of their public benefits as well as
implementing highly selective and sophisticated regulation to curb practices
deemed socially onerous. Any successful initiatives of this sort will have to
be coordinated globally, mirroring the very essence of social media (based on
globalization).

# Appendix 1: The "social media" Google 2-gram and timeline in 1969-2008

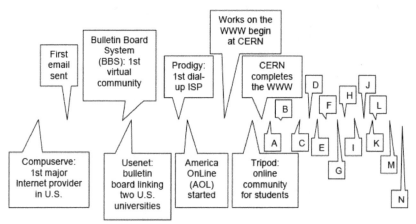

Source: Google Ngram Viewer [accessed: December 31, 2012]. Events from "The Brief History of Social Media": http://www.uncp.edu/home/acurtis/newMedia/SocialMedia/SocialMediaHistory. html [accessed: December 31, 2012].

Notes: A: Beverly Hills Internet (BHI) starts Geocities, B: Newsweek features article "The Internet? Bah! Hype alert: Why cyberspace isn't and will never be nirvana", C: The Web has 1m sites, blogging begins, SixDegrees enables profile creation and friend listing, AOL Instant Messenger develops chatting, Blackboard – online education system for teachers and students, D: Google opens up as search engine, E: Friends Reunited – first online social network founded in U.K., F: dot.com bursts, 70 m computers connected to Internet, G: Wikipedia opens up, Apple starts selling iPods, H: Friendster (a social networking site open to public and grows to 3m users in 3 months), AOL has 34 m members, I: MySpace launched (clone of Friendster), Linden Lab opens Second Life online, LinkedIn started, 3bn Web pages reached, Apple introduces iTunes, J: Facebook started by Harvard College students, MySpace outpaces Friendster in page views, online podcasting begins, Flickr image hosting website opens, Digg set up as story sharing social news website, K: Blog Early, Blog Often (BEBO) social networking site started, News Corporation (global media giant) buys MySpace, Facebook launches version for high school students, Friends Reunited (15 m member strong) sold to British ITV, YouTube begins storing and retrieving videos, more than 8bn Web pages in operation, L: MySpace most popular social networking site in U.S. (based on unique visitors), Twitter launched, Facebook made available to anyone over age 13, Google indexing more than 25bn pages, 400 queries daily, 1.3bn images and more than 1bn Usenet messages, M: Microsoft buys stake in Facebook, Facebook initiates Facebook Platform enabling third-party developers to create applications ("apps") online, Facebook launches Beacon (targeted advertising system), Apple releases iPhone multimedia and Internet smartphone, N: Facebook surpassed MySpace in monthly unique visitors, fails to buy Twitter, AOL buys Bebo (subsequently to be resold as relatively unsuccessful social media site)…

# Appendix 2: Trends in Google searches of "mass media" (blue line) and "social media" (red line) in English-language online resources in 2004-2013*

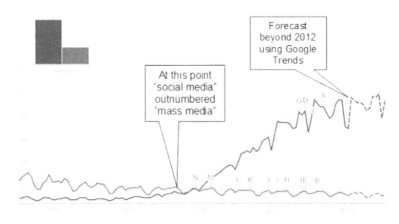

Source: Google Trends [accessed: December 31, 2012]. Note: examples of Google search results: A: Montreal Gazette ("Greek parties jump on social media bandwagon"), B: MarketWatch ("China Mass Media Reports)…(*) Forecasts using Google Trends.

# Appendix 3: Top fund holdings for the SOCL as of December 30, 2012

| Issuer name | Position | Value | Share of Total |
|---|---|---|---|
| Facebook Inc. | 66,578 | 1,864,184 | 14.296% |
| LinkedIn Corp. | 12,096 | 1,308,061 | 10.032% |
| Tencent Holdings Ltd. | 38,914 | 1,271,325 | 9.750% |
| Dena Co Ltd. | 32,464 | 1,191,285 | 9.136% |
| SINA Corp/China | 22,610 | 1,029,207 | 7.893% |
| Mail.ru Group Ltd. | 19,270 | 635,910 | 4.877% |
| Yandex NV | 27,418 | 598,261 | 4.588% |
| Gree Inc. | 33,889 | 589,106 | 4.518% |
| Google Inc. | 832 | 581,044 | 4.456% |
| Nexon Co. Ltd | 48,159 | 539,806 | 4.140% |

Source: http://www.bloomberg.com/quote/SOCL:US [accessed: December 30, 2012]. Highlighted in gray is the only common issuer for both indices (Google, Inc.).

# Appendix 4: Performance analysis of the Solactive Social Media Index (SOCL) vs. the Standard and Poor's 500 Index (SPX) in the period November 30, 2011-December 31, 2012

| Summary | |
|---|---|
| Portfolio description tion | "Global X Social Media Index ETF is an exchange-traded fund incorporated in the USA. The Fund seeks to track the performance of the Solactive Social Media Index (SOCL)." (Bloomberg, 2012). |
| Benchmark description tion | "Standard and Poor's 500 Index (SPX) is a capitalization-weighted index of 500 stocks. The index is designed to measure performance of the broad domestic economy through changes in the aggregate market value of 500 stocks representing all major industries. The index was developed with a base level of 10 for the 1941- 43 base period." (Bloomberg, 2012). |

| Summary | |
|---|---|
| Start Date | November 30, 2011 |
| End Date | December 31, 2012 |
| Currency | US$ |
| Frequency | Daily |
| Index categories | Total Return |

Total Return: -2.240 Benchmark: 17.189

Performance Analysis

| Performance: Daily | Portfolio (SOCL) | Benchmark (SPX) |
|---|---|---|
| Total Return 1 Month(s) | 1.01 | 0.91 |
| Total Return MTD | 1.01 | 0.91 |
| Total Return QTD | -5.36 | -0.38 |
| Total Return YTD | -0.37 | 16.00 |
| Total Return 3 Month(s) | -5.36 | -0.38 |
| Total Return 6 Month(s) | -4.75 | 5.95 |

| Summary | | |
|---|---|---|
| Total Return 1 Year(s) | -0.37 | 16.00 |
| Total Return 2 Year(s) | n/a | 18.45 |
| Total Return 3 Year(s) | n/a | 36.30 |
| **Risk: Weekly** | **Portfolio (SOCL)** | **Benchmark (SPX)** |
| Standard Deviation 1 Year(s) | 25.02 | 11.79 |
| Semivariance 1 Year(s) | 23.41 | 12.42 |
| Beta 1 Year(s) | 1.15 | n/a |
| Correlation 1 Year(s) | 0.54 | n/a |
| R-Squared 1 Year(s) | 0.30 | n/a |
| Information Ratio 1 Year(s) | -0.56 | n/a |
| Sharpe Ratio vs Risk Free 1 Year(s) | 0.01 | 1.17 |
| Tracking Error 1 Year(s) | 20.87 | n/a |

Source: calculations based on data downloaded from the Bloomberg Professional service, index definitions rom: http://www.bloomberg.com/markets/ [accessed: January 4, 2013].

# References

Al-Rodhan, N.R.F. *et al.* (2006), Definitions of Globalization: A Comprehensive Overview and a Proposed Definition, Geneva Centre for Security Policy, *Program on the Geopolitical Implications of Globalization and Transnational Security, Geneva,* Switzerland, pp. 1-21.

Bloomberg (2012):

Computer Crime Research Center (2012), definition of "cybercrime": http://www.crime-research.org/articles/joseph06/ [accessed: December 31, 2012].

Dumay, J. (2012), IC is Alive and Well Yet Still Seeking Relevance, *Editorial for the ECIC Special Issue of the Electronic Journal of Knowledge Management (EJKM), Academic Publishing International Ltd.,* Volume 10, Issue 3, Reading, United Kingdom, pp. 1-4.

Edvinsson, L., Malone, M.S. (1997), Intellectual Capital. The Proven Way to Establish Your Company's Real Value by Measuring its Hidden Brainpower, HarperBusiness (HarperCollins Publishers, Inc.), London, United Kingdom.

EFAMA – European Fund and Asset Management Association (2012), *Factbook, Trends in European Investment Funds, 10th Edition,* Brussels, Belgium, pp. 1-324.

Falkowski, M., Wiśniewski, P. (2013), Impact Investment as a New Investment Class, *Contemporary Economics (forthcoming),* Warsaw, Poland, pp. 1-25.

Fetzer, J.H. (2003), Information: Does it Have To Be True?, *Minds and Machines*, Volume 14, Issue 2, Lisbon, Portugal, pp. 223-229.

Google Ngram Viewer (2012): http://books.google.com/ngrams [accessed: December, 30, 2012].

Google Trends (2012): http://www.google.pl/trends/ [accessed: December 30, 2012].

Grant, J.E. *et al.* (2004), Introduction to Behavioral Addictions, The American Journal of Drug and Alcohol Abuse, Vol. 36, No. 5, *US National Library of Medicine*, London, United Kingdom, pp. 233-241.

Hudson, W.J. (1993), Intellectual Capital. How to Build It, Enhance It, Use It, John Wiley & Sons, Inc., New York, United States of America, pp. 1-231.

Kaplan, A.M., Haenlein, M (2010) Users of the World, Unite! The Challenges and Opportunities of Social Media, Kelley School of Business, Indiana University/Business Horizons, Elsevier, No. 52, Amsterdam, The Netherlands, pp. 59-68.

Kaplan, A.M., Haenlein, M (2012) Social Media: Back to the Roots and Back to the Future (invited comment on the theme of the special issue); Social Media: Back to the Roots (Special Issue), *Journal of Systems and Information Technology*, Emerald Group Publishing Limited, Vol. 15, No. 2, Bingley, United Kingdom, pp. 101-104.

Miller, A (2011) 6 Classifications of Social Media (Blog) http://www.prmarketing.com/blog/6-classifications-of-social-media/ [accessed: December 31, 2012].

OPC, Office of the Privace Commissioner of Canada (2012): http://www.priv.gc.ca/resource/pb-avp/pb_hb_e.asp [accessed: December 31, 2012].

Przeworski, A. *et al.* (2000), Democracy and Development: Political Institutions and Well-Being in the World, 1950-1990, Cambridge University Press, Cambridge, United Kingdom, pp. 1-336.

Roos, G. *et al.* (2005), Managing Intellectual Capital in Practice, Butterworth-Heinemann/Elsevier, Inc., Burlington, MA, United States of America, pp. 1-258.

Schlechty, P.C. (2004) Shaking Up the Schoolhouse: How to Support and Sustain Educational Innovation (Jossey-Bass Education, Imprint of John Wiley & Sons, Inc.), 1st Edition, New York, United States of America; samples available online at:http://catdir.loc.gov/catdir/samples/wiley031/00009570.pdf [accessed: December 31, 2012].

Stewart, T.A. (1997), Intellectual Capital. The New Wealth of Organizations, Double-day/Currency, New York, United States of America, pp. 1-246.

Stewart, T.A. (2001), The Wealth of Knowledge. Intellectual Capital and the Twenty-First Century Organization, Nicholas Brealey Publishing/Utopia Limited, London, United Kingdom, pp. 1-336.

Sullivan, P.H. (2000), Value-Driven Intellectual Capital. How to Convert Intangible Corporate Assets into Market Value, John Wiley & Sons, Inc., New York, United States of America, pp. 4-7.

The Social Media Guys (2010), online research reports available on the The Social Media Guys website (http://www.thesocialmediaguys.co.uk/resources/:) http://www.thesocialmediaguys.co.uk/wp-content/uploads/downloads/2011/03/CompleteGuidetoSocialMedia.pdf [accessed: December 31, 2012].

# Introduction to Leading Issues in Social Media for Learning

## by Susan Greener

It is generally held to be true that travel broadens the mind. Is it therefore the case that travelling across an ocean of social networks broadens and enriches our capacity to learn?

Many research papers suggest that with new media and new technologies for learning we are genuinely experiencing new ways to learn. Hold that thought for a moment. Have you asked yourself how you learn lately? If the answer is yes, you may have noticed some considerable changes in learning behaviour. You may find that you no longer search paper books for needed knowledge, or when you ask questions of others, they turn to mobile devices for the answer, whether or not they think they know. You may be scheduling far more meetings online than a few years back, and be calendar rather than diary dependent for the structure of your daily life. As a researcher you may be sharing your work at earlier stages for feedback from your networks, or widening your connections with researchers in your field across the globe without necessarily having to travel to international conferences.

Our learning lives have certainly been changed by our growing love affair with social technologies. But my question was about new ways of learning. If things in our learning lives are changing, then are we learning differently? Have social media begun to change our processing of information, our notions of connectivity and constructivism, our personal learning outcomes?

This may or may not be so; and it could be hard to tell for a generation as our behaviour and understanding of the impacts of social and learning technologies matures. But there are some tentative conclusions we may already draw. Social media is not a value or even culture- neutral phenomenon. Most of our most popular applications are commercially hosted and developed as part of someone's business plan. This doesn't equate them with evil, as Google likes to insist, but it does perhaps give us pause for thought as we rush into the delights and temptations of connecting with friends and colleagues, and, importantly, pull them into our designs for formal learning both in educational institutions and in the workplace.

We may wish to unpick briefly here the difference between scepticism and cynicism or fear of the unknown. Designers of learning experiences will all have met the latter two responses among colleagues; particularly if they are enthusiasts for learning technologies and striving to convince their peers of the greater learner engagement and opportunities to blur the boundaries of formal and informal learning through social networks. Research into social media and learning needs to explore and build evidence-based conclusions which help us debate the benefits and barriers associated with suchtechnology enhanced learning. A touch of healthy scepticism here would be a good antidote to the vast range of reported innovations in education which are daily reported as satisfying students and improving learning engagement and performance.

People learn if they want to and (or) if they need to. As educators we design educational experiences to address these time- honoured conditions. We focus on improving the learner experience to make it motivational and we set up academic or performance-based hurdles which have to be jumped to demonstrate learning. Social media seems to present us with some wonderful quick fixes here, if we accept that younger learners and, increasingly, older learners are acclimatising to the social media landscape, then building them into learning designs seems a popular move and should help to connect them with the tidal wave of information both learners and educators have to surf to stay up to date.

So the three specific issues we have identified for this volume in relation to learning and social media are three areas of potential risk in a wholesale welcoming of social media into the learning domain. The first has to do with the skills, behaviours and the understanding which is needed to get the best from social media, and even information and communication technologies in general. We need social media now for living in the real world and trying to make sense of it, so it clearly has a place in learning, but what, in terms of digital literacy, may prevent learners from taking a full and active part in such learning? Secondly, we need social media for professional learning and networking, to stay in touch with research, customers, suppliers, competitors and this affects any work we undertake, but does sharing increasing amounts of knowledge help? Will we need Web 3.0 machine-to-machine communication to simplify the task, and how will we know if we are getting what we want? Finally, we can design better and better activities for learners, which engage their sense of today's technology, but does this weigh them down too much in terms of cognitive load? The three papers in this section address these key issues. The reader might do well to keep in mind the original question, are these new social media enriching our capacity to learn?

ways of learning, or new ways of behaving which may or may not prove to be learning?

# The Relevancy of Digital Literacy for Malaysian Students for Learning With WEB 2.0 Technology

## Tenku Putri Norishah Tenku Shariman[1], Othman Talib[2] and Nazerin Ibrahim[1]

[1]Multimedia University, Malaysia [2]University Putra Malaysia, Malaysia

tengku.norishah@mmu.edu.my, otalib@upm.edu.my,
nazerin@mmu.edu.my

Originally published in The Proceedings of ECEL 2014

## Editorial Commentary

One way in which technology has disrupted learning processes is the unshackling of the formal learning environment. No longer do we as learners have to accept what we are given by teachers, automatically according it authority. The enquiring mind can explore freely, using not just static webpages but creating new knowledge through discussion beyond the classroom with friends, experts and wider connections.

This paper is based on these new freedoms to roam, which are of little value without the digital literacy skills required to hack our way through the jungle of knowledge, enabling us to cut through the shallow and trivial and seek out ideas worth transplanting. The authors present results of a student survey based on Ng's three factor digital literacy framework which confirms technical competency but shows room for improvement in the cognitive and socio-emotional domains vital for effective learning.

**Abstract:** E-learning has transitioned from mere retrieval of information to active participation of students who voluntarily engage in the learning process. As Riedel (2009) reported, Web 2.0 is about putting the power to learn and create in the hands of the students. Before the advent of Web 2.0, e-learning was primarily used to complement traditional pedagogical modes with an online component, whereas web 2.0 technology introduced new modes of learning, enabling greater reflection and discussion among learners as they construct knowledge online (Lau, 2012). Therefore at this stage, the role of digital literacy in e-learning is even more relevant. Digital literacy which refers to the effective and efficient use of web 2.0 technology to access and use the digital information needed for a variety of online tasks (Coiro, Knoble, Lankshear & Leu, 2008) should not be regarded as a separate set of skills, but instead embedded within and across e-learning activities and tasks. Although today's students have grown up around technology devices and most probably use these devices on a daily basis, they may not have necessarily have the digital literacy to appropriately use web 2.0 technology for constructivist e-learning activities and tasks. For this research, questionnaires were distributed among students in several universities across Malaysia to identify the digital literacy competencies of students for application in e-learning. Thus, this paper reports the findings of the study which aims to answer the following questions: (1) What are students' perceptions regarding their digital literacy competency? (2) How does digital literacy affect their e-learning with 2.0 technologies? The results revealed that even though students have high confidence in using Web 2.0 technology, they still lacked the digital literacy competencies needed to successfully accomplish e-learning tasks and activities.

**Keywords:** digital literacy, Web 2.0 technology, e-learning, technical domain, cognitive domain, social emotional domain

# 1. Introduction

*Digital technologies and new media are now prevalent in many aspects of teaching and learning. Consequently students need to develop more than just their Information and Communication Technology (ICT) skills; they need to be aware of the broader context in which these technologies and media function so they will be able to apply their ICT skills effectively and efficiently in an increasing digital world. ICT skill is not a factor whether or not students are able to be effective e-learners in universities across Malaysia because ICT has been used as a tool and a way to improve the pedagogy of teaching and learning in schools and universities across Malaysia since 1996. Furthermore the national e-Learning project, which involved the creation of web presence, web tools that promote collaboration, and web-based services to students to obtain sought-after information, was launched in 2000 (MOHE, 2011). One of the project's milestones was providing a Learning Management System to all public universities that offers e-learning applications such as Communications (96.2%), Course Delivery (96.2%), Productivity (88.5%), Content Development (80.8%), and Administration (73.1%). However, only a few of the universities (65.4%) had LMS features that encourage students' involvement, such as group work and portfolio [15]. Therefore, it is not surprising that only 4.7%*

*of students studying in Malaysia's universities indicated that technophobia is one of the problems they faced in adopting e-learning (M.A. Embi, 2011).*

*For the Internet generation university students, known as well as the digital natives (Prensky, 2011), surfing the Internet and working on computers is considered second nature in view of the fact that they have never known a world without technology or the Internet; they frequently and actively communicate, cooperate, and connect using technology in the virtual realm. One of the technologies that they often utilise is Web 2.0 applications such as blogs, Instagram, social networking and video sharing sites, among others. Moreover, the e-learning environment has changed to integrate and utilize Web 2.0 elements to create an environment and system that supports e-learning 2.0; an approach of learning that is centred on collaboration and constructive learning activities mediated by a range of Web 2.0 tools for exchanging content and sharing knowledge (Riedel, 2009; M.H. Zakaria, Watson and Edwards, 2012). Hence, Web 2.0 tools should prompt students to actively participate in e-learning activities at their respective universities.*

# 2. Problem statement

*It is undeniable that students are engaging actively with technology, however they may not be intuitively digital literate as conceived by the Internet Generation Theorists. A number of studies (Banwell and Gannon-Leary, 2000; Case, 2002; Coiro, Knobel and Lankshear, 2008; Combes, 2007; Jones, Ramanau, Cross and Healing, 2010) have brought up contrary evidence that indicates this generation may not be as adept as has been supposed in employing technology as an electronic information resource.* Unfortunately, being a digital native does not mean having innate digital literacy. Most often students are unable to discern the validity and value of information found online, or use that information appropriately; they also have few constraints on using digital technologies for sharing purposes like understanding copyright issues. *In light of these findings, the present study is significant to* identify the digital literacy competencies of students for application in e-learning. Today's students need help acquiring these abilities and behaviours.

## 2.1. Objectives and research questions

In order to answer the problem statement, the researcher had developed a few research objectives which are to determine:

- the level of digital literacy competence as perceived by students when they apply web 2.0 technology for e-learning tasks; and
- the effect of digital literacy on students' e-learning tasks with 2.0 technologies
- The research questions built from this research are as follows:
- What are students' perceptions regarding their digital literacy competency?
- How does digital literacy affect their e-learning with 2.0 technologies?

## 3. Review of literature

Computers and digital technologies have merged the previously known literacy skills, such as writing, reading or numeracy problem-solving with new literacy skills in constructing new knowledge, creating media expressions, and communicating with others, in the context of specific life situations in order to enable constructive social action; and to reflect upon this process (Passey, 2011). Digital literacy is a concept that has arisen out of the current lifestyle and online practices of the Internet Generation, like communication and interactions with advanced digital applications and devices. Lankshear and Knobel (2003) have described new literacies as new types of knowledge associated with *"digitally saturated social practices"* (p.11). For example, word processing has become a standard for writing (instead of pen and paper), emails and short messaging system has dominated modes of communication, and sites like Facebook, Twitter and Youtube have enabled users to share ideas.

Moreover, a digital literate person will adapt to new, emerging technologies faster and pick up new semiotics language for communication. According to Martin (2010), a digital literate person has the awareness, attitude and ability to appropriately use digital tools and facilities to identify, access, manage, integrate, evaluate, analyse and synthesize digital resources, construct new knowledge, create media expressions, and communicate with others. To design a pedagogy suitable for the Web 2.0 environment, educators are advised to embed constructivist theory in classroom practices that often comprise four critical conditions: (1) Multi–construction of learning process/ perspectives, (2) Contextual learning that suits to learner's needs (3) Mediated learning tools (technology) and semiotic tools (signs), and (4) Social-dialogical activity of learning (Duffy and Cunningham, 1996). Web 2.0 technology supports constructivist learning activities that encourage dialogic discourse among students to encourage students to look beyond their own views and incorporate realistic or authentic contexts for learning. As an example, project based learning with ICT has been applied to engage students in classrooms as a means to help students acquire knowledge more easily as they are the ones who are involved in the process of gathering the information from web-based resources and presenting their ideas on-line. Consequently, a digitally literate student will be easily adaptable to this constructivist based Web 2.0 learning environment because these conditions are believed to match the digital natives' philosophy of learning, whereby they have a preference to search for authentic meaning through exploration and discussion (Lankshear and Knobel, 2003).

In light of these theories, literacy is generally understood today as being inclusive of various technological, cognitive, and social skills that adapt to a "rapid and continuous process of change in the ways in which we read, write, view, listen, compose, and communicate information" (Coiro, Knobel, Lankshear and Leu, 2008). Hence, digital literacy should not be viewed from the narrow perspective of acquiring 'ICT skills and competencies', where digital literacy is reduced to knowledge of computer softwares such as MS Excel, Word, and other similar softwares commonly used in universities for teaching and learning purposes. Voogt and Pareja Roblin (2012) argue that digital literacy should not be regarded as a separate set of skills, but instead embedded within and across the other 21st century skills and core subjects. Calvani, Fini and Ranieri (2008) proposed a conceptual model to represent digital competence. As illustrated in Figure 1 below, digital competence is the ability " *to explore and face new technological situations in a flexible way, to analyse, select and critically evaluate data and information, to exploit technological potentials to solve problems or to create knowledge collaboratively, and finally, to foster awareness of individual responsibility and respect for others*" (p.161).

Similarly, at a more specific level, Ng [18] has suggested three main domains of literacy that are associated with digital literacy, which are technical, cognitive and socio-emotional as shown in Figure 2 below.

These three (3) intersecting domains involve interaction with digital based resources for decoding, reproducing and creating data. For example, the technical domain intersects with the cognitive domain because to construct and reconstruct knowledge, it necessary to navigate through digital media, and use online and offline tools to decode and convey meanings in the best sense possible (Ng, 2012). In summarizing the above discussion, being digitally literate requires the development of technical, cognitive and social emotional competencies. These three competencies encompass a set of abilities necessary for

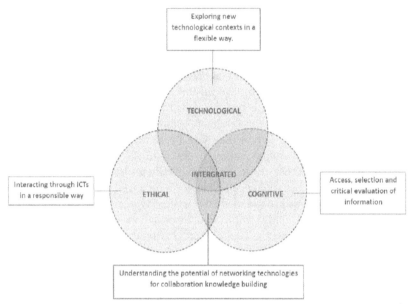

**Figure 1:**     Digital competence framework (Calvani et al, 2008)

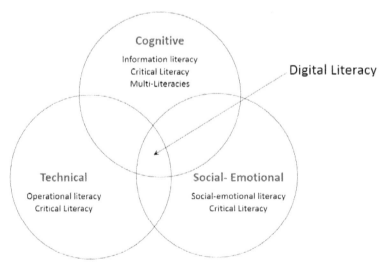

**Figure 2:**     Digital literacy model (Ng, 2012)

creating content, organizing and sharing content, reusing or repurposing content, filtering and selecting content across a variety of digital platforms, which is known as transliteracy. Other online practices such as self-broadcasting, and social networking also need to use digital technologies with cognitive, technical and social emotional competencies. Finally, all these tasks and practices require another set digital literacy ability which protects students online, like managing identity and maintaining privacy (Wheeler, 2012). As Howard Rheingold explained in his book, NetSmart (2012), access to technology is no longer an educational problem in the current Web 2.0 learning environment, but the delineation between those who know how and those who don't know how to search, sift and discern relevant information is.

# 4. Data collection

*This study was exploratory in nature, focusing on a convenience sampling of the final-year students who are pursuing their degrees at two universities in Malaysia. A survey was conducted with this group of students through a common Project Management subject which is a compulsory subject for all final-year students. Empirical data were collected through a survey questionnaire. Out of the 785 registered final-year students, 420 of them responded to the questionnaire. The general approach employed to design the questionnaire is to combine both the pre-coded and open questions. The pre-coded parts are used with a number of listed items and students are required to tick the boxes most relevant to them. A degree of openness is provided in the survey for the students to give their responses about their thoughts on digital literacy in their own words through the open-ended questions. The students' perception was measured through a list of propositions listed in the questionnaire in order to collect the relevant information regarding what they perceived as their skill and confidence in using technologies for digital literacy purposes, like filtering and selecting content, socialising and communicating, creating, organising and repurposing content as well as digital identity and digital safety.*

The first section of the questionnaire gathers demographic data pertaining to age, gender, nationality, course of study and Internet access. The second section is designed to gather information about patterns of ICT and Web 2.0 utilisation. The third section contains items that examine the respondents' digital literacy level. This section contains 18 questions on a four-point scale marked as: 1 (Basic competency), 2 (Moderate competency), 3 (High competency) and 4 (Expert Competency). The respondents were asked to perceive and self-evaluate their digital literacy level along this continuum. The measurement sub-scales used to assess digital literacy adhere to the following domains: Scale scores were obtained by summing the score for each item. The maximum possible score that a respondent could obtain was: 4 (point 4) × 18 (items) = 72. The minimum possible score that a respondent could obtain was: 1 (point 1) × 18(items) = 18. The scores from the survey would be used on a scale of 18–72 to mark the respondent as Basic, Moderate, High or Expert. Table 2 illustrates the three literacy domains and the items that indicate competency for each domain.

# 5. Data analysis

## 5.1. Profiles

The profiles of the respondents were analysed by using the SPSS descriptive analysis function. The outputs are tabulated as seen in Table 3.

Table 1    Instant digital competence assessment instrument

| Domain | Contents |
|---|---|
| Technical | 6 items focusing on examining students' understanding and abilities in using computers and the Internet in their daily lives |
| Cognitive | 6 items related to general cognitive skills, mostly linguistic or logic-linguistic capacities |
| Social-Emotional | 6 items related to three subsections focusing on protecting personal data, respecting other Net users and being aware of the digital gap |

Table 2    Level of digital literacy

| Category | Scale |
|---|---|
| Basic Competency | 18-30 |
| Moderate Competency | 31-44 |
| High Competency | 45-58 |
| Expert Competency | 59-72 |

Table 3    Demographic characteristics of respondents

| Characteristic | N | % |
|---|---|---|
| *Gender* | | |
| Male | 199 | 47.4 |
| Female | 221 | 52.6 |
| Total | 420 | 100 |
| *Age at survey time* | | |
| 22-24 | 296 | 70.5 |
| 25-27 | 118 | 28.0 |
| 28-30 | 5 | 1.19 |
| above 30 | 0 | 0.00 |
| Missing | 1 | 0.24 |
| Total | 420 | 100 |
| *Nationality* | | |
| Malaysian | 328 | 78.1 |
| Non-Malaysian | 92 | 21.9 |
| Total | 420 | 100 |
| *Technologies used to access Internet* ** | | |
| Mobile phones | 194 | 46.2 |
| Smartphones | 282 | 67.1 |
| Tablet | 202 | 48.1 |
| Lap top with built in Wi-Fi | 409 | 97.4 |
| Desktop | 56 | 13.3 |
| IPod/portable music/video devices | 35 | 8.3 |
| *Experience in using Internet technologies*** | | |
| Using search engine to locate relevant information for academic work | 420 | 100.0 |
| Using online library catalogue | 196 | 46.7 |
| Using online learning materials (e-learning) | 385 | 91.7 |
| Using social networking websites (e.g. FB) | 393 | 93.6 |

| Characteristic | N | % |
|---|---|---|
| Using instant messaging or chat (e.g. WeChat, WhatsApp) | 377 | 89.8 |
| Blogging (e.g. WordPress, BlogSpot) | 276 | 65.7 |
| Micro-blogging (e.g. twitter) | 278 | 66.2 |
| Uploading something onto Internet (video, photos) | 374 | 89.0 |
| Taking part in an online community, e.g. a "virtual world" (e.g. Second Life) | 92 | 21.9 |
| Playing Online Games such (e.g. World of Warcraft) | 263 | 62.6 |
| Watching and listening an audio visual content (e.g. music, movies) | 321 | 76.4 |
| *Web 2.0 technology Usage* | | |
| Passive User(monthly or less) | 53 | 12.6 |
| Moderate user (weekly) | 139 | 33.1 |
| Active User (use it daily) | 228 | 54.3 |
| Total | 420 | 100 |

**Respondents may check more than once and all that apply, hence there is no total count for that dimension and the count of percentage is based on 420 as 100% for each item/mobile device.

Some highlights of the demographic profiles of the respondents are as follows: Forty seven (47.6%) of the participants in this study were male and fifty two percent (52.6%) were female. Over seventy percent (70.5%) of the respondents were between 22-24 years of age and slightly less (28%) were 25-27. The remaining 1% were older than 28 and are not considered traditional students. All of the students have access and are connected to the Internet especially through laptops or smart phones. Despite being students, without their own income source, a large number of the students own mobile devices from the higher price range; as an example 67% owns a smart phone and another 48% owns a tablet. Therefore, mobile devices are presently considered a necessity for students as a convenient way of communicating and sharing or retrieving information. From their experience in using Internet technologies, we can conclude that the majority of students use the Internet for learning (92% use online learning materials provided by their lecturers and 100% use a search engine to locate relevant information needed to complete academic tasks or assignments), communication (94% use social networking sites and another 90% use the instant messaging application), and to a lesser extent entertainment (63% play online games and 76% watch and listen to audio-visual content).

## 5.2. Students' perception regarding digital literacy

To determine the level of digital literacy competence among technical students, a questionnaire was used to measure the perception of students regarding their digital literacy as they apply Web 2.0 technology for e-learning tasks. All variables were analysed by descriptive statistics (i.e. frequencies, means and standard deviations). To test the reliability, the internal consistency of the skill levels questionnaire was measured using Cronbach's alpha coefficient. The alpha for the whole sample was found to be 0.82, indicating a good level of item reliability (George and Mallery, 2003) that has exceeded the minimum alpha of 0.6 (Hair, 1998). The percentage of competency level for each literacy was compared to the Level of Digital Literacy Competence Table (refer to table 2). All the data collected were analyzed using the SPSS software and reported to determine the digital literacy competency level of Malaysian students, as perceived by students who are studying technical courses at two universities.

Based on Table 2: Level of Digital Literacy, the digital literacy level of competency among the respondents is shown in Table 5 below.

In concluding the findings, the means for all the competency levels for each respondent were calculated (Table 4.4) to advance an overall ranking of their digital literacy competency level. The analysis (Table 5) revealed that 40.5 of the respondents are in the high competency category, while 52% are in the moderate proficiency category, and 7.6% are in the basic competency category. None of the respondents fell in the expert competency category.

Based on the Table 4, according to the perception of students on their digital literacy competency, the overall level of digital literacy competency in the technical domain is high among technical students with a mean of above 3.00 for all 6 items. However, the mean for the cognitive and social-emotional domains is considered moderate overall. Although these students can be accorded the status of being tech savvy, being highly competent in using Web 2.0 technology, they still need to improve on certain digital literacy aspects in order to successfully apply their Web 2.0 technology skills for learning purposes. A few of these aspects include being able to evaluate the credibility of information sources or assist their peers effectively over the Internet. These are instances of the crucial aspects of digital literacy in the cognitive and social emotional domains that students need to grasp in order to be successful participants of e-learning at higher education institutions.

Table 4    Students' perception of digital literacy level

| Digital Literacy Domain | Mean | Standard Deviation |
|---|---|---|
| *Technical* | | |
| Technical skills in using ICT for learning online | 3.83 | 0.95 |
| Technical skills to create artefacts (e.g. presentations, digital stories, wikis, blogs) | 3.30 | 0.70 |
| Navigate the Internet without getting disoriented | 3.68 | 0.82 |
| Manage files in computer and in the cloud | 3.56 | 0.85 |
| Content creation with multi-media tools (e.g. Image editing, video editing, web page software) | 3.12 | 0.800 |
| Computer maintenance (e.g. fixing virus problem or solve other technical problems) | 3.03 | 0.89 |
| *Cognitive* | | |
| Awareness of issues related to web-based activities e.g. cyber safety, search issues, plagiarism | 2.23 | 0.87 |
| Evaluation of information sources (reliable, trustworthy, authentic or credible trustworthy or authentic) | 1.30 | 0.65 |
| Use advanced search options in search phrases (AND, OR etc) | 2.63 | 0.73 |
| Use search tools that combine multiple fields to limit the search (e.g. limiting to a date range, or to a chosen publication) | 2.57 | 0.86 |
| Search by using keywords commonly used in the discipline | 2.88 | 0.87 |
| Filter and select relevant information | 3.05 | 0.80 |
| *Social Emotional* | | |
| Awareness of copyright restrictions | 2.64 | 0.96 |
| Control of privacy, security and access permissions | 2.99 | 0.86 |
| Collaborate with peers on project work and other learning activities | 3.12 | 0.73 |
| Peer assistance over the Internet e.g. through Skype, Facebook, Blogs | 2.59 | 0.96 |
| Practice Netiquette to avoid offending people | 2.90 | 0.98 |
| Share file legally with others (e.g. using social bookmarking to organise and share information) | 3.08 | 0.70 |

Table 5    digital literacy level of competency

|  | Frequency | Percentage |
|---|---|---|
| Basic competency | 32 | 7.6% |
| Moderate competency | 218 | 52.0% |
| High competency | 170 | 40.5% |
| Expert competency | 0 | 0 |
| Total | 420 | 100 |

These findings indicate three aspects of digital literacy, namely technical, cognitive and social-emotional competence, are needed by Malaysian students in order to participate actively in Web 2.0 constructivist learning activities. Digital literacy is not a purely technical competency, and should not be dissociated from the cognitive and social-emotional aspects of literacy that are required to enhance the accomplishment of students in their academic tasks as they engage with a multiplicity of multimedia and digital technologies to "process, interact and use information and communicate in fundamentally different ways than any previous generation" (Kingsley, 2010).

# 4. Conclusion

E-learning with the use of Web 2.0 technology emphasizes on creating a community of scholars among students since it offers an assortment of tools that learners can mix and match to meet their individual learning style and get support from other participants (Rheingold, 2012) . Web 2.0 technology facilitates the individual students to collaborate, create, and share content with other students (Lau, 2012). Therefore, e-learning has progressed from its initial purpose of just delivering course materials to students and focusing on one way knowledge transfer to a more interactive, student-centred, and collaborative form of knowledge transfer.

In general, the study has ascertained that Web 2.0 technology is already in the hands of students, however further training and exposure is needed to ensure effective and productive use of ICT and Web 2.0 technology for e-learning activities. This study offers an insight about technical students' perceptions of their digital literacy competence; majority of the students are either in the high competence or moderate competence category. However, there is still space for improvement in the cognitive and social emotional domains of digital literacy. It is suggested that to achieve quality learning and successful integration of Web 2.0, the following factors have to be taken into consideration (Conole and Alevizou, 2010):

- Both instructors and students must support student-centered educational approach.
- A pedagogical approach must allow students to contribute to knowledge creation.
- The approach must be well structured and understood by both instructors and students. The students must not be confused as to what is expected of them, and to what standard.
- The processes and students output must be assessed as part of overall course assessment practices.

In conclusion, the deployment of Web 2.0 technology for e-learning in higher education institutions is a positive intervention to improve the learning process of students. Therefore, any new effort in e-learning implementation must try to accommodate to the students' differences and needs, including their digital literacy competency level. From her study, Ng (2012) revealed that most students were not as concerned about the technical aspects of unfamiliar technologies compared to planning and preparing content and integrating it with Web 2.0 to create artefacts. Consequently, the process of finding information and multimedia materials to create learning artefacts is of the upmost importance. Digital literacy is an important factor that facilitates students to improve their e-learning participation. Research in current literacy needs should not view digital literacy as a purely technical skill, or else researchers are in a delusion that online activities are divorced from social and cultural concerns (Conole and Alevizou, 2010). It is undeniable that technical skills are an advantage in e-learning; nevertheless this research clearly shows that e-learning at higher education institutes have other specific digital literacy requirements for their students, like the cognitive and social emotional domains, hence higher education institutions should incorporate digital literacy in their instruction to enhance their students' digital literacy competence.

# Acknowledgements

The authors would like to thank the Ministry of Higher Education (MOHE) for granting an Exploratory Research Grant Scheme (ERGS) to undertake the study for a period of two years (August 2012 - August 2014).

# References

Banwell, L. and Gannon-Leary, P. (2000) "JUBILEE: Monitoring User Information Behaviour in the Electronic Age", *OCLC Systems and Services*, Vol 16 , No. 4, pp. 189 – 193.

Bennett, S., Maton, K. and Kervin, L. (2008) "The 'digital natives' debate: A critical review of the evidence" , *British Journal of Educational Technology*, Vol 39, No. 5, pp. 775–786.

Calvani, A., Cartelli, A., Fini, A., and Ranieri, M. (2008) "Models and instruments for assessing digital competence at school", *Journal of E-learning and Knowledge Society*, Vol 4, No.3, pp. 183-193.

Case, D.O. (2002) *Looking for Information: A Survey of Research on Information Seeking, Needs and Behavior*, Academic Press, California.

Coiro, J., Knobel, M., Lankshear, C. and Leu, D. (Eds). (2008) *Handbook of Research on New Literacies*, Lawrence Erlbaum Associates, New York.

Combes, B. (2007) "Techno Savvy or just Techno Oriented? How do the 'Net Generation' Search for Information?" , Paper read ASLAXX BiennialConference: Hearts on Fire, Sharing the Passion, Adelaide, Australia, December.

Conole, G. and Alevizou, P. (2010) *A literature review of the use of Web 2.0 tools in Higher Education*. HEA Academy, York, UK.

George, D. and Mallery, P. (2003). *SPSS for Windows step by step: A simple guide and reference*, 4th ed., Allyn & Bacon, Boston.

Hair, J. E., Anderson, R. E., Tatham, R. L. and Black, W. C. (1998) *Multivariate Data Analysis*, 5th ed., Prentice-Hall, New Jersey.

Jones, C., Ramanau, R., Cross, S. and Healing, G. (2010) "Net generation or digital natives: is there a distinct generation entering university?", *Computer & Education*, Vol 54, No.3, pp. 722 -732.

Kingsley, K.V.(2010) "Technology-Mediated Critical Literacy in K-12 Contexts: Implications for 21st Century Teacher Education", *Journal of Literacy and Technology*, Vol 11, No. 3, pp. 2-39.

Lankshear, C. and Knobel, M. (2003) *New Literacies: Changing Knowledge and Classroom Practice*. Open University Press, Buckingham, UK.

Lau, Alwyn. (2012) "Web 2.0 as a Catalyst for Rethinking Teaching & Learning in Tertiary Education", Paper read at ASCILITE 2012, Wellington, New Zealand, November.

Livingstone, S., Bober, M. and Helsper, E.J. (2005) "Active participation or just more information? Young people's take up of opportunities to act and interact on the internet", *Information, Communication & Society*, Vol. 8, No. 3, pp. 287-314.

Martin, A. (2010) "Literacies for the Digital Age", *Digital literacies for learning*. Facet, London.

Mohd. Amin Embi. (2011) "E-Learning in Malaysian Institutions of Higher Learning: Status, Trends and Challenges", Keynote speech at International Lifelong Learning Conference (ICLLL 2011), Kuala Lumpur, November.

Mohd. Hafiz, Zakaria, Watson, J. and Edwards, S.L. (2012) "The Adoption of e-Learning 2.0 in Higher Education by Teachers and Students: An Investigation Using Mixed Methods Approach", *International Journal of e-Education, e-Business, e-Management and e-Learning*, Vol. 2, No. 2, pp. 108 -112.

MOHE. (2011) *e-Learning in Malaysian Higher Education Institutions: Status, Trends, & Challenges*, ed. Mohamed Amin Embi. MOHE Printing, Kuala Lumpur.

Ng, W. (2012) "Can we teach digital natives digital literacy?", *Computers & Education*, Vol. 59, No.3, pp. 1065– 1078.

Passey, D. (2011) *Pursuing digital literacy in compulsory education*. Stergioulas, L. H.and Drenoyianni, H. (eds.). Peter Lang, New York, pp. 117-137.

Prensky, M. (2001) "Digital Natives, Digital Immigrants Part. 1", *On the Horizon*, Vol. 9, No. 5, pp. 1 – 6.

Prensky, M. (2007) "How to teach with technology: Keeping both teachers and students comfortable in an era of exponential change", *Emerging Technologies for Learning*, Vol. 2, pp. 40 – 46.

Rheingold, Howard (2012) *Net Smart: How to Thrive Online*, MIT Press, Boston.

Riedel, C. (2009) "The Evolution of education: Empowering learners to think, create, share, and do", [online], http://thejournal.com/articles/2009/01/30/the-evolution-of-education-empowering-learners-to-think-create-share-and-do.aspx?sc_lang=en.

Rodriguez, J. (2011) "Social media use in higher education: Key areas to consider for educators", Journal *of Online Learning and Teaching*, Vol. 7, No.4, pp. 539-550. [online], http://jolt.merlot.org/vol7no4/rodriguez_1211.htm

Rowlands, I., Nicholas, D., Williams, P., Huntington, P., Fieldhouse, M., Gunter, B., Withey, R., Jamali, H.R., Dobrowolski, T., and Tenopir, C. (2008) "The Google generation: the information behaviour of the researcher of the future", *Aslib Proceedings*, Vol 60, No.4, pp.290 – 310.

Voogt, J. and Pareja Roblin, N. (2012) "Teaching and learning in the 21st century. A comparative analysis of international frameworks", *Journal of Curriculum Studies*, Vol. 44, No.3, pp. 299 - 321.

Wheeler, S. (2012) "Digital literacies for engagement in emerging online cultures", *eLC Research Paper Series*, No. 5, pp. 14-25.

# Effective Knowledge Sharing Through Social Technologies

## Jaroslava Kubátová

Palacký University, Olomouc, Czech Republic

Jaroslava.kubatova@upol.cz

Originally published in The Proceedings of ECKM 2013

## Editorial commentary

Is there a distinction between learning and sharing knowledge? Potentially of course there is a great gulf here, particularly if we consider the study of formal qualifications. However, in this well grounded paper, the author moves the debate to corporate learning and knowledge sharing. In this context, ten areas of organisational performance are identified which can benefit from learning through social technologies if the link between sharing and learning from knowledge can be made. The author explores through secondary data, originating from different world regions, the factors which may influence such a transition, and how social technologies' rapid absorption into corporate life may offer risks as well as opportunities.

**Abstract:** Social technologies available on the current Web 2.0 provide great opportunities for sharing and creating knowledge. Therefore, implementing social technologies within the framework of knowledge work entails one of the most significant activities carried out by companies today. The goal of the paper is to specify the greatest opportunities and also threats brought by the use of social technologies in terms of sharing knowledge and to recommend what kind of changes should the companies implement in order to use social technologies for knowledge sharing effectively. We have also examined if there are regional differences in the use of social technologies and how to deal with them in case of international cooperation. After a short state of the art description the terms *knowledge sharing, social technology, social media* and *social network* are defined. To achieve the goal of the paper, we have analyzed and compared four research reports from 2012: global research by the McKinsey Global Institute and three studies focused on different world regions (Europe, North America, the ASEAN countries). To carry out all the regionally focused research projects, the method of directly asking the managers was used. The results of the resultant analyses and comparisons of the research reports are further extended by the findings and predictions published by the Gartner agency at the end of 2012. In the next part of the paper we have determined the areas of company activities for which the use of social technologies is the most prospective. We have also documented to what extent companies use social technologies' potential and what kind of regional differences exist. We have assessed whether the companies are successful using social technologies and have also determined the most common causes for failure. Finally, we have presented recommendations about how to make the application of social technologies for knowledge sharing more effective. The most important factors are not those of a technological nature, but rather are arguably connected to the ways of managing knowledge workers and the behavior of the managers.

**Keywords:** social technologies, knowledge sharing

# 1. Knowledge sharing and social technologies

Knowledge, in its different forms, has been increasingly recognized as a crucial asset in modern organizations (Bonifacio, Bouquet and Cuel 2002). Knowledge sharing is some of the fundamental means through which employees can contribute to knowledge application, innovation and ultimately a competitive advantage of the organization they work for (Jackson et al. 2006). Knowledge sharing is a deliberate act by which knowledge is made reusable through its transfer from one party to another (Lee, Al-Hawamdeh 2002).

The process of knowledge sharing has been widely studied for several decades and was reflected by many knowledge management experts in their works, for example Drucker (1999), Davenport and Prusak (2000) or Nonaka and Takeuchi (1995). Nevertheless, there is still a continuing debate about the measurement of the volume of shared knowledge, because knowledge sharing can occur in many different forms (written correspondence, face-to-face communication, through networking etc.) and also knowledge as such can have various forms. Behrang, Wongthongtham and Hussain (2010) proposed a knowledge sharing measurement model, which is a function of knowledge nature and trust among workers. Fuzzification in this model is possible. Lee (2002) proposed metrics which are well trackable on-line, such as the number of links per respondent, frequency of advice seeking, the ratio of internal to external links, etc. The use of Internet-based social technologies for knowledge sharing is a new phenomenon and its reflection in scientific literature is scarce. Present-day knowledge in this field was published by Frank Leistner (2012) in his book *Connecting Organizational Silos: Taking Knowledge Flow Management to the Next Level with Social Media*.

Social technologies' entering life today was so quick that there was not enough time for a unified terminology connected to this phenomenon to originate. Therefore, let us first define the basic terms related to this topic. *Social network* is a set of relations formally created by objects (also known as knots), and reflects the relations between these objects. Objects (knots) are individuals, groups or organizations. While speaking about a *social network on the Internet*, we mean a combination of a webhosting service and a special search engine (Kadushin 2011). Internet social networks originate thanks to the available social media. *Social media* are interactive Internet platforms on which individuals and groups (users) share, co-create, discuss and modify the contents (Kietzmann, Hermkens and McCarthy 2011). In the broader sense of the word it is possible to speak about social technologies (Chui et al. 2012, p.13). *Social technologies* are used by people for the purpose of social interaction, for joint creating, extending and sharing of the contents. Social media (e.g. LinkedIn, Facebook, or Twitter), Web 2.0 tools (e.g. blogs, wikis, discussion forums, QaA pages) and collaborative tools including shared work environments (e.g. Chatter, Yammer, Work.com) can be included among social technologies defined in this way.

For the purpose of this article we consider the term *social technologies* as the most suitable for general use. For us, *social media* are particular Internet applications, and the term *social network* is used to emphasize the importance of interpersonal links and interactions of the users. External social network means a network accessible to the public (e.g. Facebook, LinkedIn, or Google+). Internal social network is a closed company network accessible only to the company's employees. External networks, however, also provide tools which can be used only by a closed group of persons, and, on the contrary, an internal network can be extended in order to have a part accessible to the public.

## 2. Areas of using social technologies in companies

The number of users of social technologies in 2012 exceeded 1.5 billion and social technologies are used by over 70% of companies in the world, out of which 90% declare that using social technologies brings them some benefits (Chui et al. 2012, p.30). We can determine ten particular areas in which the application of social technologies increases the performance of the organization thanks to sharing knowledge both among the company's employees and subjects outside the company.

## 2.1. Establishing and applying customers' opinions

Thanks to social technologies it is possible to get an overview of the customers' opinions of a particular product or brand, competition and other customer needs. These findings can then serve as a source for further decision-making within the organization. One of the approaches lies in monitoring and analyzing of what the users of social technologies express. This approach is usually denoted as *sentiment analysis*. Based on the results it is possible to immediately react and improve both the sales of the product and the brand name. Another approach lies in active communication with customers on social networks, discussion forums, etc. This way the company can attain necessary feedback on the product.

## 2.2. Collaboration on the development of a product

By the application of social technologies, companies can include a wider group of people in the development of a product than only their internal employees. One of the ways is to monitor and acquire customers' opinions. Another way is the application of crowdsourcing. This means that the company appeals to a wider group of participants (the crowd) to submit their ideas and proposals. These are then assessed (e.g. by the management, experts or again using crowdsourcing), and the best-assessed proposal is then realized.

## 2.3. Monitoring and predicting demand

Thanks to information shared on social networks it is possible to react to locally different demand for a product. In this case, information is valuable not only from the customers but also from staff, for example the sales people. Therefore it is appropriate to enable the employees to access the internal social network where they can describe the situation at their branch. Based on this information the company can quickly react in order to satisfy the customers' needs.

## 2.4. Searching for suppliers

Through social media companies can find external suppliers of both physical commodities and external coworkers for solving particular projects or problems. These can be both other companies and independent social technologies' users.

## 2.5. Marketing communication

Marketing communication is an important area of social technologies' application in marketing. Social technologies enable communication with target groups at very low expenses. The company can support the establishment of customer communities, enable their mutual communication, acquire necessary knowledge from this communication and directly influence it.

## 2.6. Creating and strengthening sales opportunities

Social technologies can support both the B2B and B2C areas. In case of B2B, sales representatives can establish mutual collaboration, find possibilities to do business with each other, acquire references and contacts to new partners. In case of B2C, social technologies' users' information about important events in their lives can be used, and they can be offered appropriate products. Strengthening a company's position on the market is connected to *social intelligence*, which is a set of activities used by the companies to ascertain strategic information about their competitors, which has been posted on social networks. It is a very complex analysis and synthesis of various information found on social networks, the result of which can be surprisingly detailed and bring an updated picture of the activities and intentions of their competitors (Harryson, Metayer and Sarrazin 2012).

## 2.7. Social commerce

Social commerce lies in the addition of sales functions to the seller's social media, or, on the contrary, in adding social features to the seller's Internet store. In the first case, for example, it can concern a discussion forum on a product created by the seller themselves. The product can be directly ordered from this forum, too. In the second case, for example, the customers can recommend a product they have bought to their friends, or enable their friends on a social network to see what they have purchased. On the contrary, they can see what their friends have bought and if they are satisfied with the product.

## 2.8. Customer care

Customer care can be significantly developed through social technologies in many ways. Social media can, for example, substitute or complement call centers. The questions of the customers and answers to them can be used to create an easy-to-use database (FAQ). Social technologies can include product-use instructions, user recommendations, etc. in various forms, for example demo videos.

## 2.9. Communication and collaboration within the organization

Social technologies can enable easier collaboration and make communication more effective, reduce time necessary for personal meetings, and contribute to sharing knowledge and good practice among employees, teams and whole organizations. Social technologies are very important to companies which have more branches in different places. Using internal social technologies, even remotely located workers can effectively collaborate in real time, create teams and share knowledge. Team members can communicate both synchronously and asynchronously. For synchronous communication they can use voice or written communication, and modify documents together. For asynchronous communication team members can use, for example, joint blogs, wikis or discussion forums, and modify their contents. With an appropriately designed social platform it is possible to attain an effect similar to a personal meeting of the team members.

## 2.10. Identifying talents and assigning the most suitable tasks to them

Social technologies have expanded the area in which companies are able to contact their potential employees. This so-called *social recruitment* is a fast-growing practice these days. Companies browse social networks (e.g. the professional network LinkedIn), and address suitable candidates that have their profiles on the network. The candidates are addressed regardless of the fact that they are actively looking for a job or not. Internal social networks of companies can be used in a similar way. The workers shall state all their knowledge on their profiles, regardless if they use it in their current positions or not, and also state what kind of projects they have worked or currently work on, etc. While creating a team for a new project, even a big company can easily find the most suitable workers. Thanks to collaborative tools that are available on social networks, it is not necessary for team members to work in the same place. The potential of using the workers' knowledge effectively is thus significantly increased.

It is obvious that using social technologies can bring the biggest benefit to those companies, whose products are based on intensive application of knowledge. An example can be professional services and consultancy, education, creating software, Internet services, entertainment industry, etc. Making knowledge work more effective represents up to two thirds of the total benefit companies can achieve by the application of social technologies. This effect has been achieved thanks to improved collaboration, coordination and communication. Knowledge workers who must maintain comprehensive interaction with other coworkers and make independent decisions (e.g. managers, developers, lawyers, sellers and many others), spend approximately 65% of their work hours communicating and collaborating with the others. They spend almost one third of this time writing, reading and answering emails, and another one fifth of this time they gather information necessary for fulfilling their tasks (Chui et al. 2012). Thanks to the application of social networks, the time necessary for handling emails could decrease by more than a quarter, the time used for searching for and gathering information could decrease by more than a third, and internal communication could be up to 35% more effective (thanks to easier identification of knowledge bearers and quick establishment of contacts). According to a different research report from 2011 published by the Fonality company (Webtorials 2011), knowledge workers lose up to 36% of their work hours by trying to contact other persons, searching for information and organizing appointments. If these activities are replaced by social technologies' features, a knowledge worker can devote to their main work activity, which brings value to their organization, as much as two more hours per day. According to an estimate made by the McKinsey Global Institute, total work productivity of knowledge workers can, thanks to the application of social technologies, increase by up to 25%. The most significant areas that can be continuously improved thanks to the application of social technologies, and which are found across every organization, are communication, knowledge sharing and collaboration.

# 3. The application of social technologies in companies in various parts of the world

In the following part of the article we have analyzed and compared the results of three research studies dealing with the application of social technologies by companies in various parts of the world: in selected European countries, in the U.S.A. and in selected ASEAN countries.

These three world regions can be seen as the main economic competitors nowadays, however, at the same time international cooperation is strengthening. For this reason we consider regional comparison beneficial. For our purposes a secondary analysis of the available research studies was used. We have chosen research studies containing the latest data, which is important due to extremely rapid development in this area. The results of the research studies are comparable due to the fact that the methodology used in case of all three studies was the same – interviewing the managers. The research methodology is explained in the below-cited research studies. Nevertheless, these research studies are not representative surveys, but rather case studies from these different world regions.

## 3.1. The application of social technologies in selected European countries

The research was focused on the opinions of particular managers of big and medium enterprises in France, Germany, Italy, the Netherlands, Spain, Sweden, and Great Britain. These countries were selected because they are considered as the most progressive social technologies users in Europe. A total of 2,700 managers were questioned. The research was carried out jointly by the companies Google and MillwardBrown (2012). Google's interest in such research is understandable since this company also offers its social technologies solutions to other companies.

In the companies that were subject to the research the application of social technologies is relatively extensive. Three quarters of them use internal social networks and one third of them use also external social media such as Facebook, LinkedIn, Google+ a Twitter in daily work.

Among the most common purposes for which companies use social technologies are:

- Quick search for persons, knowledge and information
- Collaboration and sharing knowledge
- Extending personal contacts and building professional relations, creating communities
- Replacing email communication

Managers also think that social technologies shall have a significant impact on business strategies of the companies. They will be significant for searching for, acquiring and keeping talented workers. Managers also estimate that the application of social technologies has increased productivity by 20%. Just by decreasing the volume and contents of email communication, faster searching for coworkers and reducing travel to meetings a worker can save two hours per week. The research has also shown that workers who have access to social networks are more satisfied at work than those who cannot use them. Workers who use social networks appreciate better communication with their colleagues. Collaboration becomes more effective especially in those cases when the synergy of geographically distant workers is necessary.

Managers expect even better effects of using social networks in the future. In their opinion, a worker can save more than three hours per week while performing each of the following, up to now traditionally performed – activities:

- Reading and writing emails
- Traveling to meet clients
- Traveling to meetings and to other branches
- Internal meetings
- General discussions about company problems
- Searching for information and persons
- Fulfilling work tasks of a knowledge nature

The most common users and supporters of social technologies in European companies are senior managers. By setting their example they help develop the use of social technologies in the whole company. European managers are convinced that social technologies support the development of creativity and innovations, just like they help acquire talented coworkers. Besides that, the speed of the decision-making process increases too. Managers expect (80% out of those questioned) that in the future the use of social technologies will lead to further development of companies and improvement of team work and sharing knowledge. It will be increasingly easier to use virtual teams of workers. In general, we can expect a further increase in necessary creativity and innovations. One half of the managers also mentioned the fact that companies which do not adopt the application of social technologies, will not stay on the market.

## 3.2. The application of social technologies in the USA

Based on research (Larcker, D.F., Larcker, S.M. and Tayan, B. 2012) in which 184 top managers took part, the most frequent purposes for the application of

social technologies in the U.S.A. are:
* Communication with customers
* Promotion and sale of products
* Marketing research
* Monitoring competition
* Communication with employees and stakeholders

According to the authors of the research many companies are too slow while implementing social technologies or do not use them correctly. This can be substantiated by the fact that only 22% of the managers have stated that they understand the importance of social media for their company very well.

A general question whether the companies use social technologies was not included in this research. However, the managers were asked whether they use social media themselves for business purposes. Sixty-three percent of responders responded positively, with the main purpose was declared to be professional development (reading blogs and forums, watching videos). Based on this we can assume that managers of companies do not develop sharing and creating knowledge through social media. Local companies may realize how important personal contact between workers is, and might prefer hiring a worker directly for their company to creating virtual teams, even if this is connected to higher expenses. Companies such as Google, Facebook and others, which behave like this, probably know that it is beneficial for them. At the same time, this does not mean that they do not use social networks. For example, Facebook employees working on a related task, create groups not only in terms of organization but also as a group on Facebook. Within this group they use its features for communication and sharing knowledge. The groups are associated in a community, which ensures the possibility of more extensive sharing knowledge and communication. Nobody is allowed to create work groups on a different social medium, the reason being protection of company data. In short, not only do programmers create Facebook, but they also actively use it for their work.

## 3.3. The application of social technologies in selected ASEAN countries

Similar research (Mortensen 2012) was also carried out in the Asia-Pacific area, in selected ASEAN countries, in which 1,000 companies were researched. This research was supported by Microsoft. More than a half of the companies (56%) use social technologies, another 26% are planning to do so in the nearest future. The most important areas of using social technologies according to the managers are:

- Customer care
- Communication with partners and customers
- Employee education and development
- Sharing knowledge

However, when the managers were to answer why using social technologies is important, they also mentioned different areas:

- Growth of employee satisfaction
- Effective retention of company knowledge
- Easier information sharing
- More effective problem solution
- Improving collaboration
- Easier searching for information and experts within their organization

Nevertheless, according to responders, social technologies are not supposed to replace traditional communication means (telephones, emails), but complement them. Almost all the responders have mentioned that the strategies of applying social technologies are in the competence of higher management and top management. Therefore they sometimes get in conflict with their IT departments, especially due to the question of data safety.

## 3.4. Regional differences in the application of social technologies

The results of the individual research studies confirm the estimate of the McKinsey Institute that over 70% of companies use social technologies. However, there exist regional differences in purposes and ways of their application. From the point of sharing and creating knowledge on social networks, Europe is the most progressive region. Here we have noticed a strong inclination to social technologies' replacing traditional ways of communication including emails. Effective application of social technologies is considered a competitive advantage.

Companies in the U.S.A. use social media namely as a marketing tool and tool for communication with customers. Not even the managers themselves use social technologies as a tool of collaboration. It can be assumed that the local environment still puts a lot of emphasis on personal meetings among coworkers.

Companies in the ASEAN countries are undergoing an era of implementation of social technologies. The application of social technologies here corresponds to cultural characteristics of this area, especially to collectivism. Management of the companies understands the importance of social technologies, and considers the development of their application as their task. However, social technologies in this area, unlike Europe, are supposed to complement and extend traditional ways and tools of communication.

## 4. Estimated success rate of using social technologies and its factors

Implementation of social technologies into company processes differs from all the previous changes connected to new technologies. Thus far used technologies have been implemented, the workers trained how to use them, and this usage was enforceable. Because social technologies serve primarily for communication, sharing and creating knowledge, it is impossible to force anyone to really share their knowledge. Even if implementing social technologies in companies will continue, there is a risk of failure. According to a forecast made by the Gartner agency (2012), 80% of company activities connected to the application of social technologies planned to be realized by 2015 will fail. Two main reasons for this will be mistakes in managing knowledge workers and overestimating the importance of a technological solution at the expense of motivating the users. Companies also must be aware of the risks connected to the use of social technologies such as revealing strategic information, which could be caused both by intentional and unintentional conduct of employees on social networks.

Technically, the implementation of social technologies is relatively easy. To start using social technologies more extensively, a company needs support from the management, namely top management. It is common knowledge that the culture of every organization is significantly influenced by the conduct of its leaders. Implementing social technologies into the work of a company is an important organizational but also cultural change. In order to give the application of social technologies some sense and achieve the desired effects, all the workers must be willing to change the existing ways of working, be willing to use social technologies, openly communicate, share their knowledge and collaborate with colleagues from remote places who they do not know personally, etc. Managers must count on the fact that communication schemes in their companies will be simpler, and that employees will be able to communicate directly with each other without informing their superiors. Such changes can be started only from the top. Implementation of social networks must be endorsed by top management of the company, and the same managers must start using social technologies, as they expect all their employees to. The employees must know how and for what purpose the social technologies selected by their company are to be used, and also must understand what kind of behavior is expected of them, and how it will be supported. This means that changes in the area of motivation, evaluation and remuneration of employees must be considered in advance. The company also has to consider possible risks of using social technologies, and in connection to this, stipulate rules of its employees conduct. Companies that are able to use social technologies effectively can also expect an increased interest of young talented job applicants. For young knowledge workers the possibility to use social technologies is one of the main motivators (PwC 2012). In the future, the most attractive social technologies will be the mobile ones (those that can be used in tablets and smartphones), and will include elements of gamification. These recommendations can be applied in any world region, however, cultural differences must always be considered.

# 5. Conclusion

In this article we have proved that social technologies have, in the short period of their existence, become a phenomenon significantly influencing activities of companies. Our study and conclusions are limited by the research studies used because they are rather regional case studies and not representative surveys. In spite of that, processing these secondary data can give us an idea of the development of using social technologies in today's business world. There are a number of areas where social technologies are put to use, but the most important ones are support of communication and collaboration inside and outside of the companies. Also, the bigger the share of knowledge work on the performance of an organization is, the bigger contribution can effective application of social technologies bring. The application of social technologies is rapidly developing in all the economically significant parts of the world. However, it brings the features of cultural differences, which is important knowledge in case of intercultural collaboration. Because the application of social technologies for knowledge work is completely new, it is connected to a huge risk of failure. This can be avoided if technical solution in companies is not overestimated at the expense of necessary changes in the company culture, and the management motivates knowledge workers through their own behavior to achieve the workers' desired conduct. We consider managerial methods which support sharing and creating knowledge through social technologies as an important part of future research. To evaluate these managerial methods also the models of the measurement of the volume of shared knowledge must be further developed.

# References

Bonifacio, M., Bouquet, P., and Cuel, R. (2002) "Knowledge Nodes: the Building Blocks of a Distributed Approach to Knowledge Management", *Journal of Universal Computer Science, 8(6)*, pp 652-661.

Davenport, T. H. and Prusak, L. (2000) *Working knowledge: How organizations manage what they know.* Harvard Business Press, Harvard.

Drucker, P. F. (1999) *Management challenges for the 21st century.* HarperCollins, New York.

Gartner (2012) "Gartner Says 80 Percent of Social Business Efforts Will Not Achieve Intended Benefits Through 2015", [online], Gartner, www.gartner.com/newsroom/id/2319215.

Google & MillwardBrown (2012) "How social technologies drive business success", [online], Millwardbrown Libraries, www.millwardbrown.com/Libraries/MB_Articles_Downloads/Googe_MillwardBrown_How-Social-Technologies-Drive-Business-Success_201205.sflb.ashx.

Harryson, M., Metayer, E. and Sarrazin, H. (2012) "How 'social intelligence' can guide decisions", [online], McKinsey Quartly, www.mckinseyquarterly.com/How_social_intelligence_can_guide_decisions_3031.

Hu, C. and Racherla, P. (2008) "Visual representation of knowledge networks: a social network analysis of hospitality research domain", *International Journal of Hospitality Management, 27(2)*, pp 302–312.

Chui, M. et al. (2012) "The social economy: Unlocking value and productivity through social technologies", [online], McKinsey & Company, www.mckinsey.com/insights/mgi/research/technology_and_innovation/the_social_economy.

Jackson, S. E., Chuang, C. H., Harden, E. E. and Jiang, Y. (2006) Toward developing human resource management systems for knowledge-intensive teamwork. *Research in personnel and human resources management, 25*, pp. 27-70.

Kadushin, Ch. (2011) *Understanding Social Networks: Theories, Concepts and Understandings*, Oxford University Press, New York.

Kietzmann, J.H., Hermkens, K. and McCarthy, I.P. (2011) "Social Media? Get serious! Understanding the functional building blocks of social media", *Business Horizons* 54(3), pp 241-251.

Larcker, D.F., Larcker, S.M. and Tayan, B. (2012) "What Do Corporate Directors and Senior Mangers Know about Social Media", [online], The Conference Board Trusted Isigihts for Business Wordwide, www.conference-board.org/publications/publicationdetail.cfm?publicationid=2332.

Lee, C. K. and Al-Hawamdeh, S. (2002) "Factors impacting knowledge sharing" *Journal of Information & Knowledge Management*, 1(01), pp. 49-56.

Lee, L. L. (2000) "Knowledge sharing metrics for large organizations" *Knowledge management–Classic and Contemporary Works*, MIT Press, Cambridge, MA, pp. 403-419.

Leistner, F. (2012) *Connecting Organizational Silos: Taking Knowledge Flow Management to the Next Level with Social Media*. Wiley, Hoboken.

Mortensen, C. (2012) *Ready for the Next Level: Enterprise Social in ASEAN (Excluding Singapore)*, IDC, Singapore.

Nonaka, I. and Takeuchi, H. (1995) *The knowledge-creating company: How Japanese companies create the dynamics of innovation*. Oxford University Press, New York.

PwC (2011) "Millenials at Work", [online], PwC Managing tomorrov´s people, www.pwc.com/gx/en/managing-tomorrows-people/future-of-work/download.jhtml?WT.ac=mtp-future-hp-panel-2.

Webtorials (2011) "Fonality's 2011 Report on UC and Cloud-Based Srvices for SMBs", [online], Fonality Talking Business, http://cdnso.fonality.com/lp/whitepaper/pdf/2011_SMB_UC_Cloud.pdf.

ZadJabbari, B., Wongthongtham, P., and Hussain, F. K. (2010) „Ontology based approach in knowledge sharing measurement" *Journal of Universal Computer Science*, 16(6), 956-982.

# Integrating Twitter Into an Undergraduate Medical Curriculum: Lessons for the Future

## Annalisa Manca, Natalie Lafferty, Evridiki Fioratou, Alisdair Smithies and Eleanor Hothersall

University of Dundee School of Medicine, Dundee, UK

a.manca@dundee.ac.uk, n.t.lafferty@dundee.ac.uk, e.fioratou@dundee.ac.uk, a.smithies@dundee.ac.uk, e.hothersall@dundee.ac.uk

Originally published in The Proceedings of ECEL 2014

## Editorial commentary

Unlike the other papers in this section, this one focuses down on one specific social medium: Twitter. A case study approach is used to explore universal issues such as cognitive load and pedagogical design in the context of Higher Education. The concepts offered by Bandura in his Social Learning Theory, particularly those of reciprocal determinism and self-efficacy, are brought to bear on a key question which faces today's educators - to what extent can social media bring both engagement and improved learning to educational experience? The study brings a sense of grounded reality to the use of social media in education. Using the metrics affordances of micro-blogging, the authors explore the cognitive load and engagement of students in the learning design, dealing with negative responses not, as so many current studies, as a transitional issue (it's new, they'll get used to it), but as responses to be valued and explored.as a serious risk to be mitigated.

**Abstract:** There is increasing interest in employing social media tools for educational purposes, but few mature frameworks exist within Higher Education contexts. We present a case study discussing the pedagogic implications of using the social media tool Twitter to facilitate a learning activity as part of a public health theme of the undergraduate medical programme at The University of Dundee - #fluscenario. Whilst adopting Twitter to support novel learning activities led to a rich communication process and co-creation of knowledge, students themselves did not recognise this. Furthermore students viewed these learning activities as gimmicky and did not appreciate the wider affordances of Twitter in supporting networked learning. We argue that designing good educational activities is not always a "constructive" activity but sometimes we need to "deconstruct" what already exists in order to make sense of it. We will use Albert Bandura's social learning theory concepts and self-efficacy notion to analyse this case-study and discuss how a sound educational design can enhance self-efficacy. We will also consider "cognitive load", which is increased exponentially in an online activity as students not only have to deal with the learning content, but also with "satellite" elements such as online professionalism, digital literacy, learning a new tool and new communication system. Through our reflections educators can determine common educational uses and affordances, assess the educational value of the use of technology and social media in teaching, and identify the social and cognitive components they involve. Additional objectives are to identify learning design and scaffolding strategies that engage students and consider strategies to elucidate processes of learning in online social networks, which have a critical role in online approaches to learning.

**Keywords:** higher education, Twitter, medical education, social learning theory, self-efficacy, learning design

# 1. Introduction and background

## 1.1. Social media in higher education and medical education

There is wide adoption of technology across society as it underpins 21st century communication, entertainment, business and public services including healthcare. In higher education, technology is ubiquitous and virtual learning environments (VLEs) have been the cornerstone of e-learning delivery (Jones et al. 2012). Technology is driving change and the emergence of Web 2.0 technologies, particularly social media, have seen phenomenal growth in their use and transformed how individuals consume, share and create information. In the space of 10 years Facebook has grown from one million monthly users to, by the end of March 2014, over 1.28 billion active monthly users (Facebook 2014 and Sedghi 2014). Meanwhile since 2007, Twitter, the microblogging service, has attracted 255 million active monthly users tweeting 500 million tweets per day (Twitter 2014). Universities deploy both Facebook and Twitter as channels to promote their institutions, disseminate information and support student recruitment. Academics use them to support digital scholarship, networking and professional development. Interest is also growing across the sector in the role that social media can play in learning and teaching and especially in collaborative learning as mobile devices facilitate connectedness outside the classroom.

There is a belief that social media can significantly change the way we learn (Jones et al. 2012) as they facilitate engagement and the sharing and exchange of knowledge, implying that their integration into learning and teaching approaches could improve learning outcomes (Prestridge 2014). This is of particular relevance in medical education where alternative methods to increase interaction and facilitate communication both with and between students are being explored (Ruiz, Mintzer and Leipzig 2006; Bridges, Botelho and Tsang 2010; White, Scales and Jayaprakash 2011). However with social media still relatively new territory, uncertainties surround their application in education, particularly due to concerns around safety (New Media Consortium 2014), privacy, and patient confidentiality (Cheston, Flickenger and Chisolm 2013). Guidelines developed to support the responsible use of social media (for example General Medical Council 2013) address some of these concerns but the lack of high quality evidence from research in this field (Cheston, Flickenger and Chisolm 2013) means there is no clear consensus on how this technology might best be used. Additionally, there is a lack of guidance for the design of effective Web 2.0-based learning in a higher education setting although there have been calls for these in the literature (Sandars & Schroter 2007; JISC 2009). A report of an independent Committee of Inquiry into the impact on higher education of students' widespread use of Web 2.0 technologies (JISC 2009: 7), underlined that whilst 'advice and guidance is available to institutions, there is no blueprint for implementation of Web 2.0 technologies, and each is currently deciding its own path'.

There is evidence of the utility of social media to support learning and the formation of learning networks, emerging from massive open online courses adopting a connectivist learning approach (Milligan, Littlejohn and Margaryan 2013, Siemens 2005). However learning skills and digital literacies are key to this and the belief that undergraduates are equipped with these to support their learning may be misplaced. The JISC report (2009) highlights that while students regularly use social networking sites such as Facebook and social media sites like YouTube to engage with communities and peers in their personal lives; their value when used in support of learning is not fully understood by students. Increasingly though students are being encouraged to self-direct learning, collaborate, create connections, share and build their knowledge together in an interactive dynamic way. Co-creation and reciprocal effort are the principal processes. It is very clear that teachers need to create learning opportunities to help students develop these skills and adopt a supportive role (Harden & Crosby 2000) intervening when needed to facilitate learning and reflection and adopt appropriate learning frameworks to support this.

## 1.2. Social learning theory

The study of the connection between the environment and the learner comes from Bandura, who emphasised the role of social interaction and self-efficacy in learning. In social learning theory, human behaviour is continuously influenced by environmental events, behavioural patterns and affective and cognitive factors (Bandura 1986, 1999). As such, learning happens through interaction and collaboration with other learners, and observation of others' behaviour. Human action and learning are rooted in social systems and embedded in a fine network of sociostructural influences acting in a reciprocal fashion (Bandura 1999). Central to Bandura's work is the concept of self-efficacy: an individual's belief in their ability to succeed in producing a particular outcome (Bandura 1977). An important element to consider in any educational setting is that self-motivation is influenced by a person's efficacy expectations. When self-efficacy perceptions are strong, individuals will tend to get more involved in activities and put a greater effort in completing tasks (Bandura 1977). However personal expectations of ability are not enough to positively affect a performance, if the real capabilities are lacking. The role of the teacher becomes essential here to provide direction for learning, support and incentives to students, so that they can gradually build self-efficacy.

Every educational experience can be seen as a scaffolding structure where every component contributes to the structure and its design. Each of these components can be positioned in different directions, touching others and connecting with them. Each has a weight and a role in the structure; some being more load-bearing than others. These systems can only handle a certain amount of weight, so, when we overload them with extra material they will eventually collapse. We define these components as learning material, activities and tools which, connecting with each other, will eventually form the elements of learning, in turn providing support for further learning. All the satellite elements that can contribute to the whole educational experience also carry a cognitive weight that can eventually cause overload and subsequently a perceived failure from the learner, so affecting self-efficacy.

Any activity requiring a large amount of information to be processed by working memory may increase cognitive load (Sweller 1988). As such, cognitive overload can be triggered during a demanding learning task, where the processing capacity of the cognitive system is exceeded (Mayer and Moreno 2003). Vasile et al (2011) demonstrated a direct correlation between academic self-efficacy and cognitive load within the academic environment. Thus, in order to maximise the educational value of a learning activity, educators must ensure that the learning activity is designed to reduce the risk for cognitive load and maximise self-efficacy. Designing good educational activities is not always a "constructive" activity but sometimes we need to "deconstruct" what already exists in order to make sense of it. We will consider the case at Dundee Medical School to reflect on the design of a social media-based educational activity, using the concepts considered above to reach an insight of the educational values and affordances of technology in teaching.

# 2. Case study

This case study addresses the design and pilot of a Twitter-based educational intervention we undertook within the Public Health teaching during two consecutive academic years (2012/2013 and 2013/2014). The design of this educational activity, due to the technology use, involved educational and technological evaluations and went through an iterative process where strategies and approaches were adapted to the particular context and educational needs. We additionally used learning theory to underpin the design process.

## 2.1. Why we chose Twitter

Twitter was chosen to support this learning activity, based on the affordance that microblogging has to build communities (Kear 2011). Individuals' interests can be identified by the inclusion of hashtags (#) in tweets, allowing conversations to be followed and connections to be made around specific topics. Self-organised learning communities and collectives have emerged around these. Over 4,000 healthcare related Twitter hashtags are registered on Symplur's hashtag project which supports participation in social media for health care professionals (Symplur, no date). One example is #FOAMed (Free Open Access Meducation) (Life in the Fast Lane 2014), a learning community that has emerged from the emergency medicine community which has spawned many other learning collectives across different specialties. Three of the authors (AM, EH, NL) were also familiar with using Twitter to support their own lifelong learning, actively participating in Twitter networks and chats. Furthermore it offered an opportunity to observe whether students might gain an insight into the medical education and FOAMed communities on Twitter and the wider benefits these might offer to support their learning.

## 2.2. Learning activity design

We designed a series of short scenarios to be discussed online using Twitter to teach first year medical students about emergency planning and pandemic influenza. The scenarios, based on those originally written by Alex Talbott and Chloe Selwood on nhssm.org.uk (original version no longer online), were posted on a dedicated Flu Scenario blog in the Medical School's VLE, supplemented with resources from media websites (mostly the BBC) offering students archived footage of real events. A series of questions were used to guide the discussion in timetabled sessions dedicated to this learning activity. Participation in the flu scenario teaching was mandatory for all first year students in University of Dundee medical school. We also used a publicly accessible website (http://dundeepublichealth.wordpress.com/fluscenario/) so that staff and students from outside the medical school, and members of the public could read the background and follow or join in the conversation.

According to Bandura's theory, learners build personal efficacy expectations through four principal sources of information: (1) performance accomplishments, (2) vicarious experience, (3) verbal persuasion, and (4) physiological states (Bandura 1977). We integrated these four elements into the design of the #fluscenario educational activity, incorporating elements in a way that the risk for cognitive overload was addressed, while facilitating students' self-efficacy and engagement with the task (Table 1). After evaluating the first #fluscenario experience, some variations were introduced in the 2013 activity to address some concerns related to students participation and enjoyment of the learning experience (Table 1).

Table 1   How Bandura's self-efficacy concept underpinned the educational design of #fluscenario

| Sources of self-efficacy and definition | Meaning in the educational design context | How it was addressed in 2012 | How it was addressed in 2013 |
|---|---|---|---|
| **1. Performance accomplishment** Based on personal mastery. When a learner successfully accomplishes a task, personal expectations raise, while repeated failures lower them. This is the most influential source of information of self-efficacy because it is based on authentic experience. Once the level of self-efficacy is established, it can also positively influence self-motivation, when the learner finds through experience that difficult tasks can be mastered through sustained effort (Bandura 1977). | Aim to give students the best learning experience, modelled around students' learning needs, taking account of their pre-existing knowledge and the context in which the new knowledge will be acquired and then assimilated in learning. Learning activities should be created to boost students' knowledge and sense of achievement, giving possibilities for self-direction of learning, coupled with constructive and discursive feedback. Help students take ownership of their own learning by identifying their learning needs before the activity, and outcomes after. | Questions to guide the discussion Choice was offered between media for participation Positive feedback from tutors | As 2012 plus: Storify (gives a sense of accomplishment to the task) (see, for example https://storify.com/DundeePublicH/fluscenario-week-1) "Summary of learning" tweet |
| **2. Vicarious experience** Based on 'inferences from social comparison' (Bandura 1977: 197). Students can learn by observing and interacting with others, creating new knowledge from experience. This happens with self-efficacy expectations as well. | Encourage group performance and communication Set level of activity so students will succeed | Tutors and facilitators are prolific Twitter and Blog users. Students were referred to their online spaces and facilitators shared their experiences with Twitter. | No change |

*Continued*

Table 1    (Continued)

| Sources of self-efficacy and definition | Meaning in the educational design context | How it was addressed in 2012 | How it was addressed in 2013 |
|---|---|---|---|
| **3. Verbal persuasion**<br>Based on verbal encouragement from tutors, mentors and peers. This can be the most readily available source of self-efficacy, however, because it is not directly based on experience, it can easily be discredited. Beware of raising expectations beyond capabilities (Bandura 1977) | Accountability of the teacher - good moderation skills in a twitter chat and private emailing to encourage participation<br>Tutor should show positive leadership and engagement with the discussion in all formats<br>Consider peer support from enthusiastic students | Students were contacted via email if they were not participating<br>Tutors moderating all formats - replying to all contacts | No change |
| **4. Physiological states**<br>Emotional states can influence the level of perceived personal competence. In particular, stressful situations, by causing emotional arousal, can negatively affect self-efficacy because they tend to debilitate performance.<br>A key element of this dimension is that 'diminishing emotional arousal can reduce avoidance behavior' (Bandura, 1977: 199) | Ensure anxiety about new situations (e.g. a new learning environment) are addressed in advance<br>Help students overcome fear and anxieties due to the assessment or the use of social media for learning. Common areas of anxiety are expressing opinions publicly and online professionalism issues.<br>Require prior discussion or training to reduce their impact. | Introduction to Twitter prior the activity<br>Tutors online and face-to-face presence | No introduction to Twitter due to timetabling constraints<br>Otherwise as 2012 |

# 3. Methodology

This case study aims to evaluate the intervention and inform professional practice and future evidence-based decisions (Baxter & Jack 2008). The qualitative case study method has developed within the social sciences and is aimed at capturing the complexities of a single case within its context (Baxter & Jack 2008). We use a variety of data sources to explore a phenomenon through different lenses, which allows observing and understanding it from different perspectives (Baxter & Jack 2008).

## 3.1 Data collection and analysis

We collected and analysed data combining different strategies and methods, permitting triangulation. The data mainly consists of a large corpus of text deriving from the Twitter discussion involving students, tutors and external participants. Email and blog comments were not included in this analysis. A post-hoc evaluation questionnaire was completed by 99 (54%) students in 2012, and by 44 (35%) in 2013. The quantitative responses are briefly summarised below, with qualitative components included in subsequent analysis. Students who participated through Twitter used the #fluscenario hashtag. Any public tweet made using this hashtag was collected using a Twitter Archiving Google Spreadsheet (TAGS) (Hawksey 2013). Any student who sent tweets using a "private" account did not have their data retained and so was automatically excluded from the study. Analysis of this educational activity was approved by the University of Dundee Research Ethics Committee.

Student participation was analysed through social network analysis (SNA), a method using visual representation of data to obtain information about the relationships within a social network. When a social network is visualised, the social agents (or "nodes") are usually represented by points and their connections (or "ties") by lines linking one or more nodes. Student learning is influenced by the quantity and quality of connections in a network and by the students' position in the network, which is determined by the reciprocal transfer of information to and from other students (Hommes, Rienties, de Grave et al. 2012). The TAGS tool used for the Tweets collection and storage is connected to a conversation explorer, TAGSExplorer (Hawksey 2011). This tool automatically creates an interactive visualisation of the collected tweets, which proved to be particularly useful to perform SNA. Initial content analysis was performed through using text analytics software (https://www.leximancer.

com). We sought evidence of learning and reflection by identifying key words within the corpus of the tweets that indicated the main concepts of discussion. Additionally, observation of the pattern of ties in the TAGSExplorer graph, in combination with information obtained from Leximancer, allowed inferences of how and how much students referred and replied to contributions from the other participants.

# 4. Findings

Student participation in 2012 and 2013 is summarised in Table 2. Participation via Twitter, measured by either percentage taking part, or number of tweets, increased from 2012 to 2013. SNA identified 227 individuals and 5215 connections in 2012 (19th Nov to 8 Dec), and 258 individuals and 1939 connections in 2013 (5thNov to 8th Dec) (Figure 1). This data highlights a decreased interaction in 2013.

The image shows 258 nodes and 1939 edges (the "lines", representing a connection between nodes). TAGSExplorer creates a dynamic representation of the conversation, which can be re-played to reproduce what was actually happening in a particular moment. Follow the QR codes or URLs to replay the conversations.

A visual representation of the main themes emerging from #fluscenario 2012 can be seen in Figure 2, showing how words representing the key concepts have been used repeatedly, and how these words are linked to other conceptually-related words (evidenced by the lines between the circles). Students were

Table 2    Participation data for both cohorts

|  | 2012 | 2013 |
| --- | --- | --- |
| Total number of students in year | 184 | 127 |
| Students participating via Twitter (%) | 160 (87) | 119 (94) |
| Students participating via email (and/or VLE in 2012) (%) | 19 (10) | 5 (4) |
| Students who refused to participate at all (%) | 5 (3) | 3 (2) |
| Total number of tweets | 2,987 | 3,965 |
| Mean number of tweets per student (range) | 13.8 (1-88) | 21.2 (1-105) |

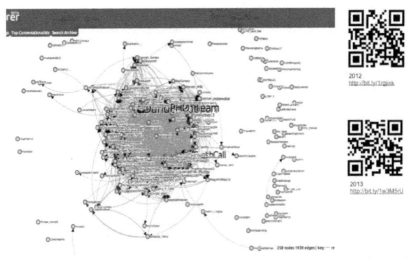

2012
http://bit.ly/1rgjoxk

2013
http://bit.ly/1w3M5rU

Figure 1    representation of the #fluscenario 2013 conversation and social
network created by TAGSExplorer

clearly engaging in on-task discourse by replying or referring to contributions from peers. Thus they were constructing new knowledge. This inference
is reinforced by individual comments, and parallels the connections between
students seen in the SNA. Similar patterns can be seen in the 2013 data (not
shown).

In contrast with the findings above, responses to the evaluation questionnaire were generally negative. Around half of students (54% in 2012, 48% in
2013) disagreed with the statement "the structure of this activity was helpful
to my learning". 47% in 2012 and 32% in 2013 disagreed that "using Twitter helped me consolidate my learning." In 2013, an additional question asked
students to compare the Twitter scenario with other teaching. 36% report no
difference, and 27% considered it worse than other methods.

Fewer students responded to a question specifically asking what students
disliked about the activity (Figure 3), but the overall impression was that students found the character limit very difficult to deal with. Strikingly, a number of students did not use the material as intended, with 22% in 2012 and
14% in 2013 admitting that they had not used the VLE or blog to access any
materials.

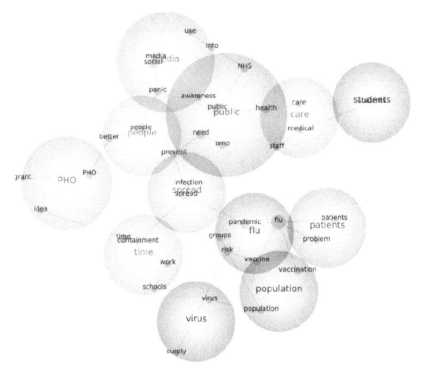

**Figure 2**   Overview of the main concepts emerging from the whole corpus of tweets during scenarios (2012), obtained through an analysis made with Leximancer Software. Words with >100 uses are shown as large coloured circles (themes), smaller circles indicate commonly associated words, while lines indicate where words are used close to each other

# 5. Discussions and conclusions

Our results mirror recent literature (Badge, Saunders and Cann 2012; Junco, Elavsky and Heiberger 2013) highlighting the pedagogic potential of online social networking tools. Our experience shows that Twitter can be successfully used as a discussion tool in educational interventions where students participate in a network of learning. However, triangulating the evidence showed that

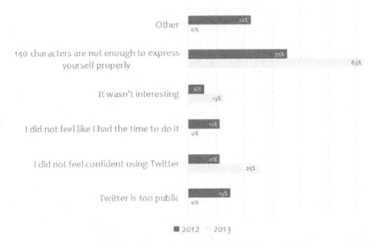

**Figure 3**   Summary of student feedback for 2012 vs 2013: reasons why students did not enjoy the activity (n=58 for 2012, n=8 for 2013)

despite high levels of participation and the discussion appearing to address the key questions posed, the level of interaction was not that high. In the 2013 cohort this was particularly so, with lower numbers of conversational threads and many of the students tweeting as if speaking into a crowded room. Furthermore the students' perceptions of the learning activity were not overly positive with either cohort.

A critical issue here is to uncover the reasons of an intervention's impact (Pascarella 2006). An air of reluctance was evident amongst some students surrounding the adoption of Twitter, due to their perception that it was a social media tool and not something that should be used in learning and teaching. Lowe and Laffey (2011) have previously highlighted there can be reluctance around the use of technology which can result in decreased interactivity.

The cognitive load in the task was underestimated. Low engagement with the task in part of the cohort may be due to a number of factors. The impact of the 140 character limit of Twitter clearly generated stress for some students. The intensive nature of a Twitter chat can be overwhelming to newcomers, requiring significant cognitive effort to follow and participate the treads of conversation. Some of the authors (AM, EH, NL) reflecting on their own experience of Twitter chats were reminded of their own initial lack of confidence in active participation. Self-efficacy built-up gradually by "lurking" - reading but not actively contributing - and then joining in conversations and receiving positive and reinforcing outcomes from the chat experiences. The absence of an introductory session to Twitter in 2013 may account for the larger number of this cohort lacking confidence in using Twitter and have led to increased overload due to processing the intensity of new information in the chat activity whilst also learning a new tool. Furthermore, some students find the requirements of digital professionalism (General Medical Council 2013) difficult to understand, and resent the incursion of staff into "their" online space, fearing censure (rightly or wrongly).

#fluscenario was designed to influence what Kirkwood and Price (2013) have described as a "qualitative change in learning": promoting reflection thus producing deeper learning. To achieve this, we need to account for the indirect ways in which social technology impacts students' involvement and learning acting on their interpersonal experiences (Pascarella 2006). For example considering ways to allow students to be "lurkers" through promoting reflection (Megele 2014). Badge, Saunders and Cann (2012) highlight the need to understand the social network within which communication is taking place, and to cultivate connections with the networks of lower-performers, which may help address the other challenges of helping students to see the benefits. Megele (2014) suggests an introductory workshop and hands-on session in the IT suite, given the intensity of the activity to follow. We intend to develop this next academic year and also involve student led approaches to introduce their peers to Twitter.

The existing broad literature on understanding student development reflects the importance of recognising the processes underpinning learning in order to design engaging educational activities. When using social media this is even more true as educators need to carefully evaluate the way in which such technology might affect the intervention itself and ultimately students involvement and outcomes. Introducing technology in educational interventions should be *"derived from an identified educational need or aspiration"* (Kirkwood and Price 2013 p20) rather than *"technology-led"*, this is why using social media in education requires a framework where precise attention is given to the design process and the means of its use are applied with consistency. We believe that thorough evaluation of educational strategies using social media, will allow further developments to be "evidence based", thus gaining the confidence of both teaching staff and students.

# References

Badge, J.L., Saunders, N.F.W., Cann, A.J. (2012). Beyond marks: new tools to visualise student engagement via social networks. *Research in Learning Technology*, Vol 20, pp 1-14.

Bandura, A. (1977). Self-efficacy: Toward a unifying theory of behavioral change. *Psychological Review*, Vol 84, No. 2, pp 191-215.

Bandura, A. (1986). *Social foundations of thought and action: A social cognitive theory.* Englewood Cliffs, NJ: Prentice-Hall.

Bandura, A. (1999). Social cognitive theory: An agentic perspective. *Asian Journal of Social Psychology*, Vol 2, pp 21-41.

Baxter, P. and Jack, S. (2008). Qualitative Case Study Methodology: Study Design and Implementation for Novice Researchers. *The Qualitative Report*, Vol 13, No. 4, pp 554-559.

Bridges, S.M., Botelho, M.G., & Tsang, P.C.S. (2010). PBL.2.0: Blended learning for an interactive, problem-based pedagogy. *Medical Education*, Vol 44, No. 11, pp 131-131.

Cheston, C.C., Flickinger, T.E., & Chisolm, M.S. (2013). Social media use in medical education: a systematic review. *Academic Medicine*, Vol 88, No. 6, pp 893-901.

Facebook (2014) *Our Mission.* [Online] Available from: http://newsroom.fb.com/company-info/ [Accessed: 19th June 2014].

General Medical Council (2013). *Doctors' use of social media* [Online] Available from: http://www.gmc-uk.org/Doctors__use_of_social_media.pdf_51448306.pdf [Accessed: 19th June 2014].

Harden, R.M., & Crosby, J.R. (2000). The good teacher is more than a lecturer: the twelve roles of the teacher AMEE Medical Education Guide No 20. *Medical Teacher*, Vol 22, No. 4, pp 334-347.

Hawksey, M. (2011). *Twitter: How to archive event hashtags and create an interactive visualization of the conversation.* [Online] 7th November 2011. Available from: MASHe http://mashe.hawksey.info/2011/11/twitter-how-to-archive-event-hashtags-and-visualize-conversation/ [Accessed: 16th June 2014].

Hawksey, M. (2013). *Twitter Archiving Google Spreadsheet TAGS v5.* [Online] 15 February 2013. Available from: MASHe http://mashe.hawksey.info/2013/02/twitter-archive-tagsv5/ [Accessed: 16th June 2014].

Hommes, J., Rienties, B.,de Grave, W., Bos, G., Schuwirth, L., Scherpbier, A. (2012). Visualising the invisible: a network approach to reveal the informal social side of student learning. *Advances in health sciences education : theory and practice*, Vol 17, No. 5, pp 743-57.

JISC (2009). *Higher education in a Web 2.0 world* [Online] Available from: http://www.jisc.ac.uk/media/documents/publications/heweb20rptv1.pdf [Accessed: 16th June 2014].

Jones, K., Pole, R., Hole, S., Williams, J. (2012). Social Networks for Learning: Breaking Through the Walled Garden of the VLE. In Abraham, A., Hassanien, A-E., ed. *Computational Social Networks: Tools, Perspectives and Applications.* London: Springer, pp 417-444.

Junco, R., Elavsky, C.M.& Heiberger, G. (2013). Putting Twitter to the Test: Assessing Outcomes for Student Collaboration, Engagement, and Success. *British Journal of Education and Technology,* 44(2), 273-287.

Kear, K. (2011). *Online and social networking communities: A best practice guide for educators.* New York, London: Routledge.

Kirkwood, A., Price, L. (2013). Technology-enhanced learning and teaching in higher education: what is 'enhanced' and how do we know? A critical literature review. *Learning, Media & Technology,* Vol 39, No. 1, pp 6-36.

Life in the Fast Lane (2014). *FOAM* [Online] Available from: http://lifeinthefastlane. com/foam/ [Accessed: 18th June 2014].

Lowe, B., Laffey, D. (2011). Is Twitter for the birds? Using Twitter to enhance student learning in a marketing course. *Journal of Marketing Education,* Vol 33, No. 2, pp 183-192.

Mayer, R.E., Moreno, R. (2003). Nine Ways to Reduce Cognitive Load in Multimedia Learning. *Educational Psychologist,* Vol 38, No. 1, pp43-52.

Megele, C. (2014). eABLE: embedding social media in academic curriculum as a learning and assessment strategy to enhance students learning and e-professionalism. *Innovations in Education and Teaching International,* Vol 51 ahead of print [Online] Available from: http://dx.doi.org/10.1080/14703297.2014.890951 [Accessed: 18 June 2014].

Milligan, C., Littlejohn, A., Margaryan, A. (2013). Patterns of Engagement in Connectivist MOOCs. *MERLOT Journal of Online Learning and Teaching,* Vol 9, No.2, pp149-159.

New Media Consortium (2014). *NMC Horizon Report: 2014 Higher Education Edition;* New Media Consortium, Austin, USA.

Pascarella, E.T. (2006). How College Affects Students: Ten Directions for Future Research. *Journal of College Student Development,* Vol 47, No. 5, pp 508-520.

Prestridge, S. (2014). A focus on students' use of Twitter - their interactions with each other, content and interface. *Active Learning in Higher Education,* Vol 15, No 2, pp 101-115.

Ruiz, J.G, Mintzer, M.J, Leipzig, R.M. (2006). The impact of e-learning in medical education. *Academic Medicine* Vol 81, No. 3, pp 207-212.

Sandars, J., Schroter, S. (2007). Web 2.0 technologies for undergraduate and postgraduate medical education: an online survey. *Postgraduate Medical Journal,* Vol 83, No. 986, pp 759-762.

Sedghi, A. (2014). Facebook: 10 years of social networking, in numbers. *The Guardian.* [Online] 4th February Available from: http://www.theguardian.com/news/datablog/2014/feb/04/facebook-in-numbers-statistics [Accessed: 19th June 2014].

Siemens, G. (2005). Connectivism: A learning theory for the digital age. *International Journal of Instructional Technology and Distance Learning,* Vol 2, No. 1,pp 3-10.

Sweller, J. (1988). Cognitive Load During Problem Solving: Effects on Learning. *Cognitive Science,* Vol 12, No. 2, pp 257-285.

Symplur (no date). *The Healthcare Hashtag Project* [Online] Available from: http://www.symplur.com/healthcare-hashtags/ [Accessed: 19th June 2014].

Twitter (2014). *About Twitter.* [Online] Available from: https://about.twitter.com/company [Accessed: 19th June 2014].

Vasile, C., Marhan, A., Singer, F. M., & Stoicescu, D. (2011). Academic self-efficacy and cognitive load in students. *Procedia - Social and Behavioral Sciences,* Vol 12. No. 1, pp 478-482.

White, M., Scales, J., & Jayaprakash, K. (2011). What can a student-led e-learning site add to medical students ' education and professional development. *Enhancing Learning in the Social Sciences,* Vol 3, No. 3, pp 1-16.

# Introduction to Leading Issues in Social Media for Society

*by Asher Rospigliosi*

The impact of social media on contemporary society is an area where many voices are contesting the narrative, and where we all have an opinion. The rapid global adoption of the internet as a means of telling, finding and sharing is cause for celebration and concern in fairly equal measure.

*"Our societies are increasingly structured around the bipolar opposition of the Net and the Self"* (Castells, 1996 p.3)

In the debate between those who fear the loss of our freedoms through a panopticon of surveillance (Keen 2015) and the advocates of a new global self organising democracy based on Twitter (Lutz & du Toit, 2014) lurk nuances that need careful academic consideration. This volume attempts to surface a range of important issues for business, for education and for society viewed as a whole. The concerns of business and learning have been looked at as discrete areas in the preceding sections. Both business and learning are part of our understanding of broad trends and are strong leading indicators of the impact of technology on processes, but for this final section we will focus on what the study of social media can tell us about society, about civic participation and engagement and finally about what social media may offer to the old and ageing.

One area where there can be little disagreement is that social media is generating enormous amounts of data. Whether big data is a paradigm shift or not, there are many pieces of content generated on services such as Twitter. There are many who would like to understand what is being said and to gain some insight into those who are voicing opinions. The field sentiment analysis, or the automated analysis of some of those big data sets is being pursued by market researchers, politicians, security services and sociologists.

The analysis of the conversations on social media can provide evidence of citizens' engagement, or lack of engagement, in the processes of governance and politics. We offer here two papers, not only trying to quantify but also to analyse the role of social capital as it manifests in participants' social networks. These papers give access to a rapidly emerging and important analysis of e-democracy.

If technology is often considered the prerogative of the young, we finish the book with a consideration of how social media is able to enrich the life of the elderly. In a fascinating study from a Brazil, the final paper shows, in rich detail, a future that looks to benefit from many of these leading issues in social media.

Castells, M. (1996). *The information age: Economy, society, and culture. Volume I: The rise of the network society.*

Keen, A. (2015). *The Internet is not the answer: why the Internet has been an economic, political and cultural disaster - and how it can be transformed.* London, Atlantic Books.

Lutz, B., & du Toit, P. (2014). *Defining Democracy in a Digital Age: Political Support on Social Media.* Palgrave Macmillan

# Twitter based Analysis of Public, Fine-Grained Emotional Reactions to Significant Events

## Martin Sykora, Thomas Jackson, Ann O'Brien, Suzanne Elayan and A. von Lunen

Centre for Information Management, Loughborough University, UK

M.D.Sykora@lboro.ac.uk, T.W.Jackson@lboro.ac.uk, A.O-Brien@lboro.ac.uk, S.Elayan2@lboro.ac.uk, A.F.G.Von-Lunen@lboro.ac.uk

Originally published in The Proceedings of ECSM 2014

## Editorial commentary

The emerging field of sentient analysis applied to publicly available tweets has stimulated much debate among sociologists Questions about who has access, and how representative tweets are of broader society are current and important. While market researchers may uncritically represent twitter sentiment, as customer insight, in the study of society the value of sentiment analysis is less clear. Bringing a fine grained analytical nuance in their paper Sykora et al, attempt to weigh up public response to emotive issues. A large dataset of of more than one and half million tweets are dissected for the feelings shown by the the public to the deaths of public figures, to tube strikes in London and to the 12th anniversary of September 11th 2001.

The natural language processing used here, shows how much care is needed to attempt analysis of feelings. These subtle distinctions in public responses make fascinating reading.

**Abstract:** Due to the real-time nature and the value of social media content for monitoring entities and events of significance, automated sentiment analysis and semantic enrichment techniques for social media streams have received considerable attention in the literature. These techniques are central to monitoring social-media content, which is now becoming a significant business with commercial, institutional, governmental and law enforcement interest into its applications. Prior work in sentiment analysis has particularly focused on negative-positive sentiment classification tasks. Although numerous approaches employ highly elaborate and effective techniques with some success, the sentiment or emotion granularity is generally limiting and arguably not always most appropriate for real-world problems. In this paper a newly developed ontology based system is employed, to semantically enrich Tweets with fine-grained emotional states in order to analyse the subjective public reactions to a wide selection of recent events. The approach detects a range of eight high-level emotions and their perceived strength (also known as activation level), specifically; anger, confusion, disgust, fear, happiness, sadness, shame and surprise. A set of emotional profiles for different events is obtained and an in-depth analysis of the emotional responses is presented. Recent events, such as the 2013 horsemeat scandal, Nelson Mandela's death, September 11th remembrance anniversary, and recent tube strikes in London, are analysed and discussed. The feasibility and potential benefits of automated fine-grained emotional event response analysis from social-media is illustrated and linked to future work.

**Keywords:** Social Media, Twitter, Sentiment Analysis, Basic Emotions, Natural Language Processing, Ontology

# 1. Introduction

Automated sentiment analysis and semantic enrichment (e.g. geo-location inference, named entity recognition, topic classification, etc.) of social media text streams, such as Tweets and Facebook status updates, is receiving considerable attention in the literature. This is largely motivated by the insights and value that such datasets were shown to provide (Chew and Eysenbach, 2010; O'Connor et al., 2010; Tumasjan et al., 2010; Lansdall-Welfare et al., 2012; Abel et al., 2012). It has also been evidenced that during times of natural crises and terrorist incidents Twitter is often the first medium through which the news breaks and through which individuals express their initial impressions and emotions relating to the events (Beaumont, 2008; Cashmore, 2009; Sakaki et al., 2010; Cheong and Lee, 2011; Glass and Colbaugh, 2012). Social-media streams in general allow for observing large numbers of spontaneous, real-time interactions and varied expression of opinion, which are often fleeting and private (Miller, 2011). Miller (2011) furthermore points out that some social scientists now see an unprecedented opportunity to study human communication, which has been an obstacle up until recently. O'Connor et al. (2010) demonstrated how large-scale trends can be captured from Twitter messages based on simple sentiment word frequency measures. The researchers evaluated and correlated their Twitter samples against several consumer confidence and political opinion surveys in order to validate the approach, and have pointed out the potential of social-media as a rudimentary yet powerful polling and survey methodology. Motivated by such work this paper will specifically focus on automated fine-grained emotion analysis (also known as advanced sentiment analysis) over a number of recent events, ranging from the European horsemeat scandal to the recent tube strikes in London. As far as the authors are aware this study is novel in the range of heterogeneous events analysed and the range of emotions detected. Most literature in the sentiment analysis field has looked at polarity sentiment (i.e. negative – positive sentiment) classification only, with a few exceptions (Bollen et al., 2011; Lansdall-Welfare et al., 2012; Choudhury and Counts, 2012). In this paper a recent technique called EMOTIVE developed by Sykora et al. (2013) is employed. EMOTIVE identifies eight basic fine-grained emotions from sparse text, namely; anger, disgust, fear, happiness, sadness, surprise (also known as Ekman's basic emotions – Ekman and Richard, 1994), plus confusion and shame. Through this, novel insights towards a fine-grained emotional composition of reactions to events discussed over Twitter are provided in this paper.

The remainder of the paper is organised as follows. Section 2 introduces some background and prior work in the sentiment analysis field and gives brief method details. Event characteristics based on Twitter features and detected emotions are presented in section 3. Section 4 analyses and discusses the events further. The paper is concluded in section 5.

# 2. Background and Methodology

A recent, in-depth overview of prior academic work in the sentiment analysis field is provided in Thelwall et al. (2012). The approach used in this paper (Sykora et al., 2013) broadly falls under the lexicon / linguistic analysis approach, from the three approaches presented in Thelwall et al. (2012) – except that we draw on emotion terms from within an ontology with a richer semantic representation than commonly used emotion term-lexicons. Although numerous approaches employ highly elaborate and effective techniques with some success, the sentiment or emotion granularity is generally limiting. Specifically, there are three main problems with existing approaches. (1) Notions of affect and sentiment have been rather simplified in current state-of-the-art, often confined to their assumed overall polarity (i.e. positive / negative), Thelwall et al. (2012). (2) Another problem with polarity-centric sentiment classifiers is that they generally encompass a vague notion of polarity that bundles together emotion, states and opinion (Bollen et al., 2011). (3) There is no common agreement about which features are the most relevant in the definition of an emotion and which are the relevant emotions and their names (Grassi, 2009). In the emotion analysis employed in this paper, sentiment is fine-grained based on the widely accepted Ekman's emotions (Ekman and Richard, 1994) from social psychology, while other work on emotions was also considered (Plutchik 1980; Drummond, 2004; Izard, 2009) and is further discussed in Sykora et al. (2013). Only explicit expressions of emotions are extracted and ambiguous emotional expressions, such as certain moods and states that are not expressing emotions are ignored on purpose, as opposed to Bollen et al., (2011), Lansdall-Welfare et al. (2012), and Choudhury and Counts (2012). The EMOTIVE ontology employed in this paper was designed to detect a wider range of well recognised human emotions, for instance 'surprise', 'disgust', or 'confusion', but at the same time differentiate emotions by strength (e.g. 'uneasy', 'fearful', 'petrified'). In addition to the basic emotions, the ontology also covers and handles negations, intensifiers, conjunctions, interjections. It contains information on the perceived strength (also known as activation level) of individual emotions and whether individual terms and phrases are slang or used in standard English. Finally emotions and their associated POS (Parts-of-Speech) tags are also taken into consideration when these would aid to resolve ambiguity. In Sykora et al. (2013) our technique was evaluated and compared to Choudhury and Counts (2012) and Thelwall et al. (2012) – SentiStrength 2 – in terms of emotion detection and emotion strength scoring, respectively. Good results, comparable with state-of-the-art were achieved and a high f-measure for emotion extraction on an initial test dataset was reported (see sub-section 2.2).

## 2.1. Data Collection

The datasets analysed within this paper were continuously retrieved from Twitter, using the standard REST Twitter Search API to access the datasets (see https://dev.twitter.com/docs/using-search). The retrieval occurred during the related time-period of an event and a search-term or hashtag, known to be extensively used by the Twitter community for that event was chosen by a microblogging expert. For most events of interest data collection would occur during the days / time-period of the event, or the days immediately following the event in order to collect the related reactions, chatter and emotions. Often the selected term or hashtag used for the data collection would also be trending, i.e. according to Twitter trends. The maximum possible number of tweets, given the API limitations and compatible with Twitter's terms of service, was automatically retrieved using custom developed scripts. In total 1,570,303 tweets were collected and analysed (see sections 3 and 4).

## 2.2. Fine-Grained Emotion Extraction

Due to enforced brevity of messages (e.g. 140 characters or fewer on Twitter), textual content commonly encountered on social media is often not grammatically bound nor constructed properly and contains extensive use of slang, short-hand syntax, incorrect spelling, repeated letters, repeated words, inconsistent punctuation, odd Unicode glyphs, emoticons and overall a high proportion of OOV (Out-Of-Vocabulary) terms. Hence it has been suggested that a retrained NLP pipeline for sparse, informal text is necessary to effectively process such language (Ritter et al. 2011). The approach used to extract the fine-grained emotions from tweets is described in detail within Sykora et al. (2013). Essentially the approach has two parts and is based on (1) a custom Natural Language Processing (NLP) pipeline, which efficiently parses tweets and classifies parts-of-speech tags, and (2) an ontology, in which emotions, related phrases and terms (including a wide set of intensifiers, conjunctions, negators, interjections) and linguistic analysis rules are represented and matched against. Hence rules inferred from the semantics within the ontology are applied to each tweet to evaluate a tweet's emotional content, and certain elements, such as negators or intensifiers (increase or decrease an emotion) are only picked up if they are likely related to emotions; sentence boundaries or alternatively token proximity help to define whether an element is related. The ontology contains activation levels or emotion strength scores associated with various expressions. For instance, the example tweet "I am totally scared:-(!!! this is v upsetting. Am I riotphobic?" contains emotions of fear and sadness with scores of 9 and 4 respectively, given the scores for totally [+1] scared [+4], phobic [+4] and v [+1], upsetting [+3]. The activation levels were devised and based on prior work, see Sykora et al. (2013) fore details. An initial evaluation of the system achieves excellent results, with an f-measure of .962, precision of .927 and recall of 1. The recall is likely to be lower on larger test datasets containing higher proportion of OOV slang, yet the high recall on the test dataset is strongly indicative of good coverage of expressions. A comparison with Choudhury and Counts (2012) and Thelwall et al. (2012) performed in Sykora et al. (2013) showed that the emotion detection performs better, and in the latter case in line with state-of-the-art approaches.

# 3. Emotions and Event Characteristics

This section presents the analysis of emotional expression for 28 separate data-sets relating to 25 distinct events over a total collection of 1,570,303 tweets. Table 1 summarises the datasets and presents details on how many tweets were collected for each specific hashtag / search terms (i.e. 'Dataset' column in table), what percentage of those contained emotions, over what time-period the data retrieval took place and basic background information on the related event (please visit http://emotive.lboro.ac.uk/resources/ECSM2014 for a full list of links to specific event related articles). As can be observed from table 1, the five most emotional datasets relate to #jacinthasaldanha (37.91%), #ChineseNewYear (36.13%), #royalprank (23.17%), 'Daniel Pelka' (21.54%) and #2DayFM (20.43%). The hashtags #jacinthasaldanha, #royalprank and #2DayFM all refer to the same event, in which a nurse (Jacintha Saldanha) committed suicide after being the victim of a public (2Day FM radio station) prank (#royalprank). The emotional outpouring on Twitter over her needless and tragic death was enormous. The torture and death of the four-year-old boy, Daniel Pelka, was also met with outrage and significant outpouring of highly emotionally charged tweets. #ChineseNewYear (31st Jan 2014) was nat-urally filled with mostly positive emotions and New Year wishes. However, quite often tweets carry relatively low emotional content, which seems to be due to the nature of the event / topic discussed in tweets. On average 12% of tweets contain explicit emotions (standard deviation being 9%).

Despite some datasets containing relatively low proportion of emotional tweets, no dataset has less than 291 emotional tweets (avg. being 4,670), with the exception of Anjem Choudary. Only 57 tweets with explicit emotions were available for Anjem Choudary (i.e. 5% out of 1,047 tweets). Figure 1 illustrates how a useful emotional 'footprint' can nevertheless be generated, despite the low count of emotional tweets. Specifically, figure 1 presents the distribution of the proportion of emotions among eight basic, fine-grained emotions for #woolwich (incident in which a UK soldier was murdered in broad daylight in London) and Anjem Choudary (a controversial religious figure who was given air-time on BBC after the event, and was accused of hate speech and declined to condemn the attack on the soldier). The distribution of emotions is intuitive and can be interpreted in a straight forward manner in relation to #woolwich.

The emotions most frequently associated with Anjem Choudary were extreme anger and disgust. Intuitively, the proportion of anger is much higher

**Table 1** Overview of the collected and analysed datasets and their relationship to events

| Dataset | Total (N) | Emotional Tweets (%) | Event | Event Type | Time Period |
|---|---|---|---|---|---|
| helicopter crash | 25,387 | 13.99% | Helicopter crashes into crane in central London (16th Jan) | accident | 16 Jan–17th Jan 2013 |
| #september 11 | 88,739 | 9.62% | September 11th 2013 anniversary | anniversary | 11th Sep–12th Sep 2013 |
| #twintowers | 28,168 | 16.32% | September 11th 2013 anniversary | anniversary | 11th Sep–12th Sep 2013 |
| #Chinese NewYear | 22,466 | 36.13% | Chinese New Year, 31st Jan 2014 | cultural event | 31st Jan–1st Feb 2014 |
| #bankholiday | 7,862 | 11.71% | Bankholiday – public holiday in the UK | daily life | 24th May 2013 |
| #sleep | 36,139 | 3.65% | An eight day long period | daily life | 23rd Oct–31st Oct 2013 |
| #tired | 79,253 | 4.49% | An eight day long period | daily life | 23rd Oct–31st Oct 2013 |
| #James Gandolfini | 11,975 | 18.92% | Death of actor James Gandolfini | death | 20th Jun–23rd Jun 2013 |
| Ariel Sharon | 90,603 | 8.18% | Death of the ex-prime minister of Israel | death | 11th Jan–15th Jan 2014 |
| Nelson Mandela | 108,794 | 12.51% | Death of Nelson Mandela | death | 5th Dec–9th Dec 2013 |
| 'Daniel Pelka' | 11,708 | 21.54% | Sentencing of the killers in the brutal murder of school boy Daniel Pelka | death / murder | 1st Aug–5th Aug 2013 |

*Continued*

**Table 1** *(Continued)*

| Dataset | Total (N) | Emotional Tweets (%) | Event | Event Type | Time Period |
|---|---|---|---|---|---|
| **#RoyalMail** | 4,309 | 6.75% | Privatisation of the British Royal Mail, 12th Sep announcement | economic / controversial | 12th Sep 2013 |
| **#tubestrike** | 41,176 | 8.47% | London February tube strike by RMT and TSSA unions | economic / controversial | 5th Feb-7th Feb 2014 |
| **#LFW** | 43,509 | 4.27% | London Fashion Week | fashion event | 17th Feb-18th Feb 2014 |
| **Anjem Choudary** | 1,047 | 5.44% | Controversial comments from a radical cleric on BBC | hate speech incident | 24th May 2013 |
| **#2DayFM** | 10,898 | 20.43% | Royal prank by Australian 2DayFM - suicide of Nurse Jacintha Saldanha | incident / death | 7th Dec-14th Dec 2012 |
| **#jacinthasaldanha** | 1,216 | 37.91% | Royal prank by Australian 2DayFM - suicide of Nurse Jacintha Saldanha | incident / death | 7th Dec-14th Dec 2012 |
| **#royalprank** | 10,459 | 23.17% | Royal prank by Australian 2DayFM - suicide of Nurse Jacintha Saldanha | incident / death | 7th Dec-14th Dec 2012 |
| **g8 summit** | 32,676 | 4.24% | 39th G8 Summit in UK on 17th-18th June | political / controversial | 16th Jun-20th Jun 2013 |
| **#iPhone5C** | 8,824 | 3.90% | Announcement of new iPhone on 10th Sep | product release | 11th Sep-12th Sep 2013 |
| **#iPhone5S** | 14,638 | 5.70% | Announcement of new iPhone on 10th Sep | product release | 11th Sep-12th Sep 2013 |
| **gta5** | 130,748 | 4.22% | Release of computer game GTA 5 on 17th Sep | product release | 17th Sep-18th Sep 2013 |

| Dataset | Total (N) | Emotional Tweets (%) | Event | Event Type | Time Period |
|---|---|---|---|---|---|
| #NSA | 381,402 | 5.08% | National Security Agency PRISM surveillance program (initially leaked early Jun) | scandal | 13th Jun-15th Jul 2013 |
| #prism | 106,432 | 4.96% | National Security Agency PRISM surveillance program (initially leaked early Jun) | scandal | 13th Jun-15th Jul 2013 |
| Horsemeat | 56,970 | 7.47% | Horsemeat missold as beef (issue came to light on 15th Jan) | scandal | 16th Jan-18th Jan 2013 |
| #ClosingCeremony | 87,943 | 11.55% | London 2012 Olympics - Closing ceremony | sport event | 12th Aug-17th Aug 2012 |
| #paralympics | 27,993 | 13.97% | London 2012 Olympics - Paralympic games (29th Aug - 9th Sep) | sport event | 4th Sep-6th Sep 2012 |
| #woolwich | 98,969 | 12.63% | Attack and murder of Drummer Lee Rigby in Woolwich, by extremists | terror incident / murder | 23rd May-24thMay 2013 |

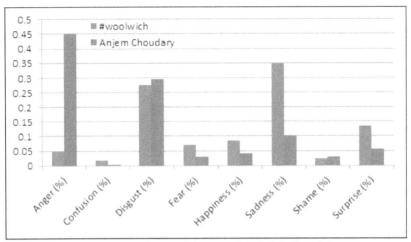

Figure 1    Basic emotions detected for #woolwich (blue) and Anjem
Choudary (red)

for Choudary than for #woolwich, whereas both contain similar levels of disgust, but sadness dominated #woolwich. Several exemplary tweets illustrate the outpouring (basic emotions are highlighted in the square brackets):

- I'm quite angry that Anjem Choudary is on Newsnight tonight - I can only imagine how furious Muslims he falsely claims to speak for must be [anger]
- And I'm angry that Anjem Choudary is aloud to preach hate in our towns and city's It's the government we should be angry with not a religion [anger]
- Anjem Choudary, gfy. Ruining the 'Choudhary' name for all of us, you complete bastard, it's sickening #woolwich [disgust]
- *@EDLTrobinson* so sad, and so wrong that ANJEM CHOUDARY can get air time saying muslims around the world will call them heroes what a twat. [sadness]

## 3.1. Overview of Event Detected Emotions

This subsection focuses on further specific example events and their emotional profiles in order to illustrate the use and highlight several nuances of our Twitter emotion detection system.

The 2013 September 11th terror attack anniversary related tweets (represented by #september11 and #twintowers) mostly contain sadness and a similar emotional distribution overall. Nevertheless, although subtle yet noticeable, it is interesting that happiness is much lower for the #twintowers than #september11 tweets. A detailed inspection of the tweets showed that #september11 was used more widely and somewhat surprisingly by people with radical and offensive opinions, who actually expressed happiness about the terror attacks of 2001, see bullet list below for some example tweets.

- Glad to say I'm from Canada #september11 [happiness]
- Yes We Are Terrorist And We Are Proud!When It Comes To Scaring Pigs #september11 *(attributed to the account @albatar_moahed, other such as @laskegah have retweeted it)* [happiness]
- We will never forget that HAPPY day #september11 really we love u "Osama" #Remember_11_September enjoy your eyes http://t.co/c8bSk-SZ0Y4 [happiness]
- I will never forget where I was on #september11 Keep your thoughts w/ the families who lost their loved ones. I am Proud to be an American! [happiness]
- Remembering 9/11& feeling blessed for the safety of my friends & family and the freedoms we all still enjoy. God bless us all. #september11 [happiness]
- I still remember like it was yesterday, watching the #twintowers tumble down on TV, hands tied, in complete state of shock and anguish. [surprise]
- This day 12 years ago, I was sitting on my coffee table in shock, 16 miles away from Ground Zero. #remember #nyc #newyork #911 #twintowers [surprise]
- I'm flying today....is that my bad luck kicking it....9-11 brings back more fear when you're flyin on it #twintowers #Remember_11_September [fear]
- I was scared shitless for my mother, the then ignorant me didn't know that Atlanta was miles away from #twintowers #sept911th [fear]
- The fact that Miley Cyrus is trending over #september11 and #twintowers is actually disgusting. [disgust]

As evidenced by our dataset, it seems that generally speaking deaths of (well known) people tend to be accompanied with relatively high level of emotional outpour. Figure 3 highlights that sadness, as expected, tends to be a well represented emotion in such events, as well as higher levels of surprise.

The figure further illustrates that in the case of the controversial former prime minister of Israel, Ariel Sharon, people expressed disgust, shame and

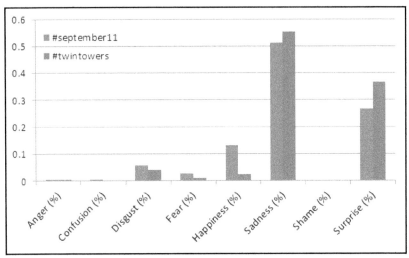

Figure 2     Basic emotions detected for #september11 and #twintowers

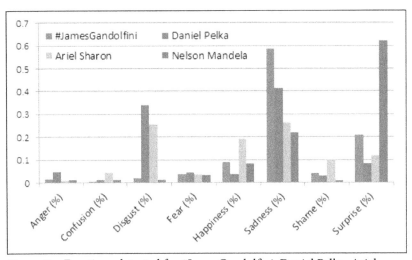

Figure 3     Emotions detected for #JamesGandolfini, Daniel Pelka, Ariel Sharon and Nelson Mandela

even happiness, which is significantly higher, although a proportion of it is in his remebrance by his supporters. The actor James Gandolfini died unexpectedly from a heart attack aged 51, hence the associated higher level of surprise. Interestingly very high proportion of tweets containing surprise were detected for Nelson Mandela, which were mostly expressions of disbelief that such a legendary leader has passed away, although he has been in frail health for a prolonged period of time.

Finally, tweets employing the hashtags and relating to the individual #JacinthaSaldanha, #2DayFM, the radio station responsible for the so-called #royalprank, which resulted in the nurses' suicide, highlight an interesting aspect about our emotion detection system.

From figure 4 it is apparent that sadness, followed by shame, dominated the emotional reaction in the immediate days following the event. Also the higher levels of sadness and shame for #JacinthaSaldanha relative to the two other hashtags point out that these reactions were marginally more prevalent in relation to the nurse. Expressions of disgust, happiness, surprise and anger on the other hand were more prevalent for #2DayFM and #royalprank relative to #Jacintha-Saldanha, which indicates that these emotions were targeted not at the victim but the radio station and tweets relating to the prank. This relative difference is especially noticeable for 'happiness', where a manual inspection of individual tweets

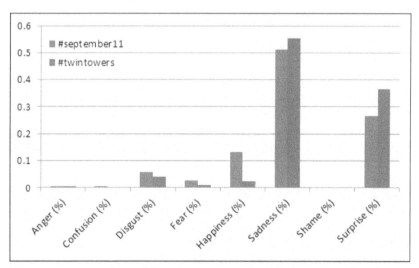

Figure 4    Emotions detected for #2DayFM, #jacinthasaldanha and #royalprank

reveals a proportion of sarcasm and irony, but at the same time people did not react with 'happiness' (including sarcasm) to the victim of the prank.

## 3.2. Correlations

An initial evaluation of correlations between emotions and basic twitter usage features (e.g. tweet @replies and tweet @mentions) was performed. Kendall's Tau β, which is generally more conservative than Spearman's rank correlation was employed on ratio summaries of the 28 topical datasets. All the significant correlations at p (two-tailed) < .001, were between; happiness–sadness (-.614), anger–confusion (.444), anger–disgust (.370), disgust–happiness (-.360), anger–mentions in tweets (-.524), anger–replies (-.386), fear–mentions in tweets (-.402) and fear–replies (-.349). The strongest association exists between happiness and sadness for the different datasets, as well as increased levels of anger which tends to coincide with increased levels of confusion and disgust. Tweet mentions (i.e. not replies, but rather mentions of other @user_accounts in a tweet) and tweet replies are also both negatively correlated with increased levels of anger and fear. Although with much lower significance levels, some other interesting correlations were found, such as a negative correlation between proportion of geo-located tweets and increased fear. These correlations are; however, unreliable due to the small dataset (28 measurements) and hence in future work we intend to extensively increase the size of analysed events and employ a thorough regression analysis.

# 4. Further Analysis and Discussion

In order to measure similarities purely based on emotional scores for the eight basic emotions between the events, hierarchical clustering was employed. The clustering method used was agglomerative between groups linkage clustering with squared Euclidean distance (values were normalised to z-scores) to generate the Dendogram in figure 5.

Reading the Dendogram horizontally from left to right, some spontaneous clusters of related events become apparent. It can be observed that #Chinese-NewYear and #bankholiday are grouped in the same cluster, which is also quite distinct from other clusters. This is due to the emotional profile for both events predominantly containing happiness (96% and 85% respectively), with little to no other emotions being detected. Other events contain more widely distributed emotional profiles which are still closely related; #royalprank, #2DayFM and #jacinthasaldanha all cluster together, for instance. #ClosingCeremony and #LFW are both events which had a similar distribution of emotions as generally positive emotions with some level of surprise. iPhone5S, which was received better than the iPhone5C model and Paralympics, cluster together. Some unexpected and sad events, such as #JamesGandolfini, #september11, #twintowers and helicopter crash all cluster together as well. Not surprisingly more controversial and sad events, i.e. tweets relating to Daniel Pelka, Woolwich attack, Horsemeat scandal and the G8 summit all fall into a cluster, which is also related to a similarly sized cluster with events 15, 26, 28, 23 and 18 (consult figure 5). Some events could not be placed into very meaningful clusters, such as Ariel Sharon and iPhone5C which have some similarity, as the iPhone5C was disappointing and attracted more specific negative emotions, similar to the profile of emotions for Ariel Sharon, yet still related to the clusters containing the other deaths (1, 11, 6 and 4). Anjem Choudary had a sufficiently different emotional profile and did not compare closely with the other clusters.

## 4.1. Limitations and Future Work

There are several limitations to the work presented in this paper. Spam on social-media streams is a major issue (Yardi et al. 2010), as it is not uncommon for hashtags to be misused, often by rogue accounts, to piggyback on a popular twitter topic and feed spam into the social-media stream. In this paper's analysis tweets were indirectly filtered to include only the ones that contained explicit expressions of emotion, as detected by EMOTIVE. This seems to be relatively effective in filtering out obvious spam and hijacked hashtag tweets, since these often don't contain subjective content, such as emotions. However, effective recognition of dubious accounts and their profiling may improve future analysis. Linked to this is the issue of profiling individual Twitter accounts to better understand demographic variables of the analysed sample, such as detecting the likely age, gender, or income level of specific user accounts. Currently available techniques unfortunately leave much to be desired, in terms of inference accuracy; however, there is ongoing research in this area (Bates et al. 2012). In this paper we did not distinguish between RTs (re-tweets) and original tweets, as there is some evidence that RTs are useful because they amplify and validate a message or opinion (Starbird and Palen 2012). Hence there is an argument to be made for their inclusion in the analysis. To address the issue of a relatively small sample size (see sub-section 3.2) we intend to generate fine-grained emotional footprints for much larger event samples in the future. We also see significant potential in investigating how emotions in long-lived events evolve over time, and how they differ between events.

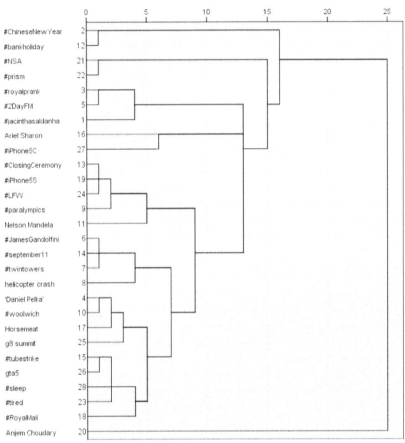

**Figure 5**    Dendogram – Agglomerative between groups linkage clustering (based on emotion scores)

# 5. Conclusion

This paper presents some novel results of emotionally annotated Twitter events with respect to the range of heterogeneous events analysed and the range of fine-grained emotions detected. Analysis of emotions was performed on over 1.5 million tweets, relating to 25 distinct events. The approach employed is a newly developed advanced-sentiment analysis technique, which automatically detects fine-grained, basic emotions (as identified in psychology literature) with an already established accuracy. Several examples of emotional profiles were given and the emotionality within tweets for different datasets discussed. Hierarchical clustering was employed to help organise the events based on emotions in tweets and it was found that events that generate similar emotional reactions on Twitter tend to also be similar in type. They can hence be organised solely based on specific fine-grained emotional information. Future work includes a larger study and analysis of emotions over time.

# References

Abel, F., Hauff, C., Houben, G., Stronkman R. and Tao, K. (2012) "Semantics + Filtering + Search = Twitcident Exploring Information in Social Web Streams", paper presented at the 23rd ACM International Conference on Hypertext and Social Media, Milwaukee, USA, June.

Bates, J., Neville, J. and Tyler, J. (2012) "Using Latent Communication Styles to Predict Individual Characteristics", paper presented at the 2nd Workshop on Social Media Analytics (SOMA KDD), Beijing, China, August.

Beaumont C. (2008) "Mumbai attacks: Twitter and Flickr used to break news", The Telegraph, http://www.telegraph.co.uk/news/worldnews/asia/india/3530640/Mumbai-attacks-Twitter-and-Flickr-used-to-break-news-Bombay-India.html [27th November 2008].

Bollen, J., Mao, H. and Pepe, A. (2011) "Modeling Public Mood and Emotion: Twitter Sentiment and Socio-Economic Phenomena", paper presented at the fifth International AAAI Conference on Weblogs and Social Media, Barcelona, Spain, July.

Cashmore P. (2009) "Mashable: Jakarta bombings - Twitter user first on the scene", [online], Mashable, http://mashable.com/2009/07/16/jakarta-bombings-twitter/ [16th July 2009].

Cheong, M. and Lee, V. C. S. (2011) "A microblogging-based approach to terrorism informatics: Exploration and chronicling civilian sentiment and response to terrorism events via Twitter", Journal of Information Systems Frontiers – Springer, Vol 13, No. 1, pp 45-59.

Chew, C. and Eysenbach, G. (2010) "Pandemics in the age of Twitter: content analysis of Tweets during the 2009 H1N1 outbreak", PLOS One, Vol 5, No. 11.

Choudhury, M. and Counts, S. (2012) "The Nature of Emotional Expression in Social Media: Measurement, Inference and Utility", Technical Report: Microsoft.

Drummond, T. (2004) "Vocabulary of Emotions", [online], North Seattle Community College, Available from http://www.sba.pdx.edu/faculty/mblake/448/FeelingsList.pdf [last viewed 9th January 2012].

Ekman, P. and Richard, J. (1994) "All emotions are basic, The nature of emotion: Fundamental questions", Oxford University Press, New York, pp 15-19.

Grassi, M. (2009) "Developing HEO human emotions ontology", Biometric ID Management and Multimodal Communication, Springer Berlin Heidelberg, pp 244-251.

Izard, C. E. (2009) "Emotion theory and research: Highlights, unanswered questions, and emerging issues", Annual Review of Psychology, Vol 60, No. 1, pp 1-25.

Lansdall-Welfare, T., Lampos, V. and Cristianini, N. (2012) "Effects of the Recession on Public Mood in the UK", paper presented at the 21st International Conference companion on World Wide Web, Lyon, France, April.

Miller, G. (2011) "Social scientists wade into the tweet stream", Science, Vol 333, No. 6051, pp 1814-1815.

O'Connor, B., Balasubramanyan R., Routledge B. and Smith N. (2010) "From Tweets to Polls: LinkingText Sentiment to Public Opinion Time Series", paper presented at the fourth International AAAI Conference on Weblogs and Social Media, Washington D.C., USA, May.

Plutchik, R. (1980) "Emotion: A Psychoevolutionary Synthesis", Longman Higher Education, 1980.

Ritter, A., Clark, S., Etzioni, M and Etzioni, O. (2011). "Named Entity Recognition in Tweets: An Experimental Study", paper presented at the Conference on Empirical Methods in Natural Language Processing, Edinburgh, UK, July.

Sakaki, T., Okazaki, M. and Matsuo, Y. (2010) "Earthquake shakes Twitter users: real-time event detection by social sensors", paper presented at the 19th International Conference on World Wide Web, Raleigh, USA, April.

Starbird, K. and Palen, L. (2012) "(How) will the revolution be retweeted?: information diffusion and the 2011 Egyptian uprising", paper presented at the ACM 2012 conference on Computer Supported Cooperative Work, Seattle, USA, February.

Sykora, M., Jackson, T. W., O'Brien A. and Elayan, S. (2013) "EMOTIVE Ontology: Extracting fine-grained emotions from terse, informal messages", IADIS International Journal on Computer Science and Information Systems, Vol 8, No. 2, pp. 106-118.

Thelwall, M., Buckley, K. and Paltoglou, G. (2012) "Sentiment Strength Detection for the Social Web", Journal of the American Society for Information Science and Technology, Vol 63, No. 1, pp 163-173.

Tumasjan, A., Sprenger, T. O. and Welpe, I. M. (2010) "Predicting elections with twitter: What 140 characters reveal about political sentiment", paper presented at the fourth International AAAI Conference on Weblogs and Social Media, Washington D.C., USA, May.

Yardi, S., Romero, D., Schoenebeck, G. and Boyd, D. (2010). "Detecting spam in a Twitter network", First Monday, Vol 15, No. 1, Online Journal.

# Civic Conversations and Citizen Engagement – A New Framework of Analysis for Web 2.0 Mediated Citizen Participation

## Nick Ellison and Johanne Orchard-Webb

Department of Social Policy and Social Work, University of York, York, UK
School of Environment and Technology, University of Brighton, UK

nick.ellison@york.ac.uk, J.Orchard-Webb@brighton.ac.uk
Originally published in The Proceedings of ECSM 2014

## Editorial commentary

Whose voice gets heard in civic discussion? Social media is often cited as a paradigm shift in contemporary political debates. This paper avoids the naive optimism of those who heralded the Arab Spring as a change to the way that communities decide what they want. Instead Ellison and Orchard-Webb propose a new framework for analysing who is engaged in 'civic conversation' and who is not. Drawing on a number of current studies, synthesised in their own research proposal, the authors explore the impact of social media on important contemporary issues such as tokenism, low levels of voter participation and consultation fatigue. The paper draws practical and realistic conclusions about the strengths and weaknesses of social media in current citizen participation.

**Abstract:** This paper outlines a research agenda that introduces a distinctly sociological framework of analysis for understanding the role played by social media (in the English context) in re-shaping the nature of localized political/civic engagement between citizens and local authorities. Amidst heated contemporary policy debates about the shifting roles and responsibilities of local government and subsequent citizen-state relations, it is timely to ask if Web 2.0 platforms such as Facebook and Twitter afford opportunities for new forms of interaction – characterized here as 'civic conversations'. The critical framework we propose explores the deployment of these platforms in terms of their potential to encourage distinctive forms of participation that might bridge the divide that has emerged in recent years between citizens as consumers of local services and citizens as local democratic actors. This framework has been informed by both initial evidence of such civic conversations in a nationwide survey of English local authorities (Ellison and Hardey, 2013) and also the day-to-day policy and practice challenges emerging from detailed local authority case study scoping (in 2013) with regard to relations between social media use, citizen engagement and localized political praxis. Specifically this framework asks - if such civic conversations exist - what impact, if any, might they have upon stubborn citizen engagement issues such as accessibility, depth of representation, tokenism, poor citizen feedback, consultation fatigue, democratic deficit and inequalities of power within state-shaped platforms of engagement? In this paper we outline: the theoretical debates from which this approach to analysis emerges; the social policy and broader sociological questions that constitute the framework; and finally we highlight themes from initial empirical findings concerning the risks, opportunities and practical implications of this emergent form of citizen-state interaction.

**Keywords:** social media; citizen engagement; local government; civic conversations

# 1. Introduction

This paper introduces a framework of analysis to help inform policy development and research questions concerning the relationship between a rapidly maturing social media ecology (Future Identities Report, 2013) and the shifting nature of citizen/(local) state relations within a public sector austerity and localism context (Lowndes and Pratchett, 2012). More specifically, the framework has been developed to explore the potential and risks of the use by local government of social media platforms to engage local citizens in the development of what Ellison and Hardey, (2013) describe as 'civic conversations'. As an innovative point of entry into the evaluation of rapidly shifting and contested local citizen-state relations the concept of 'civic conversations' is used to illuminate hitherto under-researched social processes concerning the nature and consequence of a meso-space of engagement that we argue may exist between the citizen as service consumer and the traditional narrow engagement of citizens with liberal democratic institutions, for example, through local or national elections (Ellison and Hardey, 2013).

The next section of the paper outlines the dominant areas of investigation researched by the academy in relation to social media and political engagement in order to reveal the areas that might be usefully explored through the alternative framework of 'civic conversations'. Here we make the argument based on the survey of all English local authorities by Ellison and Hardey (2013) that there is an under-researched and indeed under-utilized potential meso-space of low-level, but nevertheless important 'civic conversations' between local government and citizens. It is our belief that such open-ended conversations on local political/civic issues, via social media, require greater critical attention in order to begin to address the neglect by both the academy and policy-makers of these less formally constituted episodes of public participation in relation to their impact upon citizenship and civic engagement (Ellison and Hardey, 2013). This discussion is followed by a more detailed consideration of the proposed framework to illustrate the policy relevance of this analysis in the context of broader debates concerning a neo-liberal post-political consensus in local government (Swyngedouw, 2008), and degraded local politics (Harvey, 1989; Featherstone *et al.*, 2012). The paper concludes with themes emerging from detailed local government/voluntary sector scoping meetings in 2013 in three English local authorities for a future research project that seeks to test this framework. This final section provides an indication of some of the challenges faced by local government in planning and delivering this new route to participation, but also the questions and concerns this route raises for local communities in terms of responsibilization of citizens and equity of engagement and influence.

## 2. Political citizenship in a mediated society - a synthesis of recent key debates

Research exploring the democratic potential of social media and citizen-state relations has been dominated by two streams of investigation in recent years. The first is concerned with the practicalities and efficiencies of social media as an additional information-providing platform or service delivery medium with evident links to how this contributes to a form of citizenship dominated by practices of consumption (i.e. the citizen consumer) (Newman and Clarke, 2009). This academic and policy focus reflects the fact that 73% of UK Internet users access some form of government service online (Dutton and Blank, 2011). The second focus has been to report on and critique experiences of large-scale government e-democracy models such as national and regional scale consultations, e-petitions and online voting mechanisms (Lindner and

Riehm, 2010; Miller, 2009). This model has evolved with the advent of Web 2.0 technologies which are held to offer a more 'open source' (many-to-many) configuration of political engagement with the potential for more deliberative political exchange (Dahlberg, 2001; O'Reilly, 2010; Rheingold, 2000) but perhaps relies on a form of libertarian 'active citizenship' to give it motility. This model is critiqued for its exclusionary practices and the risk of post-political citizenship (Loader and Mercea, 2011; Pajnik, 2005). While these are all important elements of the relationship between the state and citizens, as mediated by social media and Web 2.0 technologies, there is much less said about the day-to-day potential for civic conversations at a local government level (Ellison and Hardey, 2013). We argue that exploring the link between this evolving mode of participation and local government/citizen conversations is key to a more nuanced critical analysis of civic engagement and praxis in England today.

The more utopian aspect of recent thinking about the role of the Internet can be seen in the early research by Norris (1999) and in more reflective but still optimistic work more recently by Dahlgren (2009), Coleman and Blumler (2009) and Zavestoski et al, (2006), all of whom have argued the case for the Internet's democratizing potential. Others have since argued that the naïve optimism of early academic champions and web entrepreneurs was founded on a misplaced faith in the alleged common values of 'transparency', 'universal access' and 'freedom of voice' shared by internet-based communications and aspirations for a progressive Habermasian style deliberative democracy (Dean, 2003; Pajnik, 2005). Nevertheless, this early optimism has been reinvigorated by the arrival of Web 2.0 technology and in particular social media platforms such as Facebook and Twitter (O'Reilly, 2010). The use of social media as a catalyst for acts of real world democratic protest during the Arab Spring in Tunisia, Egypt and Libya 2011/12 have been widely commented upon in this vein (Dutton, 2013; Foresight Future Identities, 2013). Moreover, it has been argued that this second generation technology offers distinctive and new conceptions of the democratic potential of the Internet centered around the networked citizen-user rather than a public sphere model (Dahlgren, 2009; Papacharissi, 2010). This leads some observers (Loader and Mercea, 2011) to wonder if this new model will largely be incorporated into existing everyday power relations, or if indeed through this broader conception of democratic citizenship – 'a less dutiful … more personalized and self-actualizing notion of citizenship' (Loader and Mercea,

2011: 761) – there are opportunities to challenge dominant discourses and privileged positions.

Pajnik (2005) warns us critical reflection upon the scope of citizenship shaped by a mediated society is central to these debates. Certainly, a number of academic observers have argued that the deployment of the e-democracy model in particular articulates a very thin understanding of political citizenship that is tied to voting and elections only (Coleman and Blumler, 2009). In addition, it is observed that this model of communication also fails to attract the attention of under-represented groups (Lindner and Riehm, 2010) thus replicating the issues of democratic deficit and inequalities of access that plagues real world political participation (Taylor, 2007). Perhaps a more integral concern for the capacity of social media to enable political dialogue is the dominant use of the web as a marketplace shaped by market laws rather than a place of democratic politics which it is argued encourages consumer attitudes and a search for individualized solutions to problems rather than fostering association or collective political action (Wellman *et al.* 2003). Yet Ellison and Hardey (2013: 13) would argue that this is not the only potential outcome with evidence in their research of social media facilitating 'interaction between local councils and citizens, this interaction taking the form of more or less extended 'conversations' hosted, but not dominated by local authorities'. By opening up the analysis of this space to previously absent or unobserved forms of engagement the critical reflection of citizenship at the local scale is expanded to consider whether civic conversations erode or compound these individualized and exclusionary trends, or if the social media model is evolving to allow for new more inclusive and open political dialogue.

## 3. Civic conversations – towards a new framework of analysis

Civic conversations between citizens and local government are characterized by their informal, flexible, open-ended and day-to-day nature (Ellison and Hardey, 2013). These are dialogues about local civic issues ranging from service quality, through the social justice implications of service cuts, to wider issues of democratic representation and the structure of local governance. The policy, planning and political implications for this form of engagement lead to currently unanswered (social) policy questions in the English context that form the outline of this analytical approach and prompt the following questions. When and where (i.e. which social media platforms and in which communities) are civic conversations emerging and why? What are the issues triggering these conversations? Who does and does not partake in this dialogue (in terms of both citizens and members of local government), and why? What challenges/ barriers do both local government personnel and citizens face in order to engage in this form of conversation? What new expectations or demands does this create for local politicians, civil servants and citizens in terms of the practical delivery and future forms of local civic engagement and participation? What is the impact for both citizens and local government of (not) engaging in this space? How does this form of engagement complement, supplement, hybridize or displace traditional routes to participation such as town hall meetings? Finally, and importantly, what do these answers mean for the equality of engagement in local politics?

By exploring in detail contemporary examples of local government use of social media to engage citizens the authors seek to understand further the critical space between the optimism of some libertarian commentators and the cautionary tales of the post-political counter-argument. Building on the thesis developed by Ellison and Hardey (2013) the proposed research project will explore the social power implications, practical possibilities and challenges that are likely to be associated with civic conversations at local level. While Ellison and Hardey (2013) found through their survey of all 352 English councils that local authorities are largely failing to engage with social media in any substantive manner, they also found some clear pre-figurative examples of social media use that amounted to what they describe as an 'embryonic form' (p.1) of civic conversation. They detected in certain local authorities Facebook interactions that had the character of bottom-up, less formally constituted open-ended conversations between local government personnel and citizens. Given the context of a broadly degraded local politics (Evans *et al.,* 2009), the rapid increase in use of social media in a liquid modern (Bauman, 2000) or networked society (Castells, 2011) and central state pressures to employ localist agendas, the research questions outlined above have been developed to explore whether civic conversations might offer a new response to familiar difficulties associated with citizen engagement and, if so, whether they might lead to new practices of social and political citizenship and a rearticulation of citizen-state relations.

# 4. Testing the 'civic conversations' analysis: emerging themes

*"Developing Civic Conversations? Exploring social media use and citizen participation in English local government"* is a research bid that has been co-developed by a partnership of local authority communications practitioners, third sector leaders and the authors. The objective of this project is to test the civic conversations framework via in-depth case studies to map and analyse the contemporary use of social media by three English local authorities (LA) in order to gain an understanding of their potential impact on the nature of citizen engagement, emerging forms of 'active' citizenship and shifting citizen-state relations in the context of the British government's current localist agendas.

In building the research partnership and through initial scoping meetings with the partners it has become evident that, owing to an absence of contemporary evidence upon which to base policy decisions, there is a real appetite for gaining a fuller understanding of the engagement potential of local authority social media use and the relations and cultural norms this disturbs or develops within local politics. Below we outline emerging themes from the project scoping meetings with local authority and third sector partners, and reflect on what these might mean for the 'civic conversations' analysis detailed above. We also consider how these compare to the results of recent large scale local government surveys on the use of social media by local government for citizen engagement purposes in both England (Spurrell, 2012) and Australia (Purser, 2012).

In common with the Spurrell (2012) and Purser (2012) surveys our partners have all indicated they are using social media to engage citizens in a number of forms (predominantly via Twitter and Facebook), but are aware (in line with the Ellison and Hardey (2013) findings) that they are not fulfilling the potential of this medium of engagement. One partner acknowledged that as a sector local government is largely stuck in 'broadcast' mode and not fulfilling what he described as its 'transformative potential'. One concern raised in scoping meetings in this respect has been that a great deal of social media communication is still originating from the local government communications teams. Partners felt a barrier to a more progressive employment of social media can often be caused by a fear within local government about who 'manages' social media communications and controls the 'message'. This is highlighted in other surveys and wider commentary as being a direct barrier to accessing the full potential of open and transparent dialogue between local councils and citizens

(Purser, 2012; Shewell, 2011; Spurrell, 2012; The Young Foundation, 2010). That said in all three case studies both council officers and councillors currently use social media (and there is an appetite to spread the extent of this use), however, there is an anxiety about the potential difficulties created when that goes 'wrong', with examples of councillors making inappropriate comments in online public forums and the damage limitation subsequently required. Despite these control barriers the existing areas covered by social media use already includes the political process itself with one council introducing web-streaming of local authority formal meetings and a Twitter wall at the meeting to extend the dialogue via questions from Twitter users. While in another LA recently introduced live uncensored Facebook 'Question and Answer' sessions with local Councillors has generated considerable interest from local citizens. It was evident throughout the initial scoping that social media will play a role in future efforts to address local government concerns regarding citizen disengagement and disenfranchisement from the local political process. The Purser (2012: 8) Australian survey showed 25% of councils 'believed that social media would specifically assist them to engage with hard to reach segments of the community including youth, those with disabilities, seniors and time poor families'. All of our partners are looking to gain insight into which citizens within their diverse demographic are using this form of engagement and why – and perhaps more importantly who is not, and why. While all three case studies can see an increase in the scale of their social media following, the concern at this stage is that their followers are the usual vocal white middle class groups that have transferred their political interests and energies to social media platforms. This evidently needs further critical attention to explore how social media might be eroding or embedding pre-existing barriers to engagement.

In terms of extending who is using social media beyond the communications team partners noted that as a younger, more 'media-savvy' generation of councillors came forward, fears about the potential damage to the council's reputation from loose or inappropriate comments were beginning to diminish. Indeed our partners confirmed that they expect social media to play an increasing role in local politics, which provides further evidence of the growing impact that a 'digital by default' Generation C (Future Identities Report, 2013; Shewell, 2013) is having on the nature of local government-citizen dialogue. However, this shift is clearly by no means a painless or even process with examples described of different political cultures experiencing early clashes. For example, LA and third sector partners described resistance from some older council members and the tensions created as new political norms associated with increased transparency, pace, and accessibility of social media communications emerge.

Partners described how the discomfort of some LA members with Web 2.0 cultural norms became explicit in examples where the political conversation was not initiated or hosted by the local council but instead through neighbourhood websites. The fear for some third sector partners is that local government social media use, if it is controlled too tightly, will simply reproduce the practices of poor citizen engagement that has plagued local government in the UK for some time (Evans and Jones, 2008). Of course, political/cultural clashes have also emerged where councils/councillors have received aggressive and personal attacks on Twitter or Facebook – the traditional rules of courtesy and diplomacy that shape (some) off-line political debate appearing to them to be absent in the world of informal online conversations (see Pajnik, 2005 and Sennett, 2012). Learning how to handle this in an open and positive way is clearly a challenge for participants of this form of interaction. And yet all partners have provided examples of where this challenge had been handled well, or where the use of social media by the council to communicate with citizens had a very 'humanising' effect where more formal modes of engagement had often alienated citizens. This was an observation echoed in the Purser (2012) survey and also in UK case studies described by BDO Local Government (2012).

Interestingly all three case studies from a council and third sector perspective observed that practical emergency communications via social media between the LA and citizens (for example during localised floods and snow blocked roads) was acting as a catalyst for further engagement at a more political and strategic level. This element of engagement around the delivery of services is an experience the third sector partners in particular are building upon in all areas of service delivery and needs-based consultation. For example, one third sector partner explained that they are increasingly finding that normal partnership modes of engagement based around traditional forms of democratic dialogue are quickly becoming moribund as citizen volunteers want more fixed time /fixed topic projects rather than the slower moving deliberations associated with lengthy consultation periods or (equally lengthy) citizens surveys. In this respect it was felt that the Internet (and social media in particular) can offer the potential for rapid engagement. Further, third sector partners expressed concerns over the time premium for 'active citizens' and the dangers of consultation fatigue. This was brought into sharp focus by the centrality of citizen engagement for the success of the UK Coalition government's localist agendas (Lowndes and Pratchett, 2012). In this respect partners were hopeful that social media based public engagement in local government decision-making would have the potential to ease some of this pressure with its more informal tone, temporal and place-based flexibility, cost-savings, ease of access to information and rapid response potential. Of course this form of engagement and the liquid modern logic of social media encourages the mixing of citizen consumer and political citizenship praxis in the style of 'new public management' that Sunstein, (2007) and others warn against. Ellison and Hardey (2013: 894) suggest that we 'accept this de facto elision' and further accept that this is a way of creating a space for 'citizens to engage if they choose to do so, hear others' views, and receive responses directly from elected members' in a prompt and timely fashion. In this way social media practice and norms may remedy some of the issues with off-line engagement that leaves citizens feeling their view has no impact upon local decision-making.

# 5. Conclusion

As we have outlined above, different assumptions exist about the types of participation that social media might facilitate (Anduiza et al. 2009; Benkler, 2006; Loader and Mercea, 2011; Pajnik, 2005). On the one hand, some observers are primarily interested in 'non-reciprocal' forms of communication such as 'e-government' and e-petitioning as means of linking citizens into the public sphere (Margetts, 2006, 2009; Wright, 2006). On the other hand, 'Habermasian' portrayals of the online world take a more dialogic view that acknowledges the potential for extensive online engagement (Dahlberg, 2001, 2011; Dahlgren, 2009; Rheingold, 2000, 2012) – a view arguably boosted by the increasingly flexible and mobile forms of communication introduced by Web 2.0 platforms such as Facebook and Twitter from 2006 onwards. However, if the e-government/e-petitioning perspective does not give too much credence to the communicative potential of social media, the Habermasian approach risks overestimating citizens' inclination for extensive, in-depth social and political dialogue (Hindman, 2009; Ellison and Hardey, 2013). Ellison and Hardey suggest that, rather than being platforms that are likely to facilitate the kind of democratic dialogue associated with civic republican conceptions of publicity (Sandel, 2010; Miller, 2000) for example, social media may have the potential to foster less 'sophisticated' but nevertheless meaningful civic conversations – flexible, open-ended dialogues about local issues. These 'civic conversations' cannot satisfactorily replace the (slow-moving) structures and institutions of liberal democracy, but can complement and add to these formal structures by providing opportunities for engagement with local authorities that could reduce existing communication barriers, particularly perhaps for 'hard to engage' groups.

Currently, the majority of local authorities are some way from being able to organize and host sustained forms of social media-driven conversation – but a few are beginning to explore the possibilities this form of communication might offer. Given that hyper-connectivity, particularly through mobile technologies, has been identified as one of the key factors shaping citizen identity and practices in the UK over the next decade (Foresight Future Identities report, 2013; Beer and Burrows, 2007), what is understood by citizenship – certainly in the local context – is likely to go beyond voting and the traditional institutions of liberal democracy (Dahlgren 2009; Coleman and Blumler, 2009; Papacharissi, 2010). It is here that civic conversations could have significant potential, although whether the fostering of such conversations among local populations is a feasible strategy for local authorities and, if it is, how it should be pursued needs to be considered carefully. Through the research proposed here attention needs to be paid to the risks associated with civic conversations, not least the well-known exclusionary tendencies associated with social media (Chadwick, 2009; Pajnik, 2005), as well as the potential they may hold for enhanced citizen participation. In developing this research project centred around the concept of civic conversations we are better able to understand if the citizen norms this facilitates encourages alternative practices of (political) citizenship. This line of enquiry introduces broader research questions concerning the potentialities of a new local politics aligned to a restructured citizen-local government relationship facilitated in part by openly engaging with citizens in a reconstituted – and 'conversational' – local public sphere.

# References

Anduiza, E., Cantijoch, M. and Gallego, A. (2009) 'Political participation and the internet' a field essay', *Information, Communication and Society*, vol 12, no 6, pp. 860-78.

Bauman, Z. (2000) *Liquid Modernity*, Polity Press, Cambridge.

BDO LLP (2012) *From housing and litter to Facebook and Twitter*, BDO LLP, London

Beer and Burrows (2007) 'Sociology and, of and in Web 2.0: Some initial considerations', *Sociological Research Online*, 12 (5): 17pp.

Benkler, Y. (2006) *The Wealth of Networks: How social production transforms markets and freedom*, Yale University Press: New Haven.

Castells, M. (2011) *Communication Power*, Oxford University Press, Oxford.

Chadwick, A. (2009) 'Web 2.0: new challenges for the study of e-democracy in an era of informational exuberance', *I/S*, 5 (1): 9-41.

Coleman, D. and Blumler, J. (2009) *The Internet and Democratic Citizenship: Theory, Practice and Policy*, Cambridge University Press, Cambridge.

Dahlberg, L. (2001) 'The internet and democratic discourse: exploring the prospects of online deliberative forums extending the public sphere', *Information, Communication and Society*, 4 (1), 615-33.

Dahlgren, P. (2009) *Media and political engagement: Citizens, communication and Democracy*. Cambridge University Press, Cambridge.

Dean, J. (2003) 'Why the net is not a public sphere', *Constellations*, 10 (1), 95-112.

Department for Communities and Local Government (2011) *The Localism Act*, available at http://www.legislation.gov.uk/ukpga/2011/20/introduction/enacted (October, 2013).

Dutton, W.H. (ed.) (2013) *The Oxford Handbook of Internet Studies*. Oxford University Press, Oxford.

Dutton, W. H. and Blank, G. (2011) *Next generation users: The internet in Britain, Oxford Internet Survey 2011 Report*, Oxford Internet Institute, Oxford.

Ellison, N. and Hardey, M. (2013) Developing Political conversations? *Information, Communication and Society*, 16 (6): 78-98 Evans, J., and Jones, P. (2008) 'Rethinking sustainable urban regeneration: ambiguity, creativity, and the shared territory', *Environment and Planning*, 40: 1416-1434

Evans, J., Jones, P., and Krueger, R. (2009) 'Organic regeneration and sustainability or can the credit crunch save our cities?', *Local Environment,* 14 (7), 683-698

Featherstone, D., Ince, A., MacKinnon, D., Strauss, K., and Cumbers, A. (2012) Progressive localism and the construction of political alternatives. *Transactions of the Institute of British Geographers,* 37: 177-182

Foresight Future Identities (2013) *Final Project Report.* The Government Office for Science, London. Habermas, J. (1998), *The structural transformation of the public sphere*, Polity Press, Cambridge.

Harvey, D. (1989) *The Condition of Postmodernity*, Polity Press, Cambridge.

Hindman, M. (2009) *The myth of digital democracy.* Princeton University Press, Princeton.

Lindner, R. and Riehm, U. (2010) 'Broadening participation through e-petitions? Results from an empirical study on petitions to the German parliament', unpublished paper, Fraunhofer Institute for Systems and Innovation Research, Karlsruhe, Germany.

Lowndes, V. and Pratchett, L. (2012) Local governance under the Coalition Government: austerity, localism and the "Big Society", *Local Government Studies*, 38 (1), 21-40.

Loader, B. D. and Mercea, D. (2011) Introduction networking democracy? Social media innovations and participatory politics, *Information, Communication and Society*, 14 (6), 757-769.

McCann, K. (2012) *Should communications teams relax control of social media?* The Guardian, Tuesday 7th February, 2012. Available online at: http://www.guardian.co.uk/local-government-network/poll/2012/feb/07/poll-relinquish-control-over-social-media [Accessed on 16.4.2013].

Margetts, H. (2006) 'E-government in Britain – a decade on', *Parliamentary Affairs*, 59 (2): 250-65.

Margetts, H. (2009) 'The Internet and public policy', *Policy and Internet*, 1 (1): 1-21.

Miller, D. (2000) *Citizenship and national identity*, Polity Press, Cambridge.

Miller, L. (2009) 'e-Petitions at Westminster: the way forward for democracy?' *Parliamentary Affairs*, 62, (1), 162–177

Newman, J. and Clarke, J. (2009) *Publics, Politics and Power: Remaking the Public in Public Services*. Sage, London.

Norris, P. (1999) 'Who surfs? New technology, old voters and virtual democracy', in E.C. Kamark and J.S. Nye (eds.) *Democracy.com? – Governance in a network world*. Hollis, New Haven.

O'Reilly, T. (2010) 'Government as a Platform', in D. Lathrop and L. Ruma (Eds.), *Open Government: Collaboration, Transparency and Participation in Practice*, O'Reilly Media, Sebastopol.

Office for National Statistics (2011) *Internet Access - Households and Individuals, 2011*. Released: 31 August 2011 Pajnik, M. (2005) 'Citizenship and mediated society', *Citizenship Studies*, 9 (4), 349-367

Papacharissi, Z. (2010) *A Private Sphere: Democracy in a Digital Age*, Cambridge: Polity Press.

Purser, K. (2012) *Using Social Media in Local Government: 2011 Survey Report*, Australian Centre of Excellence for Local Government, University of Technology, Sydney.

Rheingold, H. (2000). *The Virtual Community: Home-steading on the Electronic Frontier*, MIT Press, Cambridge, MA.

Rheingold, H. (2012) *Netsmart: how to thrive online*, MIT Press, Cambridge, Mass.

Sandel, M. (2010) *Justice: What's the right thing to do?*, Penguin Books, London.

Shewell, J. (2011) 'Social media in the public sector', *Whitepaper 14*, Public Relations Whitepaper Series, DWPub, Daryl Willcox Publishing, Brighton.

Shewell, J. (2013) *Stepping up to the challenge of digital*, Brand Republic, January 2013, Haymarket Business Media, London.

Spurrell, D. (2012) *An opportunity or a threat? How local government uses social media today.* The Guardian, Tuesday 7th February, 2012. Available online at: http://www.guardian.co.uk/local-government-network/2012/feb/07/local-government-social-media-today [Accessed on 22.1.2013]

Sennett, R. (2012) *Together. The rituals, pleasures and politics of cooperation*. Penguin Books, London

Sunstein, C. (2007) *Republic.com 2.0*, Princeton University Press, Princeton.

Swyngedouw, E. (2008) *Where is the political?* University of Manchester Working Paper, Available from: http://www.socialsciences.manchester. ac.uk/disciplines/politics/research/hmrg/activities/documents/Swyngedouw.pdf [Accessed: 28 August, 2010]

Taylor, M. (2007) 'Community Participation in the real world: Opportunities and pitfalls in new governance spaces', *Urban Studies*, 44, (2), 297-317

The Young Foundation (2010) *Listen, Participate, Transform. A social media framework for local government.* A Local 2.0 think-piece. The Young Foundation, June 2010.

Wellman, B., Quan-Haase, A., Boase, J., Chen, W., Hampton, K., Diaz, I. and Miyata, K. (2003) 'The social affordances of the internet for networked individualism', *Journal of Computer-Mediated Communication*, 8 (3), 0-0.

Zavestoski, S., Shulman, S. and Schlosberg,D. (2006) 'Democracy and the environment on the internet: electronic citizen participation in regulatory rulemaking', *Science, Technology and Human Values*, 31 (4), 383-408.

# Investigating Civic Engagement Behaviour on Facebook from a Social Capital Perspective

**Anne Marie Warren, Ainin Sulaiman and Ismawati Noor Jaafar**
Department of Operations and Management Information Systems, Faculty of Business and Accountancy, University of Malaya, Kuala Lumpur, Malaysia

annemw7@siswa.um.edu.my, ainins@sum.edu.my, isma_jaafar@um.edu.my
Originally published in the Proceedings of ECSM 2014

## Editorial commentary

Can Facebook change the world? Or at least, in what ways can Facebook provide a platform for discussions that may change the world? Warren et al took a survey to over 1000 respondents, drawing on a similar demographic to the sample used in the reputable Pew Internet reports. They tested factors that contribute to the social capital of these users (strength of ties, levels of trust and shared language and vision) and found a positive relationship with the level of civic engagement.

This paper explores these factors and presents a typology of civic engagement types mediated through Facebook : publications and action. Combined publishing content that stimulates interest and proposing and organising events in the real world may give us an insight into changes that go beyond discussion.

**Abstract:** The reoccurring perception that there is a civic deficit in society has heightened the need for the government, researches and other practitioners to understand more clearly the factors that encourage civic engagement behaviour. Considering that Facebook has extended considerably with over one billion users, this social media platform is a potential communication channel for people to learn, develop and sustain civic behaviour. While there are promising evidences that citizens are making concerted efforts in adopting Facebook for civic engagement, research on their civic behaviour from a social capital viewpoint in the social media context remains limited. This paper integrates the social capital theory to construct a model for investigating the motivations behind people's online civic behaviour. The study holds that the facets of social capital — social interaction ties (structural), trust (relational), shared languages and vision (cognitive), will influence citizens' civic engagement behaviour on Facebook. Empirical data collected from 1,228 Facebook users provide support for the proposed model. The results revealed that online civic engagement behaviour is established under trusting relationships, close social interactions and having common grounds on goals and languages as its conditions. Citizens are utilizing Facebook for protest-related actions, posting of issues and expressions to organise and lobby for changes necessary in addressing social issues. At the same time, increased social interactions among Facebook members help to build trusting relationships with members, creating opportunities to be civically engaged in addressing social issues. Similarly, shared languages and visions engender trusting relationships among members. The statistical analysis also indicated that online civic engagement behaviour is a multifaceted construct, consisting of online civic publication and online civic actions modes. The analyses provide support for the contention that asserts the civic potential of social media. This paper may serve as the catalyst for new directions of future research on social media activism for addressing social issues.

**Keywords:** Facebook, social networking sites, trust, civic engagement, social capital, social media.

# 1. Introduction

There is a growing concern that citizens are politically apathetic and lack of civic awareness (Bennet, 2008; Putnam, 2000). Scholars have illustrated the anaemic level of civic engagement from a political perspective, in particular among the younger generation (e.g. Macnamara, Sakinofsky, and Beattie, 2012; Loader, 2007). These reports raise the concerns about the nature of a civic society per se; are we becoming a less caring generation now than before? And more importantly, how can we foster civic engagement among citizens? In response to these concerns, Bennett (2008:21) argued for a need to 'bridge the paradigms' with new technologies or else citizens, digitally inspired or not, will remain disconnected from civic life.

Recently, there have been growing social media interactivity in ways that suggest a reinvigoration in civic engagement in the public sphere. For example, studies have suggest that Facebook is a powerful tool for political activism (Steenkamp and Hyde-Clarke 2014; Valenzuela, 2013) and for advocacy on social problems (Warren, Sulaiman and Jaafar, 2014). These works present an array of examples and prospects of a growing civic involvement of Facebook users in *addressing* social problems by educating, informing and organising themselves online to take action on issues. Thus, social media resembles a direct form for community participation where many real world civic tasks can now take place online. While the examples constitute promising evidence that citizens are adopting social media for civic engagement, little is known about the mechanisms of social media influenced civic behaviour from a social capital perspective. There are also relatively few studies on the phenomenon of civic engagement behaviour in social media as implied by Valenzuela (2013). Moreover, Correa, Hinsley and de Zúñiga, (2010) have encouraged the need to develop a richer measure of social media use for understanding civic behaviour and more importantly, what promotes online civic engagement (Valenzuela, 2013; de Zúñiga, 2012).

In response to the gaps identified and the calls for future research, this study examines how Facebook is shaping the landscape of civic engagement in social media by: (i) determining the facets of social capital (i.e. structural – social interaction ties, relational – trust and cognitive – shared languages and vision) which motivate online civic engagement behaviour (ii) examining the relationship between social interaction ties and shared languages and vision on trust; and (iii) exploring the modes of online civic engagement behaviour.

# 2. Literature Review and Hypotheses

## 2.1. Social capital, social media and civic engagement

According to Nahapiet and Ghoshal (1998:243), social capital is 'the sum of the actual and potential resources embedded within, available through, and derived from the network of relationships possessed by an individual or social unit'. Their conceptualisation of social capital consists of three dimensions, namely structural, relational and cognitive. A number of scholars applied this conceptualisation of social capital to investigate behaviour in knowledge sharing or integration (e.g. van den Hooff and Huysman 2009; Chiu, Hsu and Wang, 2006). Considering that individual's behaviour to willingly share is a product of their structural, relational and cognitive capitals, we draw on the social capital theory to investigate the influence of the facets of the three dimensions of social capital on civic engagement behaviour in social media. Moreover, the theory anchored by Nahapiet and Ghoshal (1998) has yet to be applied in examining citizen civic behaviour on social media.

Social media are online applications and technologies that enable user generated content, sharing of information, and collaboration amongst a community of users (Kaplan and Haenlein, 2010). Examples include Facebook, Twitter and YouTube. Statistics from Socialbakers (2013) indicate that social media usage remains on the rise, particular with Facebook, which has activities ranging from social (Manago, Taylor and Greenfield, 2012) to business (Brennan and Croft, 2012). Recently, there are evidences suggesting that citizens who engage in civic and political activities are frequent users of social media (Pearce and Kendzior, 2012; Bekkers et al, 2011). These civic efforts include online participation of political opinion expressions and protesting; volunteering and lobbying on social issues. Based on Ehrlich's (2000, Preface, p. vi) definition of civic engagement as a 'means working either through political or non-political processes to make a difference in a community...', the aforementioned civic efforts constitute as online civic engagement behaviour. We argue that social capital as a theory can be coupled with the diffusion of social media for addressing social problems.

From the psychology perspective, scholars have found that voluntary online participation behaviour for content sharing are contingent upon an individual's motivation and social capital factors. For example, some studies found that individuals voluntarily contribute their knowledge on electronic networks when they perceive that it augments their reputations (Tang et al., 2012; Farzan et al., 2008) and when they are structurally embedded in the network (Wasko and Faraj, 2005). Similarly, Polletta and Jasper (2001:290) argue that being an activist becomes a 'prized social identity', which supplies the 'incentive to participate'. Such findings provide support for the notion by Dinas and Gementis (2013) that intangible benefits often involve psychological gains stemming from civic efforts.

In Japan, the relational factor, trust, reduces the uncertainty entailed in their decisions to engage in civic efforts, particularly to donate money for various causes (Taniguchi and Marshall, 2012). In organisational studies, commonly shared goals is said to serve as a 'bonding mechanism' that integrates resources (Tsai and Ghoshal, 1988, p. 467). This was evident in Chiu, Hsu and Wang's (2006) study on knowledge sharing in a virtual community, where shared languages and visions increased the online content sharing behaviour. Other scholars suggested that social media can encourage identity construction for individuals and groups , which according to Dalton, Sickle, and Weldon (2009) are key antecedents of political behavior, by allowing multiple networks of social interaction for feedback, acceptance, and reinforcement of norms (Papacharissi 2010).

While some celebrate the importance and potential of social media in per-petuating online civic engagement, others argue that civic efforts should not be Facebooked or tweeted (Gladwell, 2010). As such, endorsing the ability of social media to produce pro-social behaviour can be quite a daunting task. Conversely, a number of scholars have indicated that social media use sup-plements social capital which are related to traditional forms of civic engage-ment such as engendering community activity (e.g. Lovejoy and Saxton, 2012). Thus, the fundamental question is whether the social capital developed on social media is resilient enough to stimulate members to contribute their valu-able resources such as time, money, effort and knowledge in addressing social issues, especially when no extrinsic reward is provided. Following the social capital theory proposed by Nahapiet and Ghoshal (1988), a theoretical model is developed to address the research question, see Figure 1.

## 2.2. Hypotheses

### 2.2.1. Social Interaction Ties

The first dimension of social capital is the structural dimension, i.e. social interaction ties. This study adopts Chiu, Hsu and Wang's (2006) understand-ing of social interaction ties which represents the strength of the relationships, the amount of time spent, and the communication frequency among online members. The social interaction ties on social media allow a cost-effective way of accessing a wider range of sources (e.g. Kaplan and Haenlein, 2010). Pre-vious studies have suggested that higher social interactions strengthens and maintains social ties with a larger, more diverse group, thus extending poten-tial resource exchanges (e.g. Young, 2011; Chiu, Hsu and Wang, 2006). This finding echoes the argument made by Nahapiet and Ghoshal (1988, p. 252)

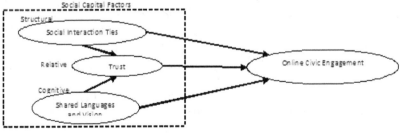

Figure 1    Theoretical model

that 'network ties influence both access to parties for combining and exchanging knowledge and anticipation of value through such exchange'. In a similar vein, a considerable number of civic engagement studies in social media have implied the importance of social interaction ties in civic participation (e.g. Valenzuela, 2013; Gibson and McAllister, 2012). Following this notion, we posit the following hypothesis:

H1: Facebook members' social interaction ties are positively associated with their level of online civic engagement behaviour.

### 2.2.2. Trust

The second dimension of social capital is the relational dimension, i.e. trust. Fukuyama, (1995:26) defines trust as 'the expectation that arises within a community of regular, honest and cooperative behaviour, based on commonly shared norms, on the part of members of that community'. There is a body of literature which contends that trust may function as a contributory factor or a catalyst for civic participation. For example, trust is encourages problem solving effectiveness (Klimoski and Karol 1976) and for civic involvement (Taniguchi and Marshall, 2012). Trust is also an influential factor in predicting e-commerce (Pavlou and Gefan 2004; Lee and Turban 2001). In this domain, users take a direct, measurable risk (of losing money), which makes trust an important construct. This risk may be less salient in other domains, such as online civic engagement on social media because no actual transaction takes place. Instead, the purpose of engagement is much dependent on the issue at hand, which is the social cause advocated and the information exchanged. As civic involvement often requires a range of different resources, especially from with people we do not know personally, such civic efforts may be instigated by trust (e.g. Graddy and Wang, 2009). Hence, we argue that trust is a salient construct in motivating online civic engagement behaviour. Following the notion that trust has the ability to reduce uncertainty and influence online participatory behaviour and that trust matters in predicting informal than formal civic work, this study proposes the following hypotheses:

H2: Trust is positively associated with the level of online civic engagement behaviour.

In another perspective, Carey, Lawson and Krause (2011:279) suggested that 'social interaction ties act as conduits for information and resource flows providing the time, opportunity and motivation to strengthen the relational aspects of the relationship. The findings from Tsai and Ghoshal (1998) resonates the statement as they found that social interaction ties had a strong effect on trust in the context of production innovation within an organisation. In addition, social capital researchers (e.g. Xu, Perkins and Chow, 2010; Kim, 2007) have indicated that trust and social ties in networks can create the context for collective problem resolution. Thus, we propose that the strength of social interaction ties among individuals is likely to increase the level of relational capital present in the context of Facebook usage for civic engagement.

H3: Facebook members' social interaction ties are positively associated with trust.

### 2.2.3. Shared Languages and Vision

The third dimension of social capital is the cognitive dimension, i.e. shared languages and vision. According to Lesser (in Chiu, Hsu and Wang, 2006:1878), 'Shared language goes beyond the language itself; it also addresses the acronyms, subtleties, and underlying assumptions that are the staples of day-to-day interactions'. When members of a group have a common perception about how to interact with one another, possible misunderstandings in their communication could be avoided (Tsai and Ghoshal, 1998). Similarly, shared vision is said to embody to be 'a bonding mechanism that helps different parts of an organisation to integrate or to combine resources' (Tsai and Ghoshal 1998: 467), thus allowing them to be more willing to contribute resources. Some scholars assert that shared values bind the members of social networks and communities, make cooperative action as much as possible (Robert, Dennis and Ahuja, 2008). On the contrary, there is a possibility that shared language could have no impact on sharing behaviour as shown by the findings of Chiu, Hsu and Wang (2006). Drawing on the earlier camp on the positive impact of having shared languages and vision on content contribution, this study holds that shared languages and vision influences people's trust and their online participatory behaviour to gain the necessary access to resources needed to achieve a common goal. Accordingly, hypotheses 4 and 5 are as follows:

H4: Facebook members' shared languages and vision are positively associated with trust.

H5: Facebook members' shared languages and vision are positively associated with their level of online civic engagement behaviour.

# 3. Research Methodology

## 3.1. Sample and Data Collection

According to a survey by GlobalWebIndex (2014), Facebook is currently the world's most popular social network. With the over 1 billion users (Facebook, 2013) base and the growing presence of activism, Facebook is a potential avenue for citizens to be involved in civic engagement. A random sample of 1,500 active Facebook users aged 15 to 40 residing in geographical areas with high social media penetration were selected. The data was collected on a face-to-face basis between June 1 and October 8, 2013. We received 1,257 responses, resulting in an 83.8 per cent response rate. 29 surveys were rejected as incomplete. Of the 1,228 completed and usable surveys, 61 per cent were female. The majority of the respondents were single (67 per cent). Most of the respondents were from the age category of 20 to 29, this result is similar to the age group findings from the Pew Internet Project's (Brenner 2013) research related to social networking.

## 3.2. Instrument development

To ensure content validity, we adapted existing scales wherever possible from the existing literature. The items were scaled on a five-point Likert scale, ranging from one (strongly disagree) to five (strongly agree). We adopted the items for the social capital factors, i.e. social interaction ties, trust and shared languages and visions from Chiu, Hsu and Wang (2006). The measurement scales for the online civic engagement behaviour construct, i.e. civic publication and civic action modes, were adapted from prior literature (Denning 2000; Gil de Zúñiga, Jung and Valenzuela, 2012; Valenzuela, Arriagada and Scherman, 2012) and validated in a series of procedures to ensure content validity, construct validity, and reliability (Straub 1989). Next, the questionnaire was pilot tested with 20 doctorial students to evaluate the phrasing and clarity of the indicators and adequacy of the domain coverage. All of the online civic engagement behaviour items were on a five-point scale: Never (1), rarely, (2), sometimes, (3), often (4), and always (5). After the pilot test, the instructions for the questionnaire were further refined prior to administration of the survey.

## 3.3. Statistical Analysis

For a more robust approach, the validity, reliability and hypotheses were assessed using two methods. Structural equation modelling (SEM) using

AMOS and linear regressions via SPSS were applied to test the five hypotheses. SEM was employed following the recommended two-stage analytical procedures by Anderson and Gerbing (1988). The first step involves the analysis of the measurement model, while the second step tests the structural relationships among latent constructs. Furthermore, two sets of linear regressions, one for trust and another for online civic engagement behaviour as the dependent variable were tested.

# 4. Research results

## 4.1. Measurement Model Analysis

### 4.1.1. Exploratory Factor Analysis

We conducted various tests to assess the construct validity and reliability of the instrument using two sequential methods: examining the exploratory factor analysis (EFA) and confirmatory factor analysis (CFA). Principle components factor analysis using varimax rotation was conducted which resulted in five factors. These explained 69.17 per cent of the variance, and all the items loaded highly on their related factors. This affirms the unidimensionality of the constructs. All item loadings were above 0.50 on their own construct (Hair et al. 2006). The reliability of the constructs measured by Cronbach's alpha, varied from 0.79 to 0.89. These values suggest that the instrument has adequate reliability (Nunnally 1978). See Table 1.

### 4.1.2. Confirmatory Factor Analysis

We conducted CFA using Analysis of Moment Structures (AMOS). The purpose of conducting CFA was to (1) validate the psychometric properties, (2) examine whether the measurement model achieved an acceptable goodness-of-fit, and (3) investigate its convergent and discriminant validity, and reliability. The ratio fit of the measurement model was 3.595, well-below the cut-off point of 5.0 (Wheaton et al, 1977). The root mean squared error of approximation (RMSEA) was 0.048, which was below the 0.08 cut-off level (Hair et al. 2006). In addition, the normed fit index (NFI=0.955), the Tucker Lewis index (TFI=0.960) and confirmatory fit index (CFI=0.967) were greater than the required value of 0.90. Finally, the goodness-of-fit (GFI=0.952) and adjusted GFI (AGFI=0.936) were greater than the threshold value of 0.90 (Hair et al, 2006). Thus, it can be concluded that the measurement model fitted the data well.

For convergent validity: (1) all indicator factor loadings should be significant and exceed 0.50 (Hair et al, 2006). Fornell and Larcker (1981) suggested two other criteria to assess convergent validity – the composite reliabilities should exceed 0.70, and the average variance extracted (AVE) for each construct should exceed the variance due to the measurement error for that construct, resulting in extractions exceeding 50 per cent of variance. As shown in Table 2, AVE values were well above the cut-off value of 0.50. The composite reliabilities (CR) were all well above 0.70 while all factor loadings in the CFA model exceeded 0.50 and were significant at p=0.001. Therefore, it is evident that the model met all three conditions for convergent validity.

We then tested the discriminant validity by comparing the square root of each factor's AVE with its correlation coefficients with other factors (Fornell and Larcker, 1981). From Table 2, we can see that all square roots of AVEs were larger than their corresponding correlation coefficients with other factors. Thus, our data reveal good discriminant validity. Based on these results, the measurement properties of the model are acceptable.

## 4.2. Hypotheses Testing

The structural model analysis result is depicted in Figure 2. Among the three facets of social capital, social interaction ties was found to have the highest coefficient path and had a positive and significant relationship with online civic engagement behaviour (H1: $\beta$ =0.31, p <0.001).Thus, supporting hypotheses H1. Similarly, this structural factor had a positive and significant impact on trust (H3: $\beta$ =0.09, p <0.05). The results also indicated that the structural

Table 2    Correlation matrix and square roots of AVEs (in bold).

|  | Trust | Social interaction ties | Shared languages and vision | Online civic engagement behaviour |
|---|---|---|---|---|
| Trust | **0.737** | | | |
| Social interaction ties | 0.484 | **0.785** | | |
| Shared languages and vision | 0.732 | 0.594 | **0.749** | |
| Online civic engagement behaviour | 0.570 | 0.537 | 0.552 | **0.763** |

and cognitive factors had significant roles in influencing the relational factor. Social interaction ties and shared languages and vision explained a fairly high amount of variance on trust ($R^2$=0.52). For hypotheses 2, trust has proved to be a greater significant predictor than shared languages and vision on for online civic engagement behaviour (H2: β =0.29, p <0.001; H5 β =0.16, p <0.01). The statistical results also indicated that shared languages and vision influences trust in a positive and significant manner (H4: β =0.67, p<0.001). Similarly, this cognitive capital significantly predicts online civic engagement behaviour (H5: β =0.16, p<0.1). The three social capital factors together explained 42 per cent of variance on online civic engagement behaviour. Overall, the model demonstrates a good fit with all fit indices within the recommended ranges. The ratio fit was 3.339, well-below the cut-off point of 5.0 (Wheaton et al, 1977). RMSEA=0.042, NFI=0.959, TLI=0.964, CFI=0.971, GFI=0.957 while the AGFI=0.941 were greater than the threshold of 0.90 (Hair et al 2006), thus indicating that the model fits the data well. See Table 3. Similarly, the findings

Table 3    **Model Fit**

| Fit indices | Recommended Value | Research Model |
|---|---|---|
| $\chi^2$/df | ≤ 5.00 | 3.339 |
| GFI | ≥0.90 | 0.957 |
| AGFI | ≥0.90 | 0.941 |
| CFI | ≥0.90 | 0.971 |
| TLI | ≥0.90 | 0.964 |
| NFI | ≥0.90 | 0.959 |
| RMSEA | ≤0.08 | 0.046 |

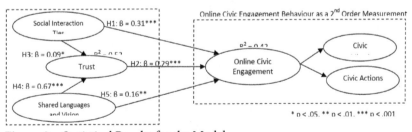

Figure 2    Statistical Results for the Model

from the multiple regression analysis resonates the significant findings from the structural model analysis. The three facets of social capital significantly positively predict online civic engagement behaviour. Both the structural and cognitive factors also influence the trust in a positive and significant manner, echoing the results from SEM.

# 5. Discussion

The overarching purpose of the research was to investigate online civic engagement behaviour from the perspective of the social capital theory. We analysed the individual impact of each dimension of social capital on civic engagement behaviour on Facebook. We looked at the effects of the structural and cognitive dimensions on trust. The empirical analysis supported the hypotheses posed and the model developed. We present the following three implicative findings:

**Finding 1.** *Social interaction ties, trust and shared languages and vision motivate online civic engagement behaviour.*

The results of this study suggest that the facets of social capital can contribute to online civic engagement behaviour. Social interaction ties factor was found to be the strongest predictor, thus indicating the importance of interactions in civic communication. This finding provides empirical support to Nahapiet and Ghoshal's (1998) argument that "the fundamental proposition of the Social Capital Theory is that network ties provide access to resources" (p. 252). The network ties on Facebook provide the opportunity for its members to combine and exchange resources, in particular to inform, clarify on issues and to comprehend the views of others in addressing social problems. In support of previous research (Xu, Perkins and Chow, 2010; Kim, 2007), trust was found to significantly influence both types of online civic engagement behaviour. The results suggests that under the perception of people being trustworthy and honest, people are more willing to use Facebook as a 'civic tool' to express concerns on social problems through links, postings, signing of petitions and coordinating events online. It also suggests that the belief that people can be relied upon and not take advantage of others will allow positive perceptions to manifest in the users' minds as a willingness to accept Facebook as a channel for civic activities. The results further revealed that commonality in communication pattern and language fosters online civic engagement behaviour. Facebook users who advocate on the same social cause

Table 1    Results of measurement model analysis

| Construct | Items | Loadings | Cronbach α | CR | AVE |
|---|---|---|---|---|---|
| Social interaction ties | I maintain close social relationships with some Facebook users. | 0.73 | 0.79 | 0.83 | 0.62 |
| | I know some Facebook users on a personal level. | 0.70 | | | |
| | I have frequent communication with some Facebook users. | 0.91 | | | |
| Trust | Facebook users will not take advantage of others even when the opportunity arises. | 0.64 | 0.86 | 0.85 | 0.54 |
| | Facebook users will always keep the promises they make to one another. | 0.79 | | | |
| | Facebook users would not knowingly do anything to disrupt the conversation. | 0.64 | | | |
| | Facebook users behave in a consistent manner. | 0.78 | | | |
| | Facebook users are truthful in dealing with one another. | 0.82 | | | |
| Shared languages and vision | Facebook users use understandable communication pattern during the discussion. | 0.73 | 0.85 | 0.84 | 0.56 |
| | Facebook users use understandable narrative forms to post messages or articles. | 0.72 | | | |
| | Facebook users share the vision of helping others solve their professional problems. | 0.81 | | | |

*Continued*

Table 1    (*Continued*)

| Construct | Items | Loadings | Cronbach α | CR | AVE |
|---|---|---|---|---|---|
| | Facebook users share the same value that helping others is pleasant. | 0.74 | | | |
| Online civic engagement behaviour: | | | 0.89 | 0.74 | 0.58 |
| *Civic publication* | Post links on social issues on Facebook. | 0.79 | | | |
| | Post photos/videos/images of issues on Facebook. | 0.86 | | | |
| | Post news on social issues on Facebook. | 0.86 | | | |
| *Civic actions* | Plan activities that address social issues on Facebook. | 0.67 | | | |
| | Send invites on social issues related event using Facebook. | 0.67 | | | |
| | Get assistance with others on social issue events on Facebook. | 0.79 | | | |
| | Sign up as a volunteer using Facebook. | 0.80 | | | |
| | Sign a petition using Facebook. | 0.72 | | | |
| | Submit a complaint to an official using Facebook. | 0.70 | | | |

would interact using the same method or tool, such as postings of messages, links and pictures on the issue on Facebook. The results resonates the findings by Xiang, Lu and Gupta (2012) that the cognitive capital has a positive influence on cohesive mannerism.

**Finding 2:** *Facebook can fulfil a variety of civic communicatory needs for problem solving.*

The results suggest that online civic engagement behaviour includes two modes, i.e. civic publication and actions. These activities include mobilizing civic behaviour such as signing of petitions, making official complaints to authorities, coordinating civic events and fostering civic awareness through postings on social problems. On this note, the present study supports previous findings (Valenzuela, 2013; de Zuniga et al, 2012) on social media usage for protest behaviour. Consequently, the findings underscore that Facebook is able provide the communicatory needs for problem solving. Thus, the argument here moves away from any suspicion that Facebook is merely a convivial tool. Also, the findings suggest that Facebook facilitates as a civic communication channel rather than pinpointing it as a cause of political action (e.g. Valenzuela 2013).

**Finding 3.** *Social capital factors are interrelated in predicting online civic engagement behaviour.*

The factors of social capital are themselves interrelated in the sense that the cognitive and structural capital engenders trust. The interconnections of these dimensions although slightly varied in previous studies were consistent with past findings by Tsai and Ghoshal (1998), and more recently by Xiang, Lu and Gupta (2012) on their study on social capital and shared mental models.

## 5.1. Theoretical Contributions and Practical Implications

This paper makes four key contributions. First, it extends the knowledge on social media usage to include online civic engagement behaviour modes for addressing social issues. The study emphasizes that social ties, trust and commonly shared language with a similar goal in mind can stimulate two types of civic modes, i.e. civic publication and actions. Second, to the best of our knowledge, this is the first study that applies Nahapiet and Ghoshal's (1998) manifestations of the three factors of social capital and applies them to the study of online civic engagement behaviour for addressing social problems on Facebook. The study reflects the important facets of social capital in studying online civic engagement behaviour in an informal social media environment such as Facebook. By considering the influence of the three factors of social capital on online civic engagement behaviour, we could avoid the bias of singling out any of the factors to be insignificant in a similar context. Moreover, the results of the statistical tests from the study adds knowledge to the trust literature by ascertaining that social ties and shared languages and vision among Facebook users can enhance the confidence levels among members. Third, we contributed to the methodology in understanding social media via the development of an instrument which measures online civic engagement behaviour in addressing social issues from a social capital perspective. Fourth, while previous research has predominately focused on the political aspect of civic engagement, the study examines the influence of social capital on civic contributions particularly in addressing problems using social media. In sum, by explicating the unique role of social capital on social media, this paper contributes to the continued development and success of social media usage for pro-social behaviour.

The results of this study also carry implications for practitioners. Social activists, the government and policy makers could use Facebook to mobilize their social causes and in an attempt to increase civic involvement among citizens, particularly the youth. In this sense, addressing social problems through social media may indeed contribute to a proliferation of a networked society and a more participatory one as suggested by de Zúñiga (2012). Corporations could also facilitate the use of social networking sites as an informal way to reinforce their corporate social responsibilities to their staff.

# 6. Conclusion and future research

This paper presented answers to the hypotheses developed and met its objectives in delivering new insights concerning how Facebook is shaping the landscape of civic engagement using the social capital theory. Civic efforts on Facebook are positively influenced by social interaction ties, trust and shared languages and vision among its users. This social media has enabled different forms of civic engagement, i.e. citizens are posting links on social issues; pictures, news and images of social issues on Facebook pages to generate awareness of these issues; members are utilizing the features of Facebook to plan events such as campaigns, connect with others through invites and sign online petitions. Social interaction ties trust and shared languages and vision are significant determinants in predicting online civic engagement behaviour on Facebook in two ways, i.e. through civic publication and civic actions. Moreover, Facebook appears to be an enabler for civic behaviour, thus, indicating that the new media can foster civic behaviour among citizens.

Despite the new insights brought by this study as discussed, the analysis has several limitations. First, by employing survey data, it is constrained to a self-report of social media use for civic engagement, which may yield inaccurate measures resulting from social desirability bias. Second, because this study is cross-sectional in nature, hence causal inferences cannot be made. As such, a longitudinal study on the phenomena of online civic engagement behaviour is recommended for future research. Third, we analysed a single social media platform, thus, the results cannot be generalized to all social media platforms. Future research could include comparison studies on different social media platforms in fostering civic behaviour, examining the actual efficacy of online civic behaviours and applying various methods to uncover the modes of civic behaviour.

Limitations notwithstanding, this study provides an initial foundation for research on the role of social capital in fostering online civic engagement behaviour in addressing social problems. The results of this study demonstrate the capability of Facebook to afford citizens of different perspectives the ability to coalesce and engage in addressing social issues through online expressions, discussions and actions. Furthermore, the results show that citizens are seeking beyond recreational use of Facebook and are harnessing the capabilities of Facebook to engage in issues they care about. There is a little doubt of the underlying possibilities that social media such as Facebook offers in fostering online civic engagement behaviour.

# References

Anderson, J. C., and Gerbing, D. W. (1988) "Structural Equation Modeling in Practice: A Review and Recommended Two-Step Approach," *Psychological Bulletin*, Vol 103 No3, pp 411-423

Bekkers, V., H. Beunders, et al. (2011). "New Media, Micromobilization, and Political Agenda Setting: Crossover Effects in Political Mobilization and Media Usage", *The Information Society*, Vol 27 No 4, pp 209-219.

Bennett, W. L. (2008) *Changing Citizenship in the Digital Age*. In W. L. Bennett (Ed.), *Civic Life Online: Learning How Digital Media Can Engage Youth*. Cambridge, Massachusetts: MIT Press, pp 1–24.

Brennan, R. and R. Croft (2012) "The Use Of Social Media in B2B Marketing and Branding: An Exploratory Study", *Journal of Customer Behaviour* , Vol 11, No .2, pp 101-115.

Brenner J. (2013) Pew Internet: Social Networking, [online],http://pewinternet.org/Commentary/2012/March/Pew-Internet-Social-Networking-full-detail.aspx.

Carey S, Lawson B. and Krause D.R. (2011) Social Capital Configuration, Legal Bonds and Performance in Buyer–Supplier Relationships, *Journal of Operations Management*, Vol 29, pp 277-288.

Chiu, C-M., Hsu M-H., and Wang T.G. (2006) "Understanding Knowledge Sharing In Virtual Communities: An Integration of Social Capital and Social Cognitive Theories", *Decision Support Systems*, Vol 42, No 3, pp 1872-1888.

Correa, T., A. W. Hinsley, de Zúñiga (2010) "Who interacts on the Web?: The Intersection Of Users' Personality and Social Media Use", *Computers in Human Behavior*, Vol 26, No 2, pp 247-253.

Dalton, R. J., Sickle, A. V., & Weldon, S. (2009) "The Individual-Institutional Nexus of Protest Behaviour", British Journal of Political Science, 40, 51-73. doi:10.1017/S000712340999038X

de Zuniga, H. G. (2012) "Social Media Use for News and Individuals' Social Capital, Civic Engagement and Political Participation", *Journal of Computer-Mediated Communication* , Vol 17, No 3, pp 319-336.

Dinas, E., and Gemenis, K. (2013) "Revisiting the Role of Process Incentives as a Determinant of University Students' Protest," European Political Science Review Vol 5, No 2, pp 225-253.

Ehrlich T. (2000) *Higher Education and Civic Responsibility*. Phoenix, AZ: Oryx Press.

Facebook. (2013) Key Facts, [online],http://newsroom.fb.com/Key-Facts.

Farzan, R., Dimicco, J., M., Dugan, C., Geyer, W., and Brownholtz, B. (2008) "Results from Deploying a Participation Incentive Mechanism within the Enterprise.," Proceedingsof the SIGCHI conference on human factors in computer systems (CHI'2008), Florence: ACM Press.

Fornell C. and Larcker D.F. (1981) Structural Equation Models With Unobservable Variables And Measurement Error: Algebra And Statistics. *Journal of Marketing Research* pp 39-50.

Fukuyama, F. (1995) Trust: The Social Virtues and the Creation of Prosperity, New York: Free Press.

Gibson, R. K. and I. McAllister (2012)"Online Social Ties and Political Engagement", *Journal of Information Technology & Politics*, Vol 10, No 1, pp 21-34.

Gil de Zúñiga, Jung and Valenzuela S. (2012) "Social Media Use for News and Individuals' Social Capital, Civic Engagement and Political Participation", *Journal of Computer-Mediated Communication*, Vol 17, pp 319-336.

Gladwell, M. (2010). "Small Change - Why the Revolution Will Not Be Tweet", [online],http://www.newyorker.com/reporting/2010/10/04/101004fa_fact_gladwell?currentPage=all.

GlobalWebIndex. (2014)"Global Internet Users Aged 16 – 64", [online],https://www.globalwebindex.net/products/report/gwi-social-january-2014.

Graddy E and Wang L. (2009) "Community Foundation Development and Social Capital", *Nonprofit and Voluntary Sector Quarterly* Vol 38, pp 392-412.

Hair Jr. JF, Black WC, Babin BJ, et al. (2006 ) Multivariate Data Analysis, NJ,USA. Prentice-Hall, Upper Saddle River.

Kaplan, A. M. and M. Haenlein (2010) "Users of the World, Unite! The Challenges and Opportunities of Social Media", *Business horizons*, Vol 53, No 1, pp 59-68.

Kim S-H. (2007) "Media Use, Social Capital, and Civic Participation in South Korea", *Journalism & Mass Communication Quarterly*, Vol 84, pp 477-494.

Klimoski R.J. and Karol B.L. (1976) "The Impact of Trust on Creative Problem Solving Groups", *Journal of Applied Psychology*, Vol 61, No.5, p. 630.

Kwak N, Shah D.V. and Holbert R.L. (2004)" Connecting, Trusting, and Participating: The Direct and Interactive Effects of Social Associations", *Political Research Quarterly*, Vol 57, pp 643-652.

Loader, B. D. (2007) *Young Citizens in the Digital Age: Political Engagement, Young People and New Media*, Routledge.

Lovejoy, K. and G. D. Saxton (2012). "Information, Community, and Action: How Nonprofit Organizations Use Social Media", *Journal of Computer-Mediated Communication*, Vol 17, No. 3, pp 337-353.

Macnamara J., Sakinofsky P. and Beattie J. (2012) "E-electoral Engagement: How Governments Use Social Media to Engage Voters", *Australian Journal of Political Science*, Vol 47, pp 623-639.

Manago, A. M., Taylor T., Greenfield P.M. (2012) "Me and My 400 Friends: The Anatomy of College Students' Facebook Networks, Their Communication Patterns, and Well-Being", *Developmental Psychology*, Vol 48, No. 2, pp 369-380.

Nahapiet, J. and S. Ghoshal (1998) "Social capital, Intellectual Capital, and the Organizational Advantage" *Academy of Management Review*, Vol 23, No. 2, pp 242-266.

Nunnally J. (1978) *Psychometric Methods*. McGraw-Hill, New York, NY.

Papacharissi, Z. (Ed.). (2010). A networked self: Identity, community, and culture on social network sites. New York, NY: Routledge.

Pearce, K. E. and S. Kendzior (2012). "Networked Authoritarianism and Social Media in Azerbaijan", *Journal of Communication*, Vol 62, No.2, pp 283-298.

Polletta, F., and Jasper, J. M. (2001) "Collective Identity and Social Movements," Annual review of Sociology), pp. 283-305.

Putnam, R. D. (2000) *Bowling Alone: The Collapse and Revival of American Society*, New York: Simon & Schuster.

Robert, L. P., A. R. Dennis and Ahuja M.K. (2008) "Social capital and Knowledge integration in Digitally Enabled Teams", *Information Systems Research*, Vol 19, No. 3, pp 314-334.

Steenkamp, M. and N. Hyde-Clarke (2014) "The use of Facebook for Political Commentary in South Africa", *Telematics and Informatics*, Vol 31, No. 1, pp 91-97.

Straub D.W. (1989) "Validating Instruments in MIS Research", *MIS Quarterly*, Vol 13, No. 2, pp 147-169.

Tang, Q., Gu, B., and Whinston, A. (2012) "Content Contribution for Revenue Sharing and Reputation in Social Media: A Dynamic Structural Model," Journal of Management Information Systems, Vol 29 No 2, pp 41-76.

Valenzuela S., Arriagada A. and Scherman A. (2012) "The Social Media Basis of Youth Protest Behavior: The Case of Chile", Journal of Communication, Vol 62, pp 299-314.

Valenzuela, S. (2013) "Unpacking the Use of Social Media for Protest Behavior: The Roles of Information, Opinion Expression, and Activism", American Behavioral Scientist, Vol 57, No. 7, pp 920-942.

van den Hooff, B. and M. Huysman (2009) "Managing Knowledge Sharing: Emergent and Engineering Approaches", Information & Management, Vol 46, No. 1, pp 1-8.

Warren, A. M., Sulaiman, A. and Jaafar, N. I. (2014), "Facebook: The Enabler of Online Civic Engagement for Activists", Computers in Human Behavior, Vol 32, pp 284-289.

Wasko, M. M., and Faraj, S. 2005. "Why Should I Share? Examining Social Capital and Knowledge Contribution in Electronic Networks of Practice," MIS quarterly, Vol 29 No 1, pp 35-57.

Wheaton B, Muthen B, Alwin DF, et al. (1977) "Assessing Reliability and Stability in Panel Models", Sociological Methodology Vol 8, pp 84-136.

Xiang C, Lu Y and Gupta S. (2012) "Knowledge Sharing In Information System Development Teams: Examining The Impact Of Shared Mental Model From A Social Capital Theory Perspective", Behaviour & Information Technology, Vol 32, pp 1024-1040.

Xu Q., Perkins D.D. and Chow JC-C. (2010) "Sense Of Community, Neighboring, and Social Capital as Predictors of Local Political Participation in China", American Journal of Community Psychology , Vol 45, pp 259-271.

Young, K. (2011) "Social ties, social networks and the Facebook experience", International Journal of Emerging Technologies and Society", Vol 9, No. 1, pp 20-34.

# Cyberseniors and Quality of Life: A Focus on Social Networking

**Leticia Rocha Machado, Anelise Jantsch, José Valdeni de Lima and Patricia Alejandra Behar**
Graduate Program in Computer Education (PPGIE) at Federal University of
Rio Grande do Sul (UFRGS), Av. Paulo Gama, Porto Alegre, Brazil

leticiarmachado@yahoo.com.br, anelise.jantsch@gmail.com,
valdeni@inf.ufrgs.br, pbehar@terra.com.br
Originally published in The Proceedings of ECEL 2014

## Editorial commentary

As a greater proportion of the world population lives longer, many societies are needing to consider the quality of life of their senior citizens. In this exciting longitudinal study from Brazil Machado et al chart the impact of social media on the physical, social, psychological and spiritual well being of a community of elders. The observed impact of social media went far beyond the use of Facebook and Skype to keep in touch with disparate family members. Health outcomes were positively stimulated by participation in online health promoting activities. The cohort reported a greater sense of engagement and participation in the broader community, as well as the expected maintenance of family ties.

While the study drew on a limited number of participants, the implication of these pioneers of growing old supported by an online network, raise aspirations for a far greater number of future beneficiaries.

**Abstract:** In the contemporary world which emphasizes the new, the different and the snapshot, we perceive an inversion of roles with regard to stages of life and appreciation of individuals. The old age in Western societies has often been linked to inactivity and biological decline. To reinforce this thought we find the cult of youth which dominates media, advertising and the contemporary society (Brandão and Silveira, 2010). Aging is not only a question of genetics and biology, but also psychological and social issues. Aging is a natural development of life and depends on the environmental conditions and the socio-cultural characteristics of seniors' lives (Freitas, 2011). Nowadays the information and communication technologies (ICT) have contributed to dissemination of knowledge through several means, and to do so ICT use digital tools. These tools allow not only research but also may provide conditions towards knowledge to be shared and socialized. Thus, these technologies may help older people to reduce isolation and loneliness, increasing their chances of keeping in touch with family and friends, including their social relationships through the use of social networks as a tool to facilitate the active aging achievement (Páscoa, 2012). In this sense the population is increasingly concerned about the quality of life. Quality of life encompasses different factors and therefore it is considered multidimensional. So, quality of life refers about biological, educational, psychological and social aspects which include new changes in society. The use of ICTs can help seniors to enjoy and include themselves in the Knowledge Society, mostly through Digital Social Networks (DSN) where they can relate with family and friends. The Digital Social Networks (DSN) foster changes in social relationships and they are a medium that enable changes in social relations, this research aims to investigate the influence of the use of DSN by elderly who are already digitally included and utilize this type of technology. We investigated the DSN influence in the quality of life of seniors. For this purpose, a survey was conducted with twelve seniors who participated in a course of digital inclusion in Brazil, during 2009 to 2013. We used the WHOQOL-bref Questionnaire of World Health Organization to evaluate the quality of life perceived by the participants. Our findings indicate that seniors were active participants in the DSN, and use it mainly to communicate with each other and exchange information as a way to maintain existing relationships and to obtain new ones. This shows that DSN can improve the quality of life for seniors.

**Keywords:** computer mediated communication, social media, Web 2.0 tools, digital social networks, Facebook

# 1. Introduction

The number of older people grows every year (Ala-Mutka et al., 2008). The World Health Organization (WHO) reported on Geneva that life expectancy has increased an average of six years around the globe. In Brazil there was an increase of eight years (WHO, 2014). These data indicate how important is to think about the quality of life in an older population. In Brazil, as in other countries, the elderly population is increasingly occupying spaces in the society. To conform to the demographic reality, seniors are participating more actively in social life. Seniors are becoming more involved in communities, and they are creating new social networks. Today we can find the elderly at different communities (face-to-face and virtual) to improve their knowledge on subjects of interest of this group (Brandão and Silveira, 2010; Páscoa, 2012).

Among the new ways of learning are the digital technologies. Older people are using more technologies like smartphones, media players, tablets and more (Chen and Chan, 2014). Despite the larger offer on new technologies, the elderly still want to learn the use of computer. Seniors see the computer as a great tool to stimulate memory and to build or to enhance new knowledge. They recognize in the computer a variety of resources for communication and interactions with family, friends and to be up-to-date. The use of tools for information technology led to virtual and social inclusion to older people, for example, by online social networks. The changes in our digital society conducted the older people to look for a space in the virtual world.

Social networks are studied in the literature since 1930. There is a wide range of theorists working on the subject. A social network is formed in different cultures and societies and generally consists of communities such as family, school, jobs etc. (Sawver, 2011). From the rise of internet in the 90s the scope of social networks has increased due to the use of communication technologies. With the improvement of internet (web 2.0) significant changes in the ways of communication and interaction occurred. By these transformations it was possible to provide tools to create virtual communities like Orkut, Facebook etc. (Varela and Ogawa, 2014). This paper aims to discuss the relationship between the use of social networks and the quality of life in a group of seniors in Brazil. The study was conducted at the Federal University of Rio Grande do Sul (UFRGS) where, since 2009, our university offered workshops of digital inclusion for older people. This paper is organized as the following: section 2 presents the concept Quality of Life and the importance of social networks to seniors; in Section 3 we present the methodology adopted in this research, and a discussion about data collected is done in section 4. Finally, section 5 presents some concluding remarks about our work and implications for education and gerontology.

# 2. Quality of life of elderly and digital social networks

The World Health Organization (WHO) defines quality of life as "the individuals' perception of their position in life in the context of the culture and value systems in which they live and in relation to their goals, expectations, standards and concerns" (WHOQOL, 1995) in accordance with three key principles: functional ability, socioeconomic status and life satisfaction (Silva et al.,

2012). Quality of life and satisfaction in old age have been related to dependency/autonomy, taking into account aging consequences. There are people who present a decline in their health status and cognition skills when aging. Others live in a healthy way until they reach advanced age (Joia et al., 2007). According to Silva et al. (2012), quality of life in old age can be understood as health maintenance in all aspects of human life: physical, social, psychological and spiritual. Understanding what the elderly think about quality of life is important for health professionals, educators, families, government, and society in order to assist them in adopting healthy practices and behaviors facing the aging process.

Research on social networking and its significance to seniors' lives has been occurring for many years. Companionship groups often act like a second family, where seniors look for occupying their free time and establishing emotional bonds. These groups serve as listening spaces and increase elderly participation in dialogues, leading them to experience feelings of being valued, avoiding the sense of isolation, reducing depression and improving self-image (Oliveira and Queiroz, 2012; Araújo et al., 2005). The nature of a social network to seniors has a strong impact on their quality of life, for those who have a large number of different types of relationships live longer, and mortality rates are highest among those with few social connections. Strong social bonds also tend to relieve depression, increase life satisfaction and stimulate interest in daily activities (Sundar et al., 2011). Technology contributes to interaction between people, especially in the case of seniors who often have limited mobility due to health problems or issues of safety in the cities. This interaction was only made possible via Internet technologies enabling synchronous or asynchronous interactions with family and friends. This way the seniors do not only receive news of their relatives, but also see and hear them, making them feel part of these people lives, despite being apart. Digital social networks (DSN) are described as online spaces where individuals introduce themselves and establish and maintain connection with others. Thus, DSN can be an alternative to provide to the elderly a greater social interaction.

Nowadays DSN are the fourth most popular activity even more than e-mail and have almost 10% of the time spent on the Internet (Lewis, 2011). With great representativeness, Facebook comes as one of the most used social networks around the world, as a meeting place for sharing, interaction, and discussion of ideas and issues of common interest. It is an informal environment where any individual including senior citizens can communicate, share and interact with the purpose of enhancing their social activity. This digital tool can be a facilitator for the active aging process. For seniors, this tool has the potential to reduce their isolation and increase interactivity with others (Páscoa, 2012). To have a better understanding about DSN and the quality of life for seniors, we present in next section the study we conducted using the WHOQOL-bref questionnaire about quality of life in a group of 12 seniors in 2013, and how they perceived the use of DSN to an improvement in their social interaction.

## 3. Methodology

Social networks have always been part of human interactions. With developments in technology these interactions have been established in other ways including the virtual environment. Seniors are considered today one of the active users of the Internet, mainly in digital social networks. For this research we used qualitative and quantitative methods focusing on the use of digital social networks by seniors and its influence in their quality of life. The twelve (12) seniors surveyed were 60 years or older and attended a course designed for digital inclusion at the Federal University of Rio Grande do Sul, Brazil, between 2009 and 2012. The course aimed to empower seniors to use different digital technologies. The continuation of the course of digital inclusion for seniors, in 2013, had as its main subject the issue quality of life during the aging process, and the goal was to work with health education. For this purpose, we used digital media for interaction including Facebook. According to Kececi and Bulduk (2012, p.160): "the main objective of health education is to provide individuals and society with assistance so that they can lead a healthy life through their own efforts and actions. Therefore, health education supports and develops all kinds of individual learning processes. Similarly, it makes changes in the beliefs and value systems of individuals, their attitudes and skill levels; in other words, it changes their lifestyles".

Throughout the course we provided materials such as videos and texts that focused on a healthy lifestyle according to the policy of active ageing (WHO, 2002), the behavioral determinants: healthy eating, physical activity, preventive behavior and social interaction. The digital social network was one of the resources used by the participants to discuss and share other materials, as well as their own experiences. In this network (Facebook), we created a closed group where only the members of our course could post and view publications. This closed group also promoted a greater interaction among participants and thus helped to strengthen emotional and social bonds. Data collection involved the use of two instruments: (1) WHOQOL-bref (WHOQOL, 1995) questionnaire focusing on quality of life in different domains and (2) social network evaluation focusing on the technology. The instruments were applied at the end of each course in 2012 and 2013. In addition, observations of interactions among participants in DSN were collected in the process.

The WHOQOL-bref questionnaire included two general questions related to quality of life and 24 questions of the original instrument. Data from the WHOQOL-bref were pilot-tested with 20 centers in 18 different countries. WHOQOL-bref consisted of four domains: physical, psychological, social relationships and environment. For the purpose of this paper, specific topics of the domain were used as "Environment" and "Social Relations" in order to relate to the use of digital social networks. In addition to the WHOQOL-bref, our study also included a questionnaire using multiple choice and essay questions focusing specifically on the use of DSN. Both instruments are complementary in analyzing the data and helped us enrich the understanding of the use of networks and their influence on the quality of life for seniors. The quantitative data were analyzed based on frequency distribution represented in percentages, average and standard deviation, and were presented in form of graphs. Qualitative data were based according to Bardin (2009) with respect to content analysis. In the next section we present the data collected for this study and their analysis.

# 4. Discussion and data analysis

Twelve seniors have participated of the research with an average of 68 years, majority with an educational level of university degree (44%), followed by secondary education (33%) and elementary education (23%). First we present data related to the use of digital social networks, followed by specific data on the quality of life ending with a joint discussion of collected information. Seniors when questioned about the use of DSN confirmed that they use it frequently (64% use social networking one or more times per week). Facebook (www.facebook.com) is the predominant DSN with 75% of use, followed by Orkut (www.orkut.com) with 11%, Tumblr (www.tumblr.com) with 11% and only 3% by Twitter (twitter.com). Facebook remains one of the most popular digital social networks considered by older audience. Data published in 2014 show that there was an increase of elderly users on Facebook. People aged 65 and over represent 45% of users in this digital social network (PEW RESEARCH, 2014). This preference is due to some factors like the resources are in the users' language; the simplicity to post content (photos, messages) and to share it; the facility to communicate easily with friends and family. As quotes one of seniors in our research that "*Facebook, because I find it less complicated to use it*". Seniors utilize DSN for communication purposes (85%), followed by leisure and work (Figure 1), and they state that the exchange of information and the possibility to meet people from the past is the great advantage of the use of digital social networks (Figure 2).

In contrast, seniors are afraid of being victims of the Internet attacks like disclosure of their personal data and privacy invasion. It is because they ignore some safety tips regarding the use of Internet. According to seniors, social networks influence people opinions (74%). Regarding to the relationships via DSN (friendship, sex), most seniors indicated that they believe that concrete relationships can occur, despite they have never gone through such experience (72%). The concrete relationships refer to those that started in the DSN and became real. In the same scenario, 14% said they do not believe that such relationship can occur and, on the other hand, 14% indicated affirmatively that they have gone through that experience (Figure 3). Data obtained about the use of DSN showed an active and participatory audience in networks, and most of seniors use it to communicate and exchange information. Relationships established on DSN reflect seniors' characteristics, because they have long-term interactions that are re-established with the support of technology. At the same time, data showed to us a public concerned about the impact of DSN in everyday life, especially about security issues like invasion of privacy and data disclosure.

Regarding to quality of life, data collected in the WHOQOL-bref (WHO-QOL, 1995) showed us a high prevalence in quality of life of seniors in different domains. To support the discussion about social networks, some aspects were highlighted in the domains "Environment" and "Social", as we will address below.

In figure 1 we can see that communication is the functionality that appeals more to the elderly. Communication plays an important role for seniors because it allows their socialization and participation with family, even with relatives of different ages. The information and communication technologies

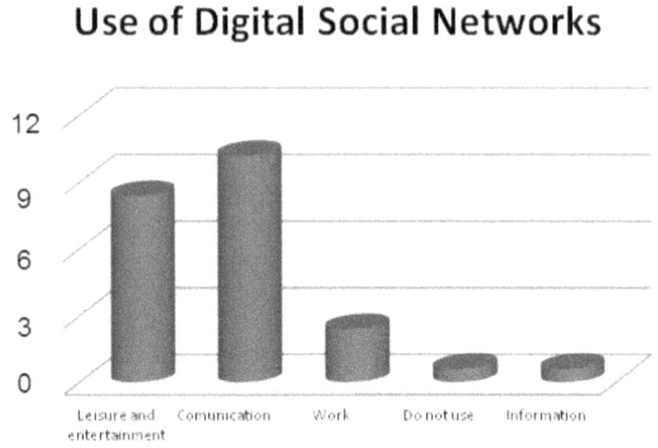

## Use of Digital Social Networks

Figure 1   Use of digital social networks by seniors

(ICT) enabled faster communication with social circles. The act of communicating can minimize the emotional and affective needs of this group (Oliveira
and Queiroz, 2012). Completing with the comment about how digital social
networks have change the life of a senior: *"Certainly, so I can see pictures of my
children who live far away, I can talk to them and send messages. Anyway, I can
stay in touch with my kids, relatives and friends "*.

How is it possible to perceive, in Figure 2, the exchange of information
(pictures, messages, videos) is one of the factors that most appeals to older
audiences on Facebook. Despite being the preference of older people exchanging information still concerns the elderly public. Inserting pictures and videos
in digital social networks is still complicated by the fear of excessive exposure.
As an elderly commented *"The fear that the use of social network leads to an
unwanted personal exposure may be an additional factor to my low utilization"*.
With these data we must examine the importance, or not, of digital social networks for maintaining and / or creating relationships in the quality of life of
this audience.

In the domain Environment, we considered three aspects: "Opportunities to acquire new information and skills" seniors showed that they are not
completely satisfied, but very satisfied (67%); with regard to *"Participation
and opportunities for recreation/leisure"*, we found 50% of satisfied seniors, fol-

## Advantages of use of Digital Social Networks

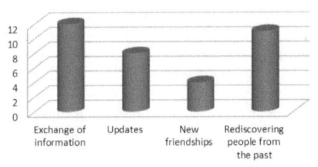

Figure 2    Advantages of the use of digital social networks

## Concrete forming relationships in Digital Social Networks

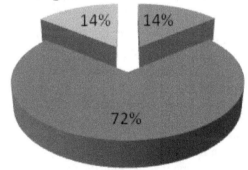

■ Yes, already built one or more friends through social networks

■ Yes, but it never occurred to me

▒ Not

Figure 3    Concrete forming relationships from interactions of digital social networks

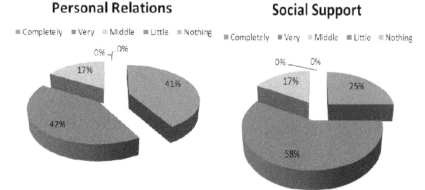

Figure 4    Domain social relation

lowed by 33% completely satisfied seniors; considering the aspect of "*Health and social care: availability and quality*" results indicate seniors' very satisfied (75%) (Figure 5). The WHOQOL-bref data collected showed to us an audience socially included, where social relationships are well established, reflecting an improved quality of life. As one of the seniors said: "*Retake the social life or enhance it*".

Regarding to the WHOQOL-bref aspect "Opportunities to acquire new information and skills", seniors showed a concern about being informed and acquiring new skills for life (Figure 5).

Although a small frequency of the use of the DSN (one or more times a week), when we compare seniors with teenagers, it is still a significant amount for an audience that did not know how to handle a computer four years ago. Digital tools allow to seniors a sense of belonging to a wider and virtual community, which allows them to come into contact with other people, with the society (DOLL, MACHADO, 2011). The risks described by seniors show a concern about safe web experience. Such perspectives are encouraged by the lack of information and clarification on the use of technology and their self-assessment as a human being that has limitations that comes with the aging process, according to them. These data were reinforced with the WHOQOL-bref results and the speech of one senior "*Like children, seniors are easily manipulated*". Seniors' speeches often lead to this: "*Communicating with friends and family, make new friends; facilitated communication, quick information; communications, reunions, entertainment and new friends*".

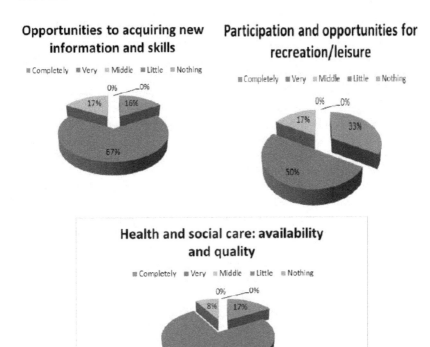

Figure 5    Domain environment

Communication is tied to the construction of social relationships with family, friends or even strangers. Seniors have confirmed that they believe in the possibility of building concrete relationships from Internet (Figure 3). Social relationships are critical to a satisfactory quality of life and the WHOQOL-bref outcomes (Figure 4) showed that there are satisfactory personal relationships in this group. These relationships are ways to get out of isolation and loneliness, and are shown in the statements of participants: *"Exit isolation ... looking for new friends... looking for hobbies and innovations; A great benefit because we are always updated and we can talk same language with grandchildren, children and relatives; Rediscovering old friends (existing friends too), keep up to date on various subjects and it is a great hobby; Distraction, friendship, be able to express our opinions, talk; Keeping contact with friends and gather with friends;*

*I participated in a meeting with friends from my hometown, scheduled by social network".* Mc Auley (2000) and Neto (2000) reported that there is a social loneliness, in which people feel unsatisfied in personal/social relationships (family, friends, etc.). This dissatisfaction harms a healthy quality of life. Therefore social loneliness can be addressed in the use of digital social networks.

The data considered here show a positive influence that the digital social networks perform in the quality of life for seniors. Our findings are described by the seniors opinion when they were asked if the DSN could help them in quality of life, and they said yes, according to comments made: *"In so far the people are dedicated to answer to all demonstrations of its own network, this includes them in a social life and produces a sense of belonging into their relationships; As I said before all of this improves health and keeps me update; I do not feel lonely because anytime I am sending or receiving wonderful messages; Yes, in so far people decrease the loneliness and keep in touch with other friends and stay updated".*

# 5. Concluding remarks

Society in general goes through many changes, both as social and cultural paradigms. In this context there is a portion of population that, unfortunately, is rarely studied: the seniors. At the same time this population is joining the society through courses, workshops, lectures or even in an active way at NGOs, unions and others. Nowadays there are many courses being offered for digital inclusion and even more seniors require learning current and popular issues. The motivation to learn for elderly people depends strongly on the purpose of the learning outcomes, and also in how much they consider themselves able to achieve these results (self-efficacy). The commitment to meaningful activities for the elderly contributes to good health and satisfaction with life and longevity (Ala-Mutka et al., 2008; Kececi and Bulduk, 2012) as is in the case of digital social networks.

This research analyzed the profile of a group of seniors who use DSN, their concerns and purposes. It was also possible to realize that DSN can greatly benefit quality of life of seniors mainly in social relationships, nearing seniors to society (family, friends, etc.), through communication and information with the world that surrounds them. As one of the seniors mentioned *"You stay connected to the world".* Every year brings new digital social networks and new features. At the same time, the elderly are increasingly present in this environment and their anxieties and motivation accompany them. Therefore it is important that studies in addition to improving the tools in digital social networks, also seek to address issues related to quality of life. It is up to educators, gerontologists and those working with digital inclusion to provide to this audience a conscious use of digital social networks, and clear doubts that seniors have, as availability of information, communication and update forms. There are many possibilities to use the DSN as a benefit to quality of life for seniors and it is a matter for professionals who work with these people to show them the possibilities and the potential of the DSN use.

# References

Ala-Mutka, K.; Malanowski, N.; Punie, Y.; Cabrera, M. (2008) *Active Ageing and the Potential of ICT for Learning*,[online], ISBN 978-92-79-09452-1, © European Communities. Avaliable from: http://ipts.jrc.ec.europa.eu/publications/pub.cfm?id=1659.

Araújo, L.F.; Coutinho, M.P.L.; Carvalho, V.A.M.L. (2005) Social representations of aging among older adults who *participate in social groups*. Psychology: Science and profession Magazine. 25 (1).

Bardin, L.(2009) *Content analysis*. 4. ed. Lisboa: Edições 70.

Brandão, M.F.; Silveira, R.M.H.(2010) Orkut and old age: and speech communitiess. In: Conto, E.S.; Rocha, T.B. (org.). *Life in Orkut: narratives and learning in social networks*. Salvador: EDUFBA.

Chen, K.; Chan, A.H.S. (2014). *Predictors of gerontechnology acceptance by older Hong Kong Chinese*. Technovation. 34. p.26-135.

Doll, J.; Machado, L. (2011). *Elderly and New Technologies*. In: Py, L.; Freitas, E.V.. (Org.). Treaty of Geriatrics and Gerontology. São Paulo: Guanabara Koogan.

Freitas, G.A. (2011) *Older adults in cyberspace: relationships and interaction in the virtual world*. Completion of course work at the Faculty of Communication and Library Science, [online], Social Communication Course: Specialization in Public Relations, Federal University of Rio Grande do Sul (UFRGS). Porto Alegre. Avaliable from: http://hdl.handle.net/10183/37567.

Joia, L.C.; Ruiz, T.; Donalisio, M.R. (2007) *Conditions attached to the degree of life satisfaction among the elderly population*. Public Health Magazine. 41(1). p.131-8.

Kececi, A.; Bulduk, S. (2012). *Health Education for the Elderly, Geriatrics*, Prof. Craig Atwood (Ed.), [online], ISBN: 978-953-51-0080-5, InTech. Avaliable from: http://www.intechopen.com/books/geriatrics/healtheducation-for-elderly-people.

Lewis, S. (2011). *Seniors and Online Social Network Use. Journal of Information Systems Applied Research* (JISAR). 4(2). p.1-15. Avaliable: http://proc.conisar.org/2010/pdf/1522.pdf.

McAuley, E.; Blissmer, B.; Marquez, D.X.; Jerome, G.J.;Kramer, A.F.; Katula, J. (2000). *Social Relations, Physical Activity, and Well-Being in Older Adults*. Elsevier. 31. p.608-617.

Neto, F. (2000) *Social psychology*. Lisboa: Open University.

Oliveira, M.Q.; Queiroz, M.B. (2012). The *"look" about elder participation in coexistence groups: contributing to the improvement of quality of life?* Journal Portal Disclosure [online], 19. Avaliable from: http://www.portaldoenvelhecimento.org.br/revista/index.php.

Páscoa, G.M.G. (2012) *The contribution of the social web - Facebook social network - to promote active aging: study case in USALBI*, [online], Dissertation of the Institute of Social and Political Sciences, Technical University of Lisbon. Avaliable from: http://hdl.handle.net/10400.5/4427.

Pew Research Internet Project. (2014). *Social Media Update 2013.* [online] january 8. Avaliable from: http://www.pewinternet.org/2013/12/30/social-media-update-2013/facebook-users/

Sawyer, R. (2011). *The Impact of New Social Media on Intercultural Adaptation.* [online], Senior Honors Projects. Paper 242. Avaliable from: http://digitalcommons.uri.edu/srhonorsprog/242

Silva, L.M.; Silva, A.O.; Tura, L.F.R.; Moreira, M.A.S.P.; Rodrigues, R.A.P.; Marques, M.C. (2012). *Social representations of the quality of life for seniors*, [online], Journal Gaúcha of Nursing. 33(1). p.109-15. Avaliable from: http://seer.ufrgs.br/RevistaGauchadeEnfermagem/article/view/24321.

Sundar, S.S.; Oeldorf-Hirsch,A.; Nussbaum, J; Behr, R. (2011). *Retirees on Facebook: can online social networking enhance their health and wellness?* In: Proceedings of the 2011 annual conference extended abstracts on Human factors in computing systems (CHI EA '11). ACM, New York, NY, USA, 2287-2292. Avaliable from: http://doi.acm.org/10.1145/1979742.1979931.

Varela, M.A.; Ogawa, K. (2014). *Social Networking Service for Helping Each Other in the Neighborhoods.* ICDS 2014 : The Eighth International Conference on Digital Society.IARIA, 2014. Barcelona. p.164-168.

WHO. World Health Organization. (2002) *Active ageing: a policy framework.* Geneve: World Health Organization.

WHO. World Health Organization. (2014) World Health Statistics 2014. [online], Geneve. Avaliable from: http://www.who.int/mediacentre/news/releases/2014/world-health-statistics-2014/en/.

WHOQOL Group (1995) *The World Health Organization Quality of Life Assessment (WHOQOL): position paper from the World Health Organization.* Soc Sci Med. 41(10). p. 1403-9.